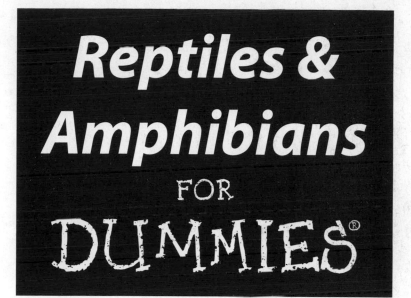

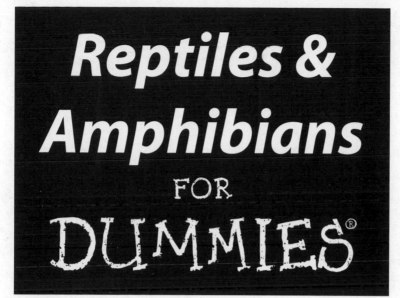

Reptiles & Amphibians

FOR DUMMIES®

by Patricia Bartlett

WILEY

Wiley Publishing, Inc.

Reptiles & Amphibians For Dummies®

Published by
Wiley Publishing, Inc.
909 Third Avenue
New York, NY 10022
www.wiley.com

JAN 2004

About the Author

Patti Bartlett began chasing lizards about 40 years ago, when her family moved to Albuquerque, New Mexico, and inviting vacant lots stretched on all sides of their house.

Those vacant lots and the lizards they contained have long since disappeared, but she still chases lizards every chance she gets. (Although the lizards are as fast as ever, the pursuer is not.)

Those lizards led to snakes, which led to turtles (the only pet you could sneak into a dorm room). Once Bartlett moved away from the desert, she discovered amphibians, a group she feels is the most beautiful of the herps. College courses in technical illustration fostered an appreciation of herps as aesthetic objects, and producing black-and-white and color artwork occupies a portion of her time (and a large portion of her workspace).

During her exploration of herps as art objects, she collected every book she could find on reptiles and amphibians. Not many of these books were available in the 1970s and 1980s, and many were purchased only for their photos, some of which were printed upside-down. Because she was living with herps that somehow ended up in almost every room of the house, she felt everyone would want to the do the same, if they only knew enough about how to take care of them. She is the author or coauthor of some 25 books on herps, as well as pet trade books on hamsters, rabbits, and basset hounds. In the meantime, she was the director of historical museums, an advertising representative for a land development company in Florida, a promotions manager for a fertility clinic, and a book editor.

Today she shares her space with her husband Dick, several dogs, and a small but very select collection of iguanas, turtles, and snakes.

Dedication

For my father, Alan Pope, and my stepmom, Ethel Pope

Author's Acknowledgments

Thanks are due the many people who helped me with this manuscript. First of all is my husband, Dick, who offered advice and assistance whenever requested. I'd like to thank my agent, Grace Freedson, whose knowledge and help made this book possible. Thanks are also due Frank Slavens; Allen Salzberg; Billy Griswold, DVM; Jim Harding; Kevin Zippel, Detroit Zoo; John Gannon, Philadelphia Zoo; Scott Pfaff, Riverbanks Zoo; Mike Goodwin, Cincinnati Zoo; Frank Indiviglio, Bronx Zoo; Marshall Meyers of PIJAC; Gerry Salmon; and Professor James Vaupel, Max Planck Institute for Demographic Research.

I'd also like to thank those hundreds of hobbyists who have shared their experiences with me over the years, and who work with herps just because they think these creatures are endlessly interesting.

Publisher's Acknowledgments

We're proud of this book; please send us your comments through our Dummies online registration form located at www.dummies.com/register/.

Some of the people who helped bring this book to market include the following:

Acquisitions, Editorial, and Media Development

Project Editor: Marcia L. Johnson

Acquisitions Editor: Tracy Boggier

Senior Copy Editor: Tina Sims

Technical Editor: Frank Indiviglio

Editorial Manager: Jennifer Ehrlich

Editorial Assistant: Elizabeth Rea

Cartoons: Rich Tennant, www.the5thwave.com

Production

Project Coordinator: Nancee Reeves

Layout and Graphics: Carrie Foster, Joyce Haughey, Michael Kruzil, Kristin McMullan, Jackie Nicholas, Brent Savage

Special Art: Richard Bartlett

Proofreaders: John Greenough, Andy Hollandbeck, Angel Perez, Kathy Simpson, TECHBooks Production Services

Indexer: TECHBooks Production Services

Special Help: Jennifer Bingham, Christina Guthrie, E. Neil Johnson

---

Publishing and Editorial for Consumer Dummies

Diane Graves Steele, Vice President and Publisher, Consumer Dummies

Joyce Pepple, Acquisitions Director, Consumer Dummies

Kristin A. Cocks, Product Development Director, Consumer Dummies

Michael Spring, Vice President and Publisher, Travel

Brice Gosnell, Publishing Director, Travel

Suzanne Jannetta, Editorial Director, Travel

Publishing for Technology Dummies

Andy Cummings, Vice President and Publisher, Dummies Technology/General User

Composition Services

Gerry Fahey, Vice President of Production Services

Debbie Stailey, Director of Composition Services

Contents at a Glance

Table of Contents

Introduction

· ·

Most reptile and amphibian owners can point with unerring accuracy to the moment they got hooked on these animals. For me, it was when I walked across the street at age 6 to the open lots west of my home in Albuquerque, New Mexico. The lots were filled with tumbleweeds, tufts of scrub grass, and a few (very few, thank goodness) scraggy, low cholla cactus. Dashing from clump to clump were blue-tailed skinks. Less active but lying quietly amidst concealing gravel patches were the sand lizards. I never knew what occupied the fist-sized tunnels, but I imagined they might be rattlesnakes.

I spent most of my summers exploring those lots, seeing what was moving; I found that I could see more lizards if I used my peripheral vision to spot their movement, and homed in on them from that. For me, those lots were paradise — who could think of anything more interesting than lizards? Then my experience expanded to include snakes and turtles and, once away from the desert, the occasional frog, and, much later, the salamanders and crocodilians.

Like me, you may want to keep these wonderful creatures yourself because, as the line from *Cabaret* says, each and every one is more beautiful than the last. But what do they need, and can the average person provide these needs? Watching animals in the caging you've set up loses its luster if the animals don't behave as they would in the wild. But providing appropriate caging is just part of keeping animals; you also need to carefully select your pets to match your lifestyle. Don't even think of buying or acquiring something that you can't take care of (or that would take huge amounts of work on your part — you'll find the routine hard to keep up).

Reptiles & Amphibians For Dummies is designed to help you decide what sort of reptile and/or amphibian is best for you and to tell you what you need to know to assure that your animal lives a normal, healthy life.

About This Book

This book deals with captive reptiles and amphibians and some of their many quirks and idiosyncrasies. Of course, not all of those little quirks are in here. I don't think that we know even *half* of them — a bunch of surprises still await the owners of these animals.

This book also deals with what most of the usually kept reptiles and amphibians need for captive care. Not all frogs need water. Not all lizards eat insects. Not all salamanders are aquatic their whole lives. The appendix in the back of the book tells you who needs what.

If you're basically proficient at herp keeping, you'll probably discover some new stuff for you in here as well. I keep learning more all the time, mainly because herpers as a group share their information. Consequently, everyone benefits, the animals in particular.

If you're the obsessive-compulsive type (which is good because we need OC types, although not as bosses), you may want to start at the beginning of this book and read right through to the end. If you have limited time and want to get a jump-start on a particular topic, riffle through these pages or look in the index (if you're not the riffling type), and dash ahead. You can absorb this book in bite-sized pieces — like while you're brushing your teeth (3 minutes) or waiting for your toast to pop up (2 minutes) or the pizza to cook (17 minutes). This book is not meant to be read while you're driving, because it's also designed to be utterly distracting.

Conventions Used in This Book

To help you pick out information from a page, I use the following conventions throughout the text to make elements consistent and easy to understand:

- ✔ Any Web addresses appear in monofont.
- ✔ New terms appear in *italics* and are closely preceded or followed by an easy-to-understand definition.
- ✔ **Bold** highlights the keywords in bulleted lists.
- ✔ Sidebars, which look like text enclosed in a shaded gray box, consist of information that's interesting to know but not necessarily critical to your understanding of the topic.

Also be aware that all temperatures are in Fahrenheit.

Foolish Assumptions

People who keep reptiles and amphibians enjoy unusual pets, and they enjoy finding out more about them. I'm assuming that's why you're reading this book. Here are a few other possible reasons:

- ✔ You've been thinking about getting a reptile or amphibian as a pet but thought these pets were too complex and too demanding. Now you're thinking that of course you can find out what you need to know right here.
- ✔ You suddenly are the owner of a reptile or amphibian, and you need to know about care basics, fast.

✔ You volunteer or work at a vet clinic, a pet store, or an animal shelter, and you've been elected as the go-to guy when problems need to be solved, like how to get the lizard to let go of your finger.

✔ Your significant other likes reptiles and amphibians, and you think the relationship (with the human, that is) is worth pursuing.

✔ Your job has gotten so demanding and so intense that you need a little nonhuman diversion to keep your perspective.

How This Book Is Organized

To help you find the information you're looking for, this book is divided into five parts. Each part includes several chapters relating to that part.

Part I: So You Want a Reptile or Amphibian?

Here's the nitty-gritty on what a reptile/amphibian is so you'll know whether this sort of pet really does appeal to you. You'll find out what a reptile is, what an amphibian is, and why they're called herps. I also take a look at the demands of various kinds of herps to help you decide which one might be right for you.

Part II: Finding Your Herp and Setting Up Shop

This part deals with where to look for the herp of your dreams. You find out what sort of caging and equipment you'll need once you acquire your pet and how to actually handle your pet. Here you also deal with the issues of outdoor caging and indoor temperature control. In addition, this part explains how to ship and travel with your herp and how to find a good pet sitter so that you can vacation worry-free.

Part III: Open Wide! Feeding, Hydration, and Health

You have your herp home in a really nifty cage. Now you have to feed him and give him water, which isn't necessarily as simple as it sounds. You also need to know how to recognize when your herp isn't well. This part tells you all you need to know about these topics.

Part IV: The Birds and the Bees, and Legalities

If you're buying an animal so you can breed it and make lots of money, hold on. Very few people actually make money when breeding herps and selling the young. But if you'd still like to breed your herps and have permanent homes for the offspring, this part tells you what you need to know to begin the process.

Part V: The Part of Tens

As important as your fingers and toes, this part has some great information for herp hobbyists. Check out this part for reasons to take your herp to a veterinarian immediately. I also include a list of ten U.S. zoos with herp collections worth seeing and ten places to turn if you can never get your fill of herp information.

Appendix

The appendix lists the most popular reptiles and amphibians and includes their scientific name, area of origin, diet, ease of care, habitat and caging needs, and behavior.

Icons Used in This Book

I identify certain bits of information throughout the book with these icons:

This icon serves as a friendly reminder — kind of a tap on the shoulder to point out the stuff you shouldn't forget.

Tips are helpful hints that show you how to benefit from the mistakes others (and I) have made before you.

This icon marks the information that only die-hard herp enthusiasts need (or care) to know. Then again, you may find these paragraphs interesting.

Watch out! This icon highlights trouble to avoid.

Part I

So You Want a Reptile or Amphibian?

The 5th Wave   By Rich Tennant

"We've had dogs all of our lives, but thought it might be nice to own a reptile for a change. We're looking for one that's good with children, won't chase squirrels, and doesn't bark when strangers come to the door."

In this part . . .

Here's the nitty-gritty on what a reptile/amphibian is so you'll know if this sort of pet really does appeal to you. You'll find out what a reptile is, what an amphibian is, and why they're called herps. You discover specific physical characteristics and behaviors about many herps. I reveal the Name Game, which is why the same animal is a blue-spotted tree runner on one list and a jeweled jungle nipper on another.

Chapter 1

Is a Reptile or Amphibian for You?

Reptiles and amphibians make unique pets. And although caring for reptiles and amphibians is going to take *some* time, it won't take *much* of your time — at least not nearly the time a warm-blooded animal would take.

Reptiles and amphibians have few emotional demands (at least on their part), but they do have occasionally exacting physical needs. Because they're in cages and can't go and get what they need in terms of clean caging, the correct temperature, clean drinking and bathing water, and the right food, they depend on you.

The type of animal you select will determine how much of a *pet* you have, in the classic, "stroke me, I like you" definition of a pet. People who have owned a tortoise for 50 years will tell you that their tortoise *is* a pet, walking up to be near them when they walk past the enclosure, standing high on his legs, and extending his head to be petted. Some iguanas hurl themselves off their perches and lumber up to you in the morning, and they seem to enjoy being rubbed on their neck and tickled. But once fed, they tend to ignore you. On the other hand, a poison-dart frog, although brightly colored and unquestionably beautiful, isn't going to recognize you and hop over to be held.

But if you're the type of person who appreciates things that are a little bit out of the mainstream, or who has always admired snakes, or if you simply have an insatiable curiosity (What does *snout-vent length* mean? How is a lizard different from a snake, and do any snakes have legs?), the chapters in this book will make you an expert — well, almost an expert — on all things related to reptiles and amphibians.

What is this subphylum thing?

All plants and animals are classified and named through a series of steps called taxonomy. The process takes a life form through Kingdom, Phylum, Class, Order, Family, Genus and Species, with prefixes adding more points of definition. There used to be just two kingdoms (yes, that old-fashioned term is still used in taxonomy): plant and animal. Now there are five, with bacteria, protozoans, and other minute life forms filling the additional kingdoms.

Each kingdom is subdivided again into phylums (about 20 phylums divvy up the animal kingdom). Reptiles and amphibians are placed with other animals in the phylum Chordata, animals that have some form of a spinal cord. Animals with a bony covering to the spinal cord are placed in a subphylum called Vertebrata. Humans are winnowed out of Vertebrata and placed in the Class Mammalia; reptiles are in the Class Reptilia, and amphibians are placed in the Class Amphibia.

Exploring the Differences Between Reptiles and Amphibians

Reptiles and amphibians are alike in some ways and different in some ways. Reptiles and amphibians are both members of the subphylum Vertebrata (see the related sidebar in this chapter for an explanation of subphylum). They share the subphylum with fishes, birds, and mammals. They're *ectothermic*, which means they're dependent on ambient (the encompassing atmosphere) temperatures for their own body temperature. They do, however, have some significant differences:

- ✔ **Skin:** Reptile skin is dry and has scales, which are actually small folds in the skin, while amphibians have moist skin laden with mucous glands.

- ✔ **Eggs:** Reptiles lay dry eggs on land, or they retain the eggs in their bodies until they hatch. Amphibians lay gel-surrounded eggs in water, in damp places under logs. A few high-altitude amphibian types also retain their eggs until they hatch.

- ✔ **Life cycle:** Newly hatched reptiles look like miniatures of their adult parents. Amphibians, with a few exceptions, go through metamorphosis — breathing water through gills when they're young and then developing lungs and becoming land-dwelling adults.

- ✔ **Defense:** Reptiles can defend themselves with claws and whipping tails, and they can bite. (Some snakes and two lizards, the Gila monster and beaded lizard, toss in a little extra by having venom. Although venom was designed to aid in food acquisition, not for defense, spitting cobras have upped the ante by developing the ability to spit their venom.) Amphibians have toxic skin secretions, which are used for defense, not for food acquisition, and they can bite. They do not have true claws or nails.

What's in a Name?

Collectively, reptiles and amphibians are referred to as *herps*. You may wonder what the term *herp* means — if you've spent any time with someone who likes reptiles or amphibians, you're certain to have heard this term. *Herp* comes from the Greek word *herpes,* which literally means crawling things. The term is applied equally to reptiles and amphibians. From herp comes *herpetology,* the study of crawling things. A person with formal training in herpetology is a *herpetologist.* Someone who likes herps, keeps them, and works with them but lacks the formal training is a *herper.*

All reptiles and amphibians are assigned a scientific name. This is a two-part Latin name that assigns the animal to a genus and species. This is part of the hierarchy that humans assign to all living things in order to better understand how they relate to each other, for example, how rat snakes are alike as a group as opposed to the kingsnakes. For those of you who are morbidly curious (or just plain serious herpers), I use both the Latin names and the common names for the herps listed in the appendix at the back of this book.

Many herp hobbyists prefer to deal with common names, words they can remember and spell. Common names offer a lot more latitude in describing an animal so we can remember it. But a common name can be as ephemeral as a tax refund.

An old trick, long known in the animal dealer profession, is that a dealer invents a common name when he/she is trying to sell something. For example, a shipment comes in from South America that contains something new — a lizard, one of the ameivas that has blue spots along the side. The dealer looks at the lizard and thinks, "Well, it has blue spots, it's from the jungle, and it runs, so I'll call it the blue spotted jungle runner." The dealer puts the "blue-spotted jungle runner" on his list of animals for sale and hopes that pet stores (retailers) will order from the wholesale list, and hobbyists will order from the retail list, and that all of them will want the "new" blue-spotted jungle runner.

A week goes by, and not many of the lizards have sold. Time is money, so the dealer squinches up his eyes and gives the lizard a more enticing name: the jeweled jungle nipper. Lo and behold, the name change works, and the lizards fly out of the dealer's shop as if they had wings. Six months from now, when a new shipment of the same lizards comes in, if jeweled jungle nippers don't sell, maybe ocellated ameivas will.

That's why scientific names come in handy — they don't change.

Take Your Pick: Reptile or Amphibian

How can you tell which herp you want to buy? If you like creatures that revel in dampness, get an amphibian. If you want an animal that likes life dry, get a reptile. But you need to consider other factors, as I discuss in the following sections.

Getting acquainted with amphibians

If you like damp environments (or if you want a pet who likes things wet), you want an amphibian (see Figure 1-1). Because they breathe partially through their skin, amphibians must have moist, clean caging, which requires careful monitoring and frequent cleaning to avoid ammonia buildup or a bacterial bloom, or your pet dies a nasty death. See Chapter 4 for more information on amphibians. The following list explains some factors to consider if you want an amphibian:

Figure 1-1: The African clawed frog is an undemanding amphibian pet. Here, an albino waits for a meal in an aquarium.

✔ **Caging:** Amphibians need caging that can hold moisture but can be easily cleaned. In most cases, this means an aquarium, usually a 15- to 20-gallon size. Moisture is provided through water (the tank itself or a container within it is filled with water), or the substrate in the tank (sphagnum moss or dampened paper towels) is moistened. You can supply additional moisture with a hand-held sprayer or a misting system.

You'll want to add a screen top to the terrarium/aquarium, but you don't need to worry about adding lighting or keeping the tank or its inhabitants warm. Amphibians like it cool; the tiger salamanders, for instance, trudge through snow as early as February to reach the ponds where they hope to meet a mate, which says something about amphibians' tolerance of cold temperatures and their sex drive.

Because amphibians are quiet creatures, they won't tear up an elaborately planted terrarium the way a lizard or snake might. The smaller amphibians, like the brightly colored dart frogs, look like animated jewels in a fern- and moss-bedecked tank.

Cleaning an amphibian tank is an important aspect of keeping these creatures alive. The smaller the amphibian, the less waste it produces, and the less work it is to maintain the tank. You have to tear down and reconstruct a 20-gallon dart frog enclosure maybe twice a year (although the water dish will need to be cleaned daily). In contrast, a bullfrog's enclosure needs daily water changes or filtration and twice-a-week partial water changes, and the moist sphagnum in a tiger salamander's cage needs rinsing at least every other day. (See Chapter 7 and 8 for more information on indoor and outdoor caging, and the appendix for specific care tips on amphibian species.)

✔ **Feeding:** Amphibians eat insects, small fish, and earthworms. All are readily purchased from bait stores or pet stores; the insects and earthworms can be mail-ordered. Crickets need to be housed in an extra aquarium. You can toss a few into each amphibian's cage as needed. Mealworms come packaged in a plastic container with a snap-on lid; store them in your refrigerator or move them to their own hideaway filled with oat bran and rolled oats — at last there's a way to use up that oatmeal! — with a few slices of apple for moisture. I buy earthworms in lots of 500 from a hunting/fishing supply firm and store them in a refrigerator. (See Chapter 11 for more on diets for amphibians.)

Size: Amphibians that are generally seen in pet stores are usually beautifully colored and fairly small in size. You can certainly go out and find big amphibians. Some of the aquatic caecilians, for example, will easily reach a 2-foot length, but few people want a retiring pet with the animation and appearance of a gray rubber hose. The pet store amphibians range in size from the fist-sized horned frog to the 3-inch-long red-spotted newt to the thumbnail-sized dart frog. You can certainly find more exotic amphibians. Your store can order them for you, or you may want to see what an expo can offer (see Chapter 5 for more info on finding and buying the amphibian of your dreams). Their easy-to-handle sizes mean the animals require less food. Amphibians don't require the amount of food a larger, more active creature, such as a green iguana, needs.

Cost: Amphibians are inexpensive. The dart frogs as a group run about $40 to $60 each, but this is at the high end for all amphibians. The more unusual horned or tomato frogs cost around $50, but the vast majority of amphibians range from $15 to $20.

Amphibians breathe, to a lesser or greater degree, through their skin. This is why they need moist, very clean caging, why the cages must be cleaned so frequently, and why you must wash your hands before handling them (see Chapter 6). Most skin diseases in amphibians are fatal (see Chapter 12 for health info). As a rule, amphibians are retiring and nocturnal, which means they won't be as responsive to a human as is a tortoise (see Chapter 4). Amphibians tend to lay massive numbers of eggs; if you plan to breed your amphibian, you'll need to plan how you'll raise up to a thousand young, or you'll need to dispose of the excess eggs. (See Chapters 14, 15, and 16 for details about breeding and care of the young.)

Taking a look at reptiles

If you like dry environments, you want a reptile (Figures 1-2 and 1-3 show a couple of cuties). Dry caging means that any debris (such as fecal matter or uneaten fruit) won't immediately contaminate the cage. You don't have to change the substrate daily; once a week is enough. You don't have to worry about unseen problems, such as ammonia or bacteria. You do need to heat the cage and provide the equivalent of bright sunlight in terms of lighting. See Chapter 3 for more on reptiles as pets.

Figure 1-2:
The Eastern fox snake, like all snakes, has no eyelids, and a tail that can't be regenerated if damaged.

Figure 1-3:
The legless
Eastern
glass lizard
has eyelids
and a tail
that can be
readily
dropped
and will
regenerate.

Most people opt for reptiles, and you can understand why. Reptiles are a lot less work than amphibians. The downside, if you want to consider this a downside, is that they're more active than amphibians. They need more food than amphibians, meaning a snake will eat a mouse instead of three crickets. They need bigger cages, and the really big reptiles, such as the green iguanas, need room-sized cages.

On the plus side, reptiles can be handled without fear of wrecking their skins (except for the thin-skinned day geckos, which you can read more about in Chapter 6), and they respond well to gentle handling. The other pluses are the same as the amphibians: They're beautiful, they adapt well to captive conditions, they're easy to feed (unless you go for a big python, which needs to eat bigger prey than mice or rats), and their caging requirements are not elaborate. Even moving them from one apartment or house to another isn't difficult (see Chapter 10).

The following list explains some factors to consider if you want a reptile:

✔ **Caging:** The basic cage for a reptile is a glass aquarium used as a terrarium, topped with a secure lid. You can start with a 20-gallon tank and go up from there.

For tortoises, the cage should be at least 16 times the footprint of a turtle's shell; a 6-inch box turtle needs as a minimum a cage that's four shell-width's wide, or a foot wide, and about four times the shell's *length* in length, or 24 inches. That gives a 6-inch long box turtle a tank the size of a 20-gallon aquarium, which is okay for a month to two. For a longer period, the tortoise needs to go in an outdoor enclosure or into an indoor enclosure that's about 4 feet on a side.

Aquatic turtles need a large tank with a filtration system; add a raised piece of corkbark to one corner and add a basking light over the cork-bark so your turtle can "sun" and dry off completely. A 20-gallon tank is large enough for an aquatic turtle up to 2 inches in length; as your turtle grows, he'll need a larger filtered tank.

Snakes need a cage that is at least half as long as they are in length, and one-third of their body in width. A yellow rat snake 3 feet long needs a tank that's about 12 inches wide and at least 18 inches in length.

Lizards can go into a glass tank, but some of them (in particular the chameleons) need more air circulation and do better in a nylon or wire mesh cage.

The caging box needs a substrate, a disposable, absorbent flooring. Newspaper was the gold standard for years, but nowadays natural substrates such as mulch or sand (or any of about 15 different commercially produced pelleted or shaved substrates) are preferred because they are more absorbent, look better, provide more traction for the reptile to push against when moving about the cage, and may provide burrowing opportunities for lizards and snakes. The water dish, drip waterer, or misting system is a critical factor in reptile husbandry. Snakes, lizards, and most of the tortoises use a hidebox at night or during the day for seclusion. See Chapters 7 and 8 for more on indoor and outdoor caging, and Chapter 11 for watering tips.

✔ **Feeding:** Snakes usually eat rodents, and for the pet keeper, this means frozen mice or rats purchased from your local pet store. You can buy them in all sizes, from the newborn babies, called pinkies, to the adults. Thaw the rodents in warm water, blot off any moisture, and place them in the cage with the snake. Tortoises are vegetarians, and dine on chopped, fresh, leafy greens and vegetables and a little fruit. Box turtles eat vegetables, fruit, earthworms and, occasionally, crickets (yes, they can stalk and catch a cricket!). Aquatic turtles eat aquarium plants, leafy greens, cat chow, and thin apple slices, along with live minnows and earthworms. My aquatic turtles really liked the freshwater shrimp I could buy seasonally at my bait store, but they tore apart the shrimp so enthusiastically that I had to clean the tank and change the water within 12 hours. See Chapter 11 for feeding information.

✔ **Size:** Reptiles really do come in all sizes, from the 3-inch long sand skink (who spends his time buried in the sand in his cage) to the 8-foot-plus common boa. Bigger snakes are available, such as the Burmese python, but they get too big to be good pets (see Chapter 17). The majority of the snakes in the pet market are captive-bred rat snakes, kingsnakes or house snakes, and these rarely get up to 6 feet in length. Those boas and pythons that make good pets — pets you can easily handle — are those, like the sand boas, that stay less than 4 feet in length.

Aquatic turtles start out small. Some are the size of a half dollar when they're hatched, but they can get to a foot or a bit longer at maturity. Tortoises emerge from the egg at maybe an inch and a half long, and their adult size depends on the type of tortoise. Spurred tortoises get up to 2 feet long, while Greek and hingeback tortoises are adult at 12 inches or less.

Lizards show the same range in adult sizes. The popular bearded dragons and geckos demonstrate the practical side of owning a placid pet that stays fairly small — 15 inches for the bearded, 14 inches for the biggest gecko types, and 4 inches for the smallest geckos. The gorgeous green iguana, once a very popular pet, grows to a length of 5 feet-plus, far more lizard than most people can house or manage.

✔ **Cost:** The initial cost of a pet reptile really depends on what you buy. For snakes, the cost ranges from about $40 for a corn snake to $65 for a Kenya sand boa. For lizards, geckos run from $15 to $150, with chameleons ranging from $35 to $125. Turtles cost from $25 for a painted turtle to $45 for a box turtle to $125 for a hingeback. See Chapter 5 for acquisition tips.

Reptiles are easy to keep, because in many ways they need what we need: warmth, sunlight, potable water, and enough space to move around in. If given good housing and proper food, they rarely get sick. They are long lived, far longer than most people would guess.

Getting What You Want

Getting started with herps isn't just deciding that you want a hingeback tortoise. (Where on earth will you find one? Does anyone breed these things in captivity?) Finding and buying the right herp involves more than simply walking into your local pet store. You need to figure out what kind of herp suits your lifestyle.

Some herps can take more time than other herps, and it's always best if you know what you're getting into before you find yourself looking under logs for termites to feed your dart frogs at midnight in midwinter. You may be happier with a herp that will cheerfully eat raw vegetables. Spend some time with Chapter 2. That's where I cover what lifestyle factors (both yours and the herps') you need to consider to find the right herp for you.

Chapter 2

Deciding Which Herp Is Right for You

In This Chapter

▶ Knowing how much time this creature needs

▶ Adding up the costs of herp ownership

▶ Recognizing potential health and safety problems

So you think you want a pet herp, but you haven't decided which one. What factors should you consider? Is the initial cost the only thing you should consider? Or should you just get whatever animal appeals to you?

Most herp lovers can remember the time (or times) they yielded to temptation. ("Golly, those frogs are so beautiful and so tiny. How much trouble can a couple of little ol' dart frogs be?") Some people have even had the grace to regret it afterward. Either the animal needed facilities they could not provide or required food that was hard to get. (For example, a snail-eating lizard is outrageously hard to feed, and where do you get termites in midwinter?)

For your own peace of mind and for your herp's welfare, you need to consider a couple things before you go out and buy the first herp that catches your eye:

✔ How much you can afford to spend not only buying but also housing, feeding, and caring for your animal

✔ How much time you can — and must — devote to your herp

Of course, the answers to these questions depend on the herp you adopt. Some require more time and care, and some require less. You also need to think about the health risks that reptiles and amphibians may pose and decide whether you're willing to do what it takes to keep yourself and your pet safe. This chapter tells you what you need to know.

Before You Jump Headfirst into the Pool

As one of my friends said when he handed me his new pair of Jackson's chameleons (see Figure 2-1) to baby-sit while *he* went to Connecticut for a week, "Wow, I really like these guys, but they really require a lot of time."

Figure 2-1:
Jackson's chameleons have a lot of visual appeal but require live food and lots of it.

Realize that you're likely to *over*estimate the amount of free time you have to care for a herp — and just as likely to *under*estimate the amount of time that a herp needs. It's easy to forget your other obligations when you're looking at something you really like, like a red sports car or a water dragon. When you already have a life, a job, school, or a family, any additional demands on your time can throw everything off balance. That's why matching a herp to your lifestyle is so important. Later on in this chapter, you find information on how much time different herps require, and if you know this ahead of time, you'll be able to provide more time to your new animal friend. (You're on your own about the sports car, though.)

For instance, if you think that you can save time by eliminating caging, maybe you're right, but probably you aren't. Setting up artificial vines in your bathroom shower stall for a pair of Jackson's chameleons isn't going to save you any time, because you'll have to take the system down for your own shower and put it back up afterward. Either you're going to have to stop taking showers, or you're going to have to come up with some other labor-saving method to keep your chameleons clean and hydrated. There are easier and better ways to take care of Jackson's (see Chapter 7 for more information about caging).

What a herp eats makes a huge difference in what specific animal you chose. Some herps can be fed with food straight from your refrigerator (if you're eating a veggie-filled diet, as you should be). But even something as simple as buying food takes time, especially if you have to go someplace other than your local grocery store. Buying crickets for your chameleons every other day also gets expensive. Buying them direct from a breeder is cheaper, but *where* are you going to house a thousand crickets? In addition, the little guys never shut up!

And what if your animal gets sick? Diet is extremely important in herp care; you can cause disease by not providing the correct foods. Good diet and housing can forestall a lot of health problems, but sometimes you're going to need a veterinarian no matter how much preventive care you give. (Put a sticky note or paper clip on Chapter 12 and read that chapter soon, because it contains a lot of important herp health-related information.) Poor diet is particularly hard on herbivores because of MBD (metabolic bone disease), which is sort of ironic, because you can purchase a good, nutritionally perfect herbivore diet at your local grocery store, thus avoiding a special trip to a pet or bait store.

You've heard the downside, and you're not budging. You still want a herp. But what to choose? Do you want a reptile or an amphibian? How can you decide which of these creatures is the one for you? I've written this chapter to help you decide.

You May Have the Money, Honey, but Do You Have the Time?

One thing people like about herps is that many of them don't require daily attention. Other than making sure that the cage temperature is okay and water is available, most herps can be left alone for a day or two without any intervention on your part. (Figure 2-2 shows a favorite reptile.) Checking the temperature may be as easy as walking into the room where you keep the herps and asking yourself, "Am I comfortable in here?" If you are, then you can probably assume that the herp is comfy, too, and you can move on to other things.

Of course, the herp you choose determines the time you need to devote to its care, which involves primarily feeding and housing needs. Reptiles take less time than amphibians because their housing needs are simpler and take less monitoring. Of the reptiles, snakes seem to require the least care — they don't need feeding more than once a month or so. Turtles and tortoises are next on the care ladder, followed by lizards. Some lizards, such as herbivorous types like iguanas and bearded dragons, need daily care. Among the amphibians, salamanders and newts seem to require less care than frogs. See Table 2-1 for an idea of the maintenance requirements for some common herps.

Figure 2-2:
The corn snake stays fairly small and is available in naturally occurring colors and more than 20 breeder-derived color morphs.

Table 2-1	Rating the Maintenance of Some Common Herps		
Herp	*Low Effort*	*Medium Effort*	*High Effort*
Reptiles:			
Corn snake	✓		
Kingsnake	✓		
Painted turtle		✓	
Green iguana			✓
Greek tortoise		✓	
Amphibians:			
Horned frog	✓		
White's treefrog	✓		
Eastern newt		✓	
Tiger salamander	✓		

Taking it one day at a time

You need to run through this checklist when you look at your animals, and you need to do this on a daily basis:

✔ Is the animal visible? Is he acting normally? Being motionless is something reptiles and amphibians do very well. Motionless is okay, but lying belly up is cause for concern.

✔ Is the animal in his expected place? A snake that normally spends his days in his hidebox (a smaller box within the cage to give him a feeling of security; see Chapter 7 for more on hideboxes) but suddenly begins to spend time coiled in his water dish may have mites or some other (relatively easy-to-fix, we hope) health problems.

✔ Is the water dish full or nearly so and is the water clean? Some herps defecate in their drinking water, which means that you need to clean the water dish as soon as you see it's soiled.

✔ Is the temperature of the cage about 80 degrees? If you use an under-tank heating pad, check the thermometer you put in the cage when you set it up.

✔ Does the light go on when you turn it on? Many herps are *heliotropic,* which means that they're dependent on the "sun" (or some type of light) to get moving. If these herps — lizards and tortoises and turtles in particular — don't have light, they stay in a torpor.

✔ How much food is left from the previous day? If you're feeding an animal that eats crickets, always having a few crickets in the cage ensures that your herp has something to eat when he's hungry. If you're keeping bearded dragons or iguanas, having food left may be a sign that they're off-feed — an early sign of illness.

Performing weekly chores

With many herps, you'll need to clean the cage and clean and refill the water dish on a weekly basis — the equivalent of changing your own bed or rousting out those assorted jars, each filled with a tablespoon or so of . . . something . . . from your refrigerator.

Water dishes can grow algae and a whole host of unseen contaminants, such as protozoans (protozoans can emerge from spores normally found in soil), bacteria, and viruses. When you wash the water dish, you can often feel a slick surface lining the dish, which is why you need to clean the dish at least weekly.

When a herp in the wild defecates, the stool is left behind as the animal wanders. Contained in a cage, a herp has to live with his stool until you swoop in and clean the cage. If you're slow to clean the cage, the herp frequently walks/slithers through his stool and spreads it all over the cage, requiring more work on your part than would have been needed if you'd cleaned the spot when you first saw it. You can sort of schedule cage cleaning on a weekly basis, but you'll be better off (and your herp, too) if you spot-clean as needed.

Cha-Ching: Adding Up the Cost of Care

No matter which herp you choose, he's going to cost you more than time. You also need to budget some dollars for your new friend. In most cases, the herp's initial purchase price may seem reasonable and affordable to you, but you may be surprised by the cost of keeping the herp well fed and in good shape on a daily basis. These expenses go on and on.

Although the cost of keeping a herp over time is affected by the animal's requirements for food and caging (see Chapters 7 and 11), Table 2-2 gives you an idea of what you can expect to pay to bring a herp home from the store and to take care of it over time.

Table 2-2		Long-Term Costs of Herp Ownership		
Herp	*Purchase Price*	*Cost of Caging and Related Accessories*	*Monthly Food Costs*	*Veterinary Care*
Corn snake	$20	$50	$10	Budget $50 per year (one visit, limited medicines)
Kingsnake	$30	$50	$10	Budget $50 per year (one visit, limited medicines)
Green iguana	$15	$135	$30: first six months only (will easily be $60 after first six months)	Budget $50 per year (one visit, limited medicines)
Bearded dragon	$50	$135	$30	Budget $50 per year (one visit, limited medicines)
Painted turtle	$25	$70	$15	Budget $50 per year (one visit, limited medicines)
White's treefrog	$20	$30 to $40	$20 to 30	Budget $50 per year (one visit, limited medicines)

Herp	Purchase Price	Cost of Caging and Related Accessories	Monthly Food Costs	Veterinary Care
Horned frog	$20	$20 to $30	$10 to $30	Budget $50 per year (one visit, limited medicines)
Tiger salamander	$15	$20 to $30	$10 to $30	Budget $50 per year (one visit, limited medicines)
Eastern newt	$10	$65 to $75	$5 to $10	Budget $50 per year (one visit, limited medicines)

Taking a look at food prices

Fish gotta swim and herps gotta eat. As a rule, herps don't eat much; their appetites pale when compared to the appetite of the average teen-aged male, for instance. But herps need to eat, and they need to eat sufficient amounts of the correct diet as well (check Chapter 11 for feeding information). You can easily dole out $360 to $720 a year for a single animal, an impressive amount when you figure it out over the herp's 10- to 15-year life span. Table 2-3 shows some typical foods and their costs.

Table 2-3	Costs of Typical Herp Food	
Item	Cost	Storage site and Shelf Life
Frozen mouse	$3	Freezer; 4 weeks
Frozen rat	$5	Freezer; 4 weeks
Romaine lettuce	$1.99 a head	Refrigerator; 1 week
Bananas	49 cents per pound	Kitchen counter; 4 days
Night crawlers	$3.60 per dozen	Refrigerator; 2 weeks
Crickets	10 cents each	Separate terrarium or plastic bucket with lid; 5 days

Commercial foods are generally slightly more expensive than fresh foods. Their extended shelf life and their enhanced vitamin and mineral content are their real advantage.

Housing expenses: No need for a second mortgage

Herp keeping has come a long way since the Dark Ages of the recycled aquarium with a newspaper substrate for everyone. There's a suggested set-up for every herp type. Want a Jackson's chameleon? Get a screen cage. Want to keep a red eft, a salamander that has both terrestrial and aquatic life stages? Buy a split terrarium with land and water areas. Want to keep a lot of colubrids but you don't have a lot of room? Buy a cage rack, where the snakes are kept in shallow drawers; a cage rack with 14 drawers has a footprint of only 2 x 5 feet. (I don't particularly like cage racks, but colubrids display normal feeding and breeding behaviors and reach expected longevity in these small cages, so my dislike of these structures is probably based on how difficult it is to see or observe the animals.) Want to keep a grass skink? Set up a vertical cage with tall tufts of dried grasses that give plenty of hiding and moving-around room for this shy lizard. The options seem endless, but this variety of acceptable caging ensures that you'll be able to set up your herp's caging without busting your bank account.

A herp needs the maximum floor space you can give it. This will be the herp's world for the rest of his life, so it needs to be as large as possible.

Now that herp caging is mass produced, the cost is surprisingly low. Unless you're bringing home a 14-foot Burmese python (if this is your plan, stop and read Chapter 17 first), you can buy or even create herp caging for not a great deal of money. Just to give you a ballpark idea of the costs involved, you can estimate the cost of a basic herp setup at $50 for the caging and another $30 to $65 for associated lighting, heating, and furniture and accessory needs. (The big jump in lighting, heating, and other costs is for the herps, green iguanas, and bearded dragons that need UV lighting.)

Although Chapter 7 tells you all you need to know about the details of caging, the following sections offer a glimpse of what you need for any herp — reptile or amphibian.

The cage

Any of the following can serve as a herp cage:

- ✔ **Screen cage:** This cage offers plenty of ventilation because it has screen on all six sides. The zippered nylon screen cages start at about $40 for a cage about 24 inches x 24 inches x 18 inches and go upward from there. These are particularly good for chameleons.

- ✔ **Glass terrarium/aquarium:** This is the old, classic herp cage, easily created from an old aquarium by the addition of a screened top. Available in a variety of sizes, this style of housing works pretty well for almost all types of herp, from snakes to frogs. Unless you add a small fan to the top, however, a tank is not a good choice for a chameleon. Depending on size, the cost runs from about $20 for a 20-gallon size upward.

- ✔ **Small plastic terrarium:** One commercial brand is the Pal Pen. These are the rectangular or circular clear plastic tanks, usually 3 to 5 gallons in size, with a snap-on ventilated top. These work well as temporary housing for smaller herps, such as the sand lizards or hatchling snakes. The cost is usually under $10. Because these units are plastic, you can't add heating or lighting, which limits their usefulness.

The substrate

In caging, *substrate* is what goes on the bottom of the cage. Ideally, substrate provides traction for the animal to walk or crawl on, absorbs any liquids from spilled water or feces and urates, and gives a burrowing species, such as fire skinks and most snakes, the chance to burrow. Here are some things that can serve as substrates:

- ✔ **Newspaper** is the absolute cheapest thing. It works for snakes and some lizards and perhaps for tortoises, although it doesn't provide much traction.

- ✔ **Paper towels** are another absorbent choice, although they aren't sturdy enough for any herp bigger than hatchling size.

- ✔ **Mulch** is another inexpensive choice. It provides moderate absorption, good traction, and fairly good burrowing opportunities.

- ✔ **Pine or aspen shavings** are used by some professional breeders. They offer good absorbency and terrific burrowing but sometimes are irritating if caught in skin folds around the animal's eyes or in the mouth of herps with underslung jaws (as in sand skinks and sand boas).

Do not use cedar chips or shavings. The phenols given off by this wood are damaging to all reptiles and amphibians.

Higher-end substrates from this point include bark chips, terrarium sand, shredded hibiscus, and wheat products, which are either washable or disposable and are all more expensive than the substrates mentioned earlier.

For amphibians (such as the White's treefrog in Figure 2-3), a moisture-retaining substrate helps keep your frog's or salamander's skin moist. Examples include moistened paper towels, moistened sphagnum moss, or moistened coconut fiber. Bark substrate that has been moistened should work well, although I find it easier to count on the softness (and non-abrasion) of the sphagnum or paper towels. Dried sphagnum moss is available at your local pet store or in the nursery department of any discount or department store for about $5 for a one-pound bag. To use it, moisten it with tap water and squeeze out as much as you can with your hands.

Figure 2-3:
Captive-bred White's treefrogs don't need large cages or special heating precautions, but they do need moisture.

If you just want to keep things simple, use a double layer of dampened paper towels. They don't scratch, and nothing can stick to the amphibian's skin, so it's easy to do a quick check for fungus. (For more on fungus, see Chapter 12.) In addition, you can change a paper towel substrate in a flash without feeling that you're tossing money or time in the trash along with the substrate.

The water supply

Most herps can drink from a water dish. Snakes, being essentially all neck, can ooze over the side of a bowl 2 inches high and drink to their heart's content. Reptiles that are closer to the ground, like lizards or tortoises, need a lower bowl, an inch high or lower. For more on watering your herp, whether for drinking or for splashing around, see Chapter 11.

Playing It Safe

Although most pet herps are harmless and pose no threat to your health and safety (or anyone else's), you need to be aware of the potential for problems.

For years, herps were heralded as the perfect pet because no one was allergic to them — they don't have fur, and they don't have feathers. But, if you're worried about maybe being allergic to a herp, go to your local pet store and ask if they'll let you handle the herp you're thinking of acquiring. Wash your hands, hold the animal for about five minutes, and wash your hands again. (This is simple good hygiene to follow when herp handling; see the following information on salmonella.) See whether you develop a stuffy or runny nose in the following 20 minutes.

Probably the best-known herp disease risk is salmonella. You've probably heard of a summer picnic where everyone comes down with a salmonella infection from eating the potato salad. The causative bacterium is Salmonella, and you find it everywhere you find dirt. You also can find salmonella on your herp, which can carry it on his body. If you hold him, put him down, pick up an apple, and start munching or touch your lips, you risk a salmonella infection, just the same as if you pick up a rock, examine it, put it down, and then munch an apple without washing your hands. If you kiss your sweetie on the lips after holding your herp and then touching your lips, guess who is at risk for coming down with salmonella infection? Of course, you're not going to kiss your herp, are you? That just doesn't make any sense. But if you do, soap and water your lips and then wash your brain out for having such a dopey idea.

No, you don't have to give up hand holding and kissing just because you have a herp. But if you want to prevent spreading salmonella through these signs of affection, simply washing your hands after handling your herp minimizes any risk of salmonella infection.

Everything is a risk for people with impaired immune systems. But following normal rules of hygiene — no herp kissing and washing your hands before and after handling — should reduce the risk for these folks as well.

Other safety considerations when purchasing a herp include his temperament, his response to humans, and whether he's likely to escape from his cage. The following minitable gives some of that information.

Safety factor	*Turtle*	*Snake*	*Lizard*	*Frog*	*Salamander*
Speed of movement	Slow	Fast	Fast	Fast	Slow
Ability to escape caging	Low	High	Medium	Medium	Low
Calmness of temperament	Calm	Medium	Medium	Nervous	Calm
Positive response to humans	High	Neutral	Medium	Neutral	Neutral

Chapter 3

Reptiles 101

The immense class Reptilia (the reptiles) contains within its fold the snakes, the lizards, the turtles (including tortoises), the crocodilians, the amphisbaenians, and the tuataras. In many ways, these critters share characteristics; in many ways, they differ from each other.

All reptiles are cold-blooded, or *poikilotherms,* meaning that they depend on outside sources of heat to bring their bodies up to operating speed. A few have found canny ways to utilize their own accumulated body heat, like female pythons that incubate their eggs. All are covered by scales and shed their skin periodically (except for the crocodilians). All of them lay eggs, although some retain the eggs within their body until the young hatch, and so give birth to live young.

Slinky Snakes

Almost everyone knows what snakes are. They're long, they're scaly, and they're slinky. They lack eyelids, and some are venomous. There are about 2,400 species of snakes. Some are only a few inches in length and about the diameter of a fat pencil lead, and some are huge — longer than 30 feet and about the diameter of a beer keg. All, no matter their size, have gotten a bum rap at least since Biblical days (and probably long before that). But once you get to know these guys, you'll realize that snakes are no fiercer than any other creature and that they're sometimes more reclusive than you'd guess.

If you're looking for snakes (and somehow I'm always doing just that), you need to look where they are. You tend to mentally classify them by where they are found. Snakes found in alike habitats may not be related to each other, but when one is gazing at a large stream-fed pond, one isn't thinking so much about natricines (the water snakes) as what sort of water-lovin' snake might live here. Here are the types of snakes grouped by habitat:

- **Terrestrial and surface-active:** Typical snakes in this habitat are corn snakes, capable of climbing (and swimming, too) but preferentially terrestrial and active on the surface, rather than burrowing in the soil like the sand boas.

- **Terrestrial and fossorial (persistent burrowers):** This category includes the hognose snakes (superb diggers), the bull snakes, and the sand boas. All spend more time underground than on top of it.

- **Aquatic in freshwater habitats:** Who can resist a snake as graceful and as much at home in the water as a fish? This group includes the water snakes, heavy-bodied little grouches that they are; the elephant trunk snakes, wrinkly aquatic snakes previously restricted to Asia (but found in at least one location in Florida), and the cottonmouths, venomous but quiet enough, unless your big feet get too close.

- **Aquatic in saltwater habitats:** Talk about adaptations! You gotta love the sea snakes. Not only do the sea snakes live in marine habitats, a harsh desiccating place, but they're entirely marine except for the times they come ashore to lay their eggs. Sea snakes perfected their venom to kill cold-blooded prey, and fairly rapidly at that. The fact that their venom is very effective on warm-blooded creatures like humans is entirely coincidental (honestly — we're just too big to eat).

- **Arboreal:** A few of these can fly (glide, actually) for quite considerable distances. Crysopelia, the flying snakes from Asia, launch themselves out of trees, expand their ribcages, and glide to another, lower branch. Other snakes may not launch themselves from branches, but they're entirely at home in and spend their lives in trees. They only rarely are found on the ground. Examples of these are the beautiful emerald tree boas, the eyelash vipers, and the rough and smooth green snakes. All are extremely difficult to see when they're resting amongst tree branches, but that's part of the fun.

Some snakes are entirely harmless (to humans), a few are moderately dangerous, and still fewer are potentially lethal. Some kill their prey by constriction, some kill by *envenomation* (the injection of venom), while others merely overpower and consume their prey while it's still alive.

Snakes are all carnivorous, but depending on their type, they eat various things, including the following:

- Insects
- Worms
- Slugs and snails
- Fish

> ✔ Some reptiles and amphibians (and their eggs)
>
> ✔ Other kinds of snakes
>
> ✔ Birds and bird eggs
>
> ✔ Mammals

Snakes (all reptiles) are *ectothermic,* meaning that their body temperature is regulated by external means rather than internal controls. Certain motions, such as the shivering indulged in by incubating female pythons of some species, may help a snake elevate the body temperature a few degrees above the ambient temperature, the current temperature of the soil, air, or water.

Some snakes can change colors. Some of them change from light pinkish brown to silvery (Hog Island boas), or their sides may change at night from the orange daytime tones to a silvery nighttime color (Brazilian rainbow boas).

All snakes shed their skin at regular intervals, with the younger snakes in a rapid growth phase shedding more frequently than adult snakes that are no longer growing. The skin is usually shed in one piece, the snake hooking the skin near the face on a rock or a rough section of a fallen limb, and crawling out of the skin, turning it inside out in the process.

Come on, give me a hug! The constrictors

The hands-down favorite snakes in the pet trade are constrictors. These attractive, powerfully muscled snakes immobilize their prey by first grasping it with their mouth and then, with a burst of speed, wrapping one or more coils of their body around it — constricting it. Once the snake's coils are in place, the prey animal is killed by suffocation. With each exhalation of its prey, the snake tightens its coils until, no longer able to breathe, the prey dies. No bones are broken nor does other apparent bodily injury occur.

Actually, constriction does more than restrict breathing. The prey animal dies due to suffocation and to heart failure, coupled with back pressure from the venous system. The constriction forces the blood back through the veins and arteries. So unwinding the snake from its prey item so the prey item can theoretically breathe probably isn't going to save the prey item. The damage has already been done. (Whew. Let me loosen my collar and open a window.)

Snakes that constrict their prey include the following:

> ✔ **Boas**
>
> ✔ **Pythons**
>
> ✔ **Rat snakes**

- Kingsnakes
- Gopher snakes

The power in any one of these snakes becomes apparent when you lift them. In most cases, constricting snakes hold tightly to the handler, making lifting and moving of small to medium-sized (to about 8 feet in length) snakes a relatively easy chore.

Approach and handle constricting snakes over 8 feet in length with caution, and only when a second person is present (see Chapter 6 for handling tips).

Name your poison: Venomous snakes

Venomous snakes (cobras, coral snakes, sea snakes, and vipers to name a few) subdue their prey by biting or striking, injecting venom, and then awaiting the prey's death before consuming it. The venoms not only subdue the prey but also begin predigesting the prey's tissues. The predigestion, along with lysis or destruction of blood cells, skin, and muscle tissue, is why the hand or foot of someone who has been bitten turns black. The black color indicates tissue *necrosis,* or tissue death.

Not all venomous snakes are the same. Snakes of different families have different fang structures and different types of venom (broadly speaking, some venoms attack the blood system, and others attack the nervous system), administer the venom in different ways, and have different ways of actually securing their prey. Some venomous snakes are actually classified as harmless, or put a different way, some harmless snakes actually produce venom. The lesson to be learned here is to know your snakes.

Even snakes have common sense(s)

The snake lives in a world governed by his senses. He senses food, stays out of trouble, and finds a mate via his senses of sound, sight, smell, heat, and touch.

- **Hearing:** Despite having neither external ear openings nor tympanic membranes, snakes can hear. They do, however, hear only low-frequency sounds. The single earbone is attached to the jaw. Snakes also can sense seismic vibrations through microreceptors in their skin, so you can rightly say that your snake is very sensitive.

- **Sight:** Exactly how accurately snakes see has always been a matter of conjecture. Certainly most snakes key in on movement, but how they react to these visual cues depends both on the snake species and the individual snake.

Among the fast and active species, racers and coachwhips use a method of hunting called *periscoping*. This technique involves lifting the head above the surrounding vegetation to look for prey.

✔ **Smell:** Although nostrils are present, the most sensitive and accurate olfactory evaluations involve a snake's flickering tongue. The nose picks up the basic scent, and if that scent is judged to be worthy of further interpretation, the tongue is brought into play. It picks up tiny molecules of scent, both from the air and from the substrate, and these molecules are then delivered to the Jacobson's organ (also called the vomeronasal organ), a specialized organ in the snake's palate.

✔ **Heat:** Some snakes (pit vipers, pythons, and boas, for example) have heat (infrared) sensory pits on their face. They are used to locate and to determine the exact position of their prey or a warm-blooded predator such as humans. By instinctively evaluating the temperature messages sent by these sensory pits, snakes can strike their prey (or a warm-blooded intruder, like your hand) virtually unerringly in total darkness. Differences in readings from the pits on opposite sides of the face also tell them where a prey item is located.

✔ **Touch:** Reptiles have mechanoreceptors in their skin to tell them what's resting against them, and where that item is along the body length. If you're nervous when you pick up a snake, the snake can sense this and is more likely to bite. With a sure, unhurried, and gentle touch, you can sometimes pick up harmless snakes in the wild and not get bitten.

Posturing — defensive and otherwise

Snakes assume certain, often classic poses. Here are some of the more typical poses:

✔ When cold, a snake often finds a patch of sunshine and coils tightly in the warming rays, often flattening his body to expose more body surface.

✔ When warm, snakes instinctively seek the shade. To most effectively thermoregulate (regulate their body temperature), a snake may expose only a part of a coil or two to the sunlight, leaving the rest of his body in a crevice, burrow, or the shade of a shrub or rock. Burrowing snakes may be reluctant to expose themselves at all, instead bringing their back in contact with the underside of a sun-warmed rock (or other surface debris) beneath which they are hiding.

✔ When hungry, certain species of snakes (such as copperheads and ground boas) may indulge in caudal-luring, using the tail as a lure. The snakes that indulge in this movement have a tail tip that's a different color than the rest of their body, and during the endeavor, the snake usually coils with his head right next to his tail. The tail is then elevated and writhed (seductively — never vibrated!) in the hope that a passing amphibian or lizard will mistake the tail tip for a succulent caterpillar or worm and come within striking range. Pretty sneaky, huh?

✔ Defensive postures and motions are often assumed by snakes to indicate fright or other displeasure (see Figure 3-1). Perhaps the best-known posture is the striking stance. In this posture, the head is elevated, and the neck forms an S, giving the snake a greater reach when he strikes. Both venomous and nonvenomous snakes can assume this posture, but vipers and constricting lampropeltine snakes (such as rat, king, milk, and gopher snakes) use it most often.

Figure 3-1:
Bull snakes use a hissing defense at the slightest provocation.

Trying to look bigger is another typical snake defense. Snakes can flatten either the body or neck. Terrestrial snakes flatten themselves horizontally, and arboreal snakes distend their bodies and necks on a vertical plane, all in the name of intimidation.

Getting around without any legs

Snakes move in one or more of several ways (see Figure 3-2). They may move in waves of lateral undulations, in a straight line (rectilinear mode), or in a concertina manner. Here's some information about each method:

✔ **Lateral undulations:** The snake pushes the outer posterior edge of each curve against an object or irregularity and moves itself forward. A snake can move remarkably fast in this manner. When swimming, only the lateral undulatory mode is effective.

✔ **Rectilinear mode:** This movement is useful if a snake is on a very smooth surface, but it's not a method that allows rapid movement. To understand how a snake moves rectilinearly, you must first know just a bit about his anatomy. Most snakes have a large ventral scute (scale) that extends from side to side. These scutes or belly scales are attached at the fore edge, with the free and sharp trailing edge slightly overlapping the belly scale just behind it. The motion of each ventral scute is controlled by muscles attached to at least two pairs of ribs. These muscles afford to each ventral scute the ability to tilt, move forward and backward, or even inward and outward. By moving groups of scales simultaneously, pushing backward with some groups while pulling other groups forward, forward movement is accomplished. Some snakes climb agilely. Those such as rat snakes and liana snakes may ascend rough-barked trees in rectilinear fashion.

✔ **Concertina method:** Boas, pythons, and rat snakes can ascend smooth trees by using the concertina motion. They form a series of zigzags with their body, looking a bit like a concertina or a hand organ, and utilize irregularities from the tree trunk and their own body strength to "crawl up" the tree.

Figure 3-2:
The Southern hognose snake has an upturned rostral scale to aid in digging.

Reproducing baby snakes

Most snakes lay eggs, but about 20 percent give birth to live young. Those that lay eggs deposit the eggs in moist soil, under rocks or logs, or inside rotting tree trunks, as the eggs absorb some water during their development.

Most egg-laying snakes in temperate areas lay their eggs in spring or early summer, and the eggs hatch in late summer or early fall. Those new babies need to find food in order to have the energy to survive the winter. Live birth, or viviparity, occurs more in snakes from temperate regions than snakes from tropical areas.

The Incredibly Adaptive Lizard

Lizards are far more diverse in appearance than the snakes, but in all other aspects, they closely parallel the legless snakes. Actually, there are legless lizards too — just far fewer kinds. Lizards have adapted to every habitat you can think of — the very cold, the very hot, the very arid, freshwater and marine habitats. Lizards can live at high elevations and low elevations. In fact, lizards are found on every continent except Antarctica. When people think of lizards, these four kinds often come to mind:

- **Anoles:** Erroneously referred to as the American chameleons, these small arboreal lizards are found in backyards and vacant fields in the southeastern United States. Most anoles change colors in response to temperature or emotional factors (like fear).

- **True chameleons:** These strange-appearing Old World lizards are of moderate size. Their eyes are turreted (the eyelids have fused and the eye opening is a small central hole in the eyelid). Their toes are arranged into groups or two or three, with the "thumb" and "forefinger" paired opposite the other toes, so the feet can function like strong pincers, the better to grasp branches and hang on. Many are capable of lightning-like color changes, flashing distinct color patterns to other chameleons to signal sexual receptivity or territorial warnings.

- **Komodo dragons:** These are huge carnivorous and potentially dangerous lizards of the Lesser Sunda Islands in the Republic of Indonesia.

- **Gila monsters:** This lizard (pronounced *hee-la*) along with its co-generic (belonging to the same genus), the Mexican beaded lizard, are the world's only two venomous lizards. Almost supernatural attributes are erroneously bestowed upon these lizards. This is sad, for all are remarkable for just being themselves and doing whatever it may be that comes naturally for them.

Some like it hot: Exploring climate preferences

Like snakes, lizards are ectothermic and rely on external sources to regulate their body temperature. Some lizards are at home in far northern or far southern regions and are active at lower temperatures (both body and ambient) than their more tropical relatives. However, the greatest diversity of these creatures occurs in the subtropics and tropics. Lizards from cold areas become dormant in the winter, and the activity patterns of those in temperate areas and the tropics and subtropics are often dictated by weather patterns such as frontal systems and rainy versus dry seasons.

Although most lizards bask in the morning sunlight to quickly elevate their body temperature to optimum, and then bask periodically through the day to maintain it, some lizards seem perfectly alert and functional at normal daytime air temperatures and bask only occasionally. One such lizard is the South American mop-headed lizard, a species that dwells fairly low on tree trunks in rain forests and water's edge locations. This lizard is exposed to only the trace amounts of sunlight that filters through the forest canopy.

On the other hand, some lizards (such as racerunners, whiptails, and wall lizards) are so dependent on sunlight that they're largely inactive on cloudy days, even when the temperatures are suitably hot to permit normal activity.

Lizards have been very successful in colonizing desert regions, and some species (such as American chuckwallas and Old World spiny-tailed agamids) are able to sustain very hot temperatures. These may be found out, active, or even basking, when rock-surface or sand-surface temperatures are over 125 degrees. Such high temperatures allow these lizards to heat up quickly (a body temperature of 100 to 110 is normal) and to begin their daily foraging.

Allowing himself to overheat can be lethal to a lizard. When a lizard is in danger of overheating, he positions himself so that the least possible body surface is exposed to the sun, and he elevates himself high on his legs and lifts his toes from the hot sand to slow the rise of his body temperature.

There's no place like home: Looking at the lizard's habitat

Lizards have adapted to live essentially all over the world, but this doesn't mean that you can take a terrestrial lizard and expect him to live in an arboreal habitat, any more than you can expect a goldfish to live out of water. You have to provide the right kind of habitat for the lizard. And there are micro-habitats within habitats: rocky areas in the middle of a desert, and sandy areas in the middle of a subtropical environment. If that's what your lizard needs, you need to provide it.

Among arboreal lizards, the habitat choices vary. Some lizards (including some color-changing anoles, casque-headed lizards, and chameleons) are canopy dwellers. Others (such as the thorny-tails and the tree runners) choose to live high on tall trunks. Still others (for example, the tropical night lizards and African blue-tailed tree lizards) live lower on suitable tree trunks. Some lizards, such as the bridled forest gecko, choose slender saplings, while the closely allied and very similar collared forest gecko prefers the trunks of large buttressed trees.

Not all lizards are terrestrial or arboreal. For some, water is as much "home" as a branch is for an iguana. Crocodile tegus and crocodile lizards spend a great deal of their time in the water, and may catch their prey in the water (fish) or out of it (earthworms and insects). Marine iguanas of the Galapagos Islands dwell on cliffs and rocks near the ocean, readily enter this salty medium, and graze on submerged seaweeds.

Some lizards burrow to varying degrees to create their homes. Some burrowers, such as the fringe-toed lizards and Old World sand lizards, race across the surface of desert sands and then literally dive beneath the surface if frightened. Other lizards (the eastern glass lizard and Borneo earless lizard, for example) burrow more extensively in moist habitats, while others (including many skinks) burrow beneath surface stones in semi-arid rocky regions. Still other lizards burrow so efficiently through desert sands that they're referred to as sandfish.

Rocks are another lizard habitat. Spiny lizards or rock lizards may live on huge desert boulders. Cliff faces are often home to geckos, spiny lizards, agamas, and night lizards. Canyon lizards and some geckos are abundant on canyon faces.

Color me beautiful

Although some snakes can change color, none can alter hues with the facility of the anoles or the chameleons. The little green anoles you may find in your backyard routinely change from bright green to dark brown, and they may do so several times daily, in fact several times an hour. Many of the Old World or true chameleons are even more adept at changing color, but don't believe people when they tell you these lizards (or the anoles) can take on checkerboard patterns or paisley patterns. True chameleons can change from brown to green, often with a few shades of gray in between. Some members of the chameleon family utilize color flashes of black, yellow, turquoise, blue, or red to signal other chameleons.

Male and female chameleons may be colored so differently, especially when the females are pregnant, that they look like different species. Indeed, these colors and patterns and the associated body language all have very definite meanings that are easily read by the chameleons of the same species and either sex. Male chameleons signal to other male chameleons, "I'm here. This is my turf, so go find your own." Female chameleons signal to male chameleons, "I'm pregnant, go away," "I'm not interested," or "I'm receptive."

Sizing 'em up

Lizards vary in size from tiny geckos that are adult at only 2 inches in length to the Komodo dragon, a monitor that can attain a length of 8 feet and a weight of more than 350 pounds. Actually, the crocodile monitor of New

Guinea reputedly attains a length greater than the maximum attained by the Komodo dragon, but the former is of a far more slender build. Somewhere within these size extremes fall the other 4,500 lizard species. The most common size ranges between 5 and 20 inches in length. Most of the types in the pet market are less than a foot in length, because caging is so much less work.

What's for dinner? The lizard's eating habits

Unlike the snakes, all of which are carnivorous, lizards run the gamut of food preferences. Lizards can be carnivores (the monitor, for example), omnivores (such as tegus and many skinks), insectivores (including horned lizards and swifts), folivores (green iguanas, for example), or herbivores (such as the spiny-tailed agamids). Within each group are specialists. For example, the Australian thorny devil, flying dragons, and many horned lizards are ant specialists. Many skinks prey principally upon earthworms, and some geckos feed largely upon pollen and sap. The more specialized in diet the lizard is, the harder he's going to be to feed. For this reason, I don't recommend horned lizards as pets.

Most lizards chew their food rather thoroughly, but a few (including monitors, tegus, and Gila monsters) swallow suitably sized prey items whole.

Picking a pet

Roughly some 4,500 lizard species exist, but only a hundred or so are in the pet trade. Just because a lizard is in the pet trade doesn't mean it's a good pet — its adult size, feeding habits, or disposition may be a problem. As tempted as you may be to want to bring a certain lizard home, it is pointless to buy a lizard for a pet that requires care or food you can't provide. Neither do you want a lizard that gets too big or is too aggressive for easy handling.

Here are some lizards currently available in the pet market. Not all of these are good choices as pets, but I include them so you'll know why you don't want one.

- ✔ **Anoles:** These little sharp-nosed day-active (diurnal) lizards with clinging toepads are commonly kept as pets. They adapt readily to captivity and eat well on easily obtained foods. Most reach adulthood when they're from 4.5 to 8 inches in length, and the largest species, the knight anole of Cuba, grows to only 18 inches in length. Many anoles are color-changing arborealists, but others, normally gray or brown species that do not undergo extensive color changes, dwell low on tree trunks.

Anoles are primarily insect eaters, but many, especially the larger species, consume fruit and blossom petals as well. All lap at sweet sap and pollen, and many visit hummingbird feeders to drink the sugar water.

✔ **Green iguanas:** These animals are as cute and bright as a baby, but pose a huge caging problem as they reach adulthood and a size of 6 feet. Unless handled regularly (meaning at least once a day), these lizards become wild, biting, scratching with their claws, and whipping with their tail when approached.

These big arboreal lizards dull in color as they grow and are folivorous (leaf eaters). Captives often have bone malformations due to improper diets.

✔ **Tegus:** These big, heavy-bodied neotropical lizards eat small animals such as other lizards, birds, and rodents, along with any dead animals (carrion) they can sniff out. Fruit is also a food item. Some species get up to 4 feet in length. They need frequent handling to become and stay tame. All will use their tail, claws, and teeth in defense and to avoid being handled.

✔ **Geckos:** These animals are small, usually less than ten inches, although the personable giant gecko may reach 14 inches. They include arid-land or forest lizards from both the Old and the New World. Perhaps the best known are the day geckos and the leopard gecko. Geckos feed on insects or a fruit-honey-vitamin mixture. Most are nocturnal.

✔ **Chameleons:** These small Old World lizards can move each eye independently of the other, so one eye can keep an eye on you while the other is looking around for food. Most species are arboreal, but those in the genus *Brookesia* are largely terrestrial. Chameleons are insectivorous and require a lot of live food. Mesh caging seems to provide the air circulation these lizards need; mist the plants in the cage to provide water.

✔ **Monitors:** They vary in size from 8-inch-long insect eaters to the huge Komodo monitor that hunts and feeds upon deer and pigs and also eats carrion. Depending on the type, the adult size of those types in the pet market may be 16 inches (such as Storr's monitor) to 8 feet (water monitor), so make certain you know what you're buying. Monitors are found in Africa, Asia, Australia, Malaysia, and New Guinea.

For specific information on pet reptile species, look at the species account in the appendix.

Considering potential dangers

Lizards are, for the most part, less dangerous than many of their cousins, the snakes. There are only two venomous lizard species (the Gila monster and the related Mexican beaded lizard), and to be bitten by either, you must find one and then handle it or step on it. They aren't slender, so they're a lot less agile than a snake.

The venom glands of the Gila monster and Mexican beaded lizard are in the lower jaw. The venom is neurotoxic in action, affecting the nervous system of the animals bitten. The venom delivery system is very unsophisticated. To administer the venom, the lizard must bite and chew, and the venom is drawn into the wounds by capillary action. These lizards are potentially dangerous, protected, and normally slow-moving. They're active both during the day and at night.

Of the lizards, only the Komodo dragon attains such a size that the lizard might be life threatening to a human. But even if a lizard produces no venom and is smaller than life-threatening size, it may cause injury or discomfort to a handler.

Most lizards, especially those taken from the wild, bite, scratch, or whip a captor with their tail. Although any one of these actions is inconsequential when it involves a lizard that is only a few inches long, a bite from a lizard that is 15 or 20 inches long or larger can be painful. If the lizard is the size of an adult Nile monitor or a big male green iguana, the bite can be dangerous. Even "tame" green iguanas have been known to turn on their owners without warning, and in some cases, they did enough damage before they could be controlled that the owner had to undergo plastic surgery to correct the disfigurement caused by the lizard. Additionally, being struck by the whipping tail of a good-sized iguana or adult Nile monitor can be painful. Being struck by the spike-studded tail of a foot-long spiny-tailed agamid or a sungazer will catch your attention!

Although unintentionally hurtful, monitors have the endearing tendency to orient themselves lengthwise along the arm of their holder and to hold tightly with all four feet. When you try to remove the lizard, he will try to cling to your arm. Peeling him off your arms can leave scratches.

The jaws of a lizard that's the size of an adult spiny-tailed agamid (17 inches), bearded dragon (18 inches), or broad-headed skink (12 inches) can pinch painfully. A bite from a big blue-tongued skink (15 inches) or a caiman lizard (30 inches) can also hurt!

Lizards often don't just up and bite or tail-whip you. Through body language, they usually advise you — or any other object of their discomfort — of their intent. Some lizards (blue-tongued skinks and tegus, for example) inflate themselves, loll out their tongues, and hiss. Others (such as monitors and chameleons) flatten themselves vertically and sidle stiff-leggedly. An angry iguana vertically flattens his body and distends his dewlap, tilts his body slightly to one side, and draws his tail to one side, so just one hurried look should tell you he's about to lash out.

Some monitor species confront you, standing upright on a tripod of tail and hind legs, opening their mouth widely, and hissing loudly. Some frightened lizards face you and open their mouth widely. Blue-tongue skinks use this type of display, and the sight of their cobalt-blue tongue adds to the effect.

Other lizards may turn an abnormally dark color and stand their ground, but most, if given a half a chance, simply turn and flee! Most lizards seem to know that avoiding confrontations if at all possible is the surest way of living to become an old lizard.

Making sense of lizard senses

Lizards are endowed with all of the senses bestowed upon snakes, often with some enhancements.

Sight

Most have marvelous eyesight, seeing and appropriately responding to both moving and stationary objects that are some distance away. Most lizards also have functional eyelids. That they can see color is obvious when you watch a displaying male true chameleon respond to a second male of the same species in defense colors yet ignore a similar species clad in different colors. Like chameleons, anoles are also capable of independent eye movement, a useful skill when you're just bite-size and danger can come from any direction.

Some burrowing lizards have functional eyelids with a transparent spectacle in the lower lid that allows the lizard to see when the lids are closed. Some burrowing lizards lack functional eyes. True geckos have nonfunctional lids, and their eyes are protected by a transparent spectacle (the brille) similar to that of a snake's.

Smell

Lizards have external nostrils that are used in olfaction, but significant non-aerial particulate odors (those found on the ground or on other surfaces) are picked up by the tongue for analysis by the Jacobson's organ in the roof of the mouth. You can sometimes watch this analysis take place when the lizard flicks his tongue on a surface, a bit like he's tasting it (but he's really smelling it). Tongue-flicking is most apparent when the lizard is placed in unfamiliar territory.

Hearing

All lizards can hear, even those — or perhaps, more accurately, *especially those* — that burrow and who depend on tactile sensation, scent, and hearing to find food, keep them out of trouble, and find mates. Most lizards have external ear openings or a surface tympanum (eardrum), but in some the eardrum is covered by skin.

Touch

Lizards have a well-developed sensation of touch in the skin. Different receptors measure pressure, tension, or stretching within the skin. Tactile receptors are especially common in the epidermis, the outer layer of skin. Despite having these senses, lizards are remarkably slow to react to some painful situations, and we have no idea why.

Here's an oddball fact: No one even knows how effective painkillers are in treating burned lizards or other reptiles. Veterinarians just use the standard animal analgesics and alter the dose by weight. During 2003, a study headed by Greg Fleming, DVM, of the University of Florida School of Veterinary Medicine will be undertaken to help determine the effectiveness of pain medication on iguanas and what doses are appropriate.

Here's looking at you: Physical features of lizards

Lizards come in a wide range of physical characteristics. Lizards may be long-legged (such as casque-headed lizards and forest chameleons), no-legged (glass lizards and dibamids, for example), or any stage between these extremes. They may have well-developed hind limbs and diminutive forelimbs (such as sand skinks). They may have different numbers of toes on the forefeet than on the hind feet (sand skinks, for example).

The toes may be long, slender, and unadorned (as they are on whiptails), or they may be flanged in some manner (as they are on fringe-toed lizards and basilisks). The toe tips may be expanded into intricately designed pads that enable a lizard (such as an anole) to climb smooth surfaces, such as glass, or move in inverted position across a ceiling (as some geckos do). The toes of some lizards (such as skinks) are short and unspecialized, while those of others (such as web-toed geckos) are fully webbed to help them traverse yielding sands. The true chameleons have opposed, clumped, and bundled non-skid toes that firmly grasp branches like pincers.

Lizards may scamper, scurry, run, or jump (see Figure 3-3), or they may not move much at all. Chameleons are slow-moving lizards that depend on camouflage to avoid detection by both predator and prey. They move in halting motions, reminiscent of the breeze-blown leaves they dwell amidst.

Some lizards (Gila monsters and shingle-backed skinks, for example) have short, stump, fat-storing tails. Others have long, prehensile tails (monkey lizards, monkey-tailed skinks, and chameleons, for example), and some have tapered, standard-appearing tails.

The tails of some lizards may be easily *autotomized* (meaning broken off and then regrown). Glass lizards and many skinks are examples of lizards having this ability. To facilitate the breakage, many lizards have a *fracture plane,* a weakened area, in some caudal vertebrae. The tails of lizards lacking fracture planes can still be broken off, but usually they don't regenerate well. Regenerated tails have a supporting structure of cartilage rather than bone.

Figure 3-3:
The sand
skink has a
chisel-like
snout and a
rounded,
smooth
body. It
literally
dives into
sand and
can "swim"
from sight in
seconds.

Many species of lizards bear crests of some design on their head, nape, back, or tail. Basilisks, water dragons, iguanas, and some anoles are examples. Others, such as the skinks, are entirely devoid of such ornamentation and are so smooth that holding them can be difficult. The body scales of lizards may be tiny and granular, large and strongly *keeled* (have a ridge down the center of the scale), tubercular, smooth and nonkeeled, or combinations of these. The belly scales are often larger and of a different appearance than those on the sides and back.

Aquatic lizards usually have some degree of keeling on the tail, thought to improve the propelling power of the tail.

Basilisks, water dragons, mop-headed lizards, and sail-tailed dragons have flanged toes that allow them to run across the surface of still waters without breaking the surface tension film. If the lizards slow or the water is roiled, the lizards sink and then swim.

Color changes of those species capable of them are determined by temperature, breeding readiness, or the presence of another lizard of the same species — in plain English, stress — not by background color.

Lizards may use their tongue in aggression displays (and you thought sticking one's tongue out in defiance was a *human* trait!), to find scents, to clean the eyes and brilles, to lap up food, or even to "shoot" food. In this latter endeavor, true chameleons are the veritable champions. The tongue is often as long as the head and body of the chameleon, is coated with sticky mucus at the tip, and has a tongue-tip depression that enhances the lizard's chances of catching the prey.

The mating game

Many cues stimulate lizard breeding, with weather conditions, ambient air temperature, and the general good health of the lizards being of paramount importance.

Reproductive pheromones, those scented hormones with sexual messages, are produced by lizards that live in temperate areas following the post-hibernation skin shedding. Tropical species may be induced to breed by the advent of the rainy season, the passage of a frontal system, or other such climatic phenomena. Lizards breed in the very traditional manner. Breeding occurs following courtship displays that often involve the male's strutting, bobbing, nodding, displaying enhanced color, distending his dewlap, or rubbing the nape of female with his chin or his foreclaws. The male usually restrains the female by biting and holding her nape.

Not all lizard species have two sexes. Some whiptails and some geckos, for example, are parthenogenic, meaning that the only sex is female. They stimulate ovulation by making courtship displays to each other.

Lizards may be *oviparous,* meaning that they lay eggs, or they may be *viviparous,* meaning that they give birth to live young. If eggs are laid, gestation, the time the eggs spend in the body, is usually from two to four weeks. Incubation of the eggs takes from about 45 days to nearly a year. If live young are produced, the gestation period is usually from 50 to 120 days.

Many egg-laying lizards routinely multiclutch (lay multiple eggs at a time). Sperm retention may allow fertile eggs (or live babies) to be produced for up to several years after a successful breeding has occurred.

The sex of many lizards (and turtles, as well) is determined by the incubation temperature rather than by genetic factors, an occurrence termed TSD (temperature-dependent sex determination). In lizards, females develop at both high and low incubation temperatures, and males develop at intermediate temperatures. Adverse or unusual temperatures could theoretically play a major role in skewing sex ratios within a lizard population, but the system has worked so far. For more information on breeding lizards, see Chapters 14, 15, and 16.

Between Two Decks: Turtles

Of all the reptiles, turtles are probably the one group that everyone likes. Maybe it's because everyone has had, at one time or another, a red-eared slider in a plastic bowl. Dealing with a quarter-sized creature whose only aim in life is to cajole you out of another piece of earthworm pretty much ends any fear you might have. Most people have a certain fondness for turtles because of their childhood experiences with them.

But there's a real difference between pet turtles and turtles in the wild. Having evolved along with their environment in the wild, turtles are pretty good at staying alive in the wild. But when they're taken from their natural environment and put into our hands as pets, they become dependent on their owner for *everything*.

The head bone's connected to the backbone: Turtle anatomy

Turtles vary in size from the 3½-inch-long shell of an Asian species (the bog turtle of the eastern United States is almost as small) to the 4-foot length of the very big Galapagos and Aldabran tortoises and the 6-foot shell length of the leather-backed sea turtle. Turtles may be long-necked or short-necked and may withdraw their neck in a vertical S or fold the neck sideways under the overhanging front edge of the carapace. But all turtles have four functional legs, usually keen eyesight, a short to long tail, and a shell. In other words, turtles are turtles are turtles, and all are immediately recognizable as such.

In the United States, the term *tortoise* is used for land-dwelling turtles, while a *turtle* is a turtle that lives in water, either freshwater or the ocean.

The shell works more to discourage a predator rather than to afford complete protection. The likelihood of predatory activity is much higher when the turtles are small and a crunchy bite size, but the larger, older turtles are fodder for larger predators.

Contrary to popular belief, the shell is not hard and dead but is a living, feeling composite of specialized bones overlain with keratinous plates called *scutes*. A few turtles don't have hard shells. The soft-shelled turtles are aquatic species. Examples include the leatherback turtle (entirely saltwater) and the pig-nosed turtle from the Australia-New Guinea area (fresh to brackish water). Their shells consist of tough, leathery skin that covers the reduced number of supporting bones.

Turtles have four legs, which are modified to deal with different habitats. Turtles that are land-going, such as the Galapagos tortoise, box turtles, and spur-thighed tortoises, have feet that look like elephant feet — they're squared off at the bottom. Tortoises can easily stand up and walk, and they hold their bodies up off the ground as they walk. These turtles rarely enter water, but some box turtles plod along underwater on rare occasions.

Sea turtles are another group of easily recognized turtles, and they share a set of characteristics:

- All have flattened shells, to reduce drag while swimming.

- Their legs and feet are modified into flippers, which are great for swimming but make for poor maneuverability on land.

- Their legs are positioned on the margins of the body.

  The females must exert enormous effort to raise the body above the ground when they come ashore to lay their eggs. The males never come ashore.

Turtles that dwell in fresh water or brackish environments have slightly webbed feet but can travel considerable distances on land with no evident discomfort. Of course, those aquatic/brackish water turtles found more than a hundred yards or so from a pond or stream are probably females, intent on finding a spot to dig a nest and lay their eggs.

Turtles are toothless reptiles, but they're agile biters when the occasion warrants. Both the *mandible* (lower jaw) and the *maxilla* (upper jaw) bear a cutting edge, rather like a parrot's beak. Coupled with strong jaws, the turtle's mouth is an effective defense, and it can remove bite-sized pieces of vegetation, worms, fish, or almost anything the turtle think might be worth tasting.

Satisfying their hunger

Most terrestrial turtles chase after and consume fish, hunt down and eat grasshoppers, or nibble on grass, plants, shrubbery, and seeds. Aquatic turtles dine on plant life, insects, worms, fish, carrion, crustaceans, and hatchling birds, either pursuing their prey or eating opportunistically during the day.

Some turtles fish for their food with lures. One of the most impressive such creatures is the alligator snapping turtle. Snapping turtles as a group are chunky, craggy turtles with heavy armored shells, big heads, and an impressive beak. They can get up to 4 feet long and can live more than 25 years with good care. They're not agile turtles at any size, although the younger turtles do actively forage for insects, crayfish, earthworms, fish, and whatever living (or no longer living) animal or plant matter they think may be worth trying. As alligator snappers get older and bigger, they literally settle down. They don't need to be agile because they don't go after food — they let food come to them.

Inside the alligator snapping turtle's mouth, under the arched tongue, is a fleshy protuberance that is white or pale pink to gray. The snapper sits in the bottom of a pond or near a lakeshore. His dark shell is well concealed by the crags, rocks, and detritus on the floor of the pond. Comfortably situated, the snapper tilts his head back, opens his mouth, and lifts his tongue toward the roof of his mouth. The inside of his mouth is black .The paler lure under his tongue contrasts with the coloring of the mouth. Muscular contractions make the lure or "worm" move. As the fish darts into the jaws to investigate the lure, the jaw closes. These turtles capture about three-quarters of the fish that actually move in to bite the lure.

Finding a place in the sun

Turtles warm up by sunning themselves. Tortoises lie in the sun with their head and limbs extended and resting on the ground. The animal looks quite dead, which can be an unnerving sight unless you know what's going on. At night, tortoises may withdraw their limbs and head and sleep where they are. Others seek shelter under a bush, in a pile of brush, or inside their custom-made turtle house that you crafted for them.

Basking turtles — the sliders and cooters, the typical pet-trade turtles — crawl out of the water onto exposed logs or rocks. They stick their head high into the air and stretch their limbs out from their body, toes extended. With their dark skin exposed to the sun, body temperatures rise to performance levels (basking turtles sun or bask until their body temperature reaches a maximum of 95 degrees). The drying of the skin and shell has extra benefits: It prevents fungus infections and bacterial shell rot and dries up leeches. If a turtle's body temperature climbs above the comfort zone, cooling off is as easy as sliding off the log.

Out of sight, out of mind: Avoiding trouble

For young turtles, staying out of view is a good way to avoid becoming prey for another animal. One estimate is that 97 percent of all baby turtles die before they reach reproductive age, which is usually about 5 years. Baby turtles avoid predators by hiding in freshwater eelgrasses or floating vegetation. Baby bog turtles stay in boggy areas, where they hide in or under grass tussocks and under clumps of sphagnum moss. Most young turtles and tortoises are cryptically marked to help them blend in with their surroundings.

Adult turtles rely on alert attitudes, cryptic patterns, and secretive habits to avoid becoming prey. Alas, not one of them yet has figured out how to avoid being crushed by cars as they cross roadways. Two types of turtles add a pugnacious attitude to their repertoire of self-defense tactics:

✔ Snapping turtles open their mouth wide and sit quietly, watching their aggressor. Should the supposed predator come too close to their head, they strike out and try to grab with their mouth.

✔ Soft-shelled turtles have very long necks and are very ready to bite. If you hold one by any area other than the extreme back edge of the shell, you'll be within easy reach of the jaws.

Producing the next generation

All female turtles lay eggs in nests they dig on land, usually in moist soil. The hatching for each clutch of eggs seems to be *synchronous,* meaning the young turtles in a single nest emerge at about the same time.

When it comes time to lay their eggs, the aquatic and marine turtles emerge from the water onto land and seek a nesting spot. Some of these turtle species return to the same site each year to deposit their eggs; the site becomes a communal nesting ground where hundreds of female turtles lay their eggs each year. This behavior is typical of marine turtles and the side-neck turtles in South America. The sidenecked nesting sites are called *arribadas,* and once their location is known, animals and humans return regularly during the laying season to plunder the newest nests. For more information on breeding turtles, see the info in Chapters 14, 15, and 16.

Can you hear me now?

Turtles communicate with each other and try to communicate with you. Turtles eagerly come to the front of their tank, paddling in the water and keeping their eyes anxiously on your face, once they learn about feeding time. Tame tortoises will approach you, stand with legs straight, and extend their head to have the head and neck petted.

Tortoises bob their heads; if the other tortoise is a male, he'll respond with head bobs of his own, and eventually they may get down to butting each other with their shells (the clacking sound made travels a considerable distance) or even trying to bite each other. Desert tortoises, however, aren't ones to harbor ill feelings. Two males may fight, spend the night in the same burrow with no aggression, and continue the fight the next day.

The female tortoise, when encountering a male tortoise bobbing his head, doesn't bob back but retreats instead. Flushed with delight at finding a female, the male follows her and initiates courtship by ramming the female, scratching her shell, making grunting noises, and mounting her. He's not always successful, however. Maybe his technique is wrong, maybe the female is already pregnant, or maybe she's too young or just doesn't like the way he looks. Sexual rejection is a fact of life in the reptile world.

Never Trust the Smile of a Crocodile

Crocodilians (of which there are 22 species) are also reptiles. They're found in both subtropical and tropical regions. They're divided into two families: the alligators and caiman, and the crocodiles and gharials. Most crocodilians

---

Using magnets to keep crocodiles away

Crocodilians use magnetic cues to orient themselves, useful for a creature that may move great distances.

In Florida, recalcitrant crocodiles that *habitually* revisit human habitations are captured and relocated. Before they're turned loose, however, a magnet may be glued to the top of their head.

This interferes with the animal's homing ability, and the crocodile can't get back to where he is not welcome.

In contrast, recalcitrant alligators that hang around human habitation are classified as dangerous. They're removed and killed by a licensed alligator hunter.

---

have been hunted so persistently (for their meat and their hides and out of fear) that their populations are only remnants of what they once were. Conservation programs have brought some forms (such as the American alligator) from the verge of extinction to actual abundance, while other species seem poised to disappear forever.

Crocodilians are elongate lizardlike creatures, possessed of great strength (although they do tire quickly) and semiaquatic habits. Some choose weed-choked freshwater ponds and lakes, others prefer river habitats, and some are creatures of brackish and saltwater habitats. They're found in tropical environs worldwide, although one genus, *Alligator,* lives in the north temperate zone of Southeast Asia and the southeastern United States.

Crocodilians vary in size from the 5-foot dwarf caiman and dwarf crocodile to the 15-plus-foot American alligator and the saltwater crocodile. One of the largest saltwater crocodiles on display was Gomek, an 18 footer at the St. Augustine, Florida, Alligator Farm. (He's still there, but in stuffed form; he died at an estimated age of 70 to 80 years.) Larger crocodilians can be dangerous adversaries of humans, and some African and Australasian species are noted people eaters.

Exploring the croc anatomy, or keeping your hands to yourself

All crocodilians have four strong limbs, thick skin, a sweeping tail they use aggressively, immensely powerful jaws, keen eyesight, and an inordinate ability to utilize the tiniest patch of suitable habitat to their advantage. Because their nasal passages are separate from the mouth, they can breathe while submerged, with only the tip of the snout protruding, something a prey animal may not realize until it's too late.

Bony plates called *osteoderms* or *osteoscutes* lie under their skin. These plates are on the back, side, and head. Those on the head fuse with the skull bones to form a very strong skull. The position and number of plates affect the usefulness of their hides; the smooth belly area is used for leather goods, so the skin is generally split down the back for removal. Trade in crocodilian hides is restricted, although commercial hunting of the American alligator is allowed.

Enjoying the night life: The crocodilian lifestyle

Crocodilians are active by night and by day, but daytime activities are pretty much limited to basking. If you've been to an alligator farm, you've seen alligators lying around like overinflated pool toys, remarkable in their realistic molding. But should a duck accidentally land in the pen with the alligators, they would come to life with remarkable speed.

Crocodilians emerge from their den or seclusion area after sunset, and spend most of their night foraging. You can spot them at night with a flashlight — their eyes reflect yellow.

Sending signals croc-style: Real vibrations

Crocodilians signal visually over short distances and use sounds for longer distances. Males bellow each morning, partially to locate each other and to identify any intruders. They generally call with their bodies submerged, and the water over their back vibrates like crazy, as if it's being pelted by raindrops.

When an intruder comes into a crocodilian's turf, the at-home male lifts his head and tail partly out of the water and watches the intruder. This motion is followed by short chases, lunges, and real or not-so-real fights. The defender of the home turf inflates his body to look large. Like the mythical fire-breathing dragon, the crocodilian blows water out of his nostrils. Alligators in particular accompany this nose-blowing display by lifting their head up and smacking it on the water at the same time. This motion helps the nostril spray go farther, an impressive sight for the intruder. (Can anyone hand that gator a tissue?)

Crocodilian motherhood — laying eggs and caring for the young

Female crocodilians lay their eggs in piles of brush or rotting vegetation, to help incubate the young and speed the incubation. Anywhere from 6 to 60 eggs can be laid in a clutch, with the large species of crocodilians laying more eggs. Larger crocodilians also lay more eggs than smaller crocodilians of the same species.

The female stays with the clutch, guarding it against intruders. When the first young begin to hatch, they make peeping sounds, a little like a mix between a cat's muted snarl and the peep of a chick. The mother digs up the nest, gently mouths the eggs to help them open, and then carries the young in her mouth to water. She may stay with the young for a few months — they lounge around on her back as she floats in the water — and nobody bothers them at all.

Crocodiles rock — but not as pets!

Crocodilians are attractive creatures, with their nubby texture, sharp teeth and bright wary eyes, but they sure aren't manageable as pets. They need huge aquatic enclosures that must be kept scrupulously clean. (Even very big captive crocodilians die if their water isn't clean.) They need food and lots of it, and that means that soon their caging will need to be drained, scrubbed, rinsed, and refilled. They don't like humans, and they don't see any reason to change that attitude. They're aggressive. A few types, the Cuban crocodiles in particular, are adept at climbing even chain link fences.

Amphisbaenians

A separate grouping of about 140 species of reptiles, the amphisbaenians are often referred to as worm lizards (see Figure 3-4). Most are limbless and have barely functional eyes that are covered by skin. Four Mexican species have two strongly-clawed forelimbs so far forward on the body that the legs look more like multispiked ears than legs! They're subtropical to tropical species, found in central Florida, Mexico, South America, part of the western Mediterranean, and Africa.

Worm lizards live underground and only rarely emerge, usually being driven out of their terrestrial world by heavy rains. I've seen only one, dug up by a neighbor in his yard in St. Petersburg, Florida. It looked like a 9-inch-long pink annulated (meaning the body is segmented in rings that encircle the body) earthworm, and it moved very slowly and awkwardly. They don't live long once above ground. Worm lizards are rarely available even in specialized pet markets. Once in a while, someone will import one or two of the bigger South American types; these eat small mammals in addition to insects and worms. All are fossorial and very secretive and are better off left in the soil where they belong.

Figure 3-4:
Worm lizards are burrowers and rarely come to the surface.

Rhynchocephalia

The final grouping of reptiles is the Rhynchocephalia, or beak-headed reptiles. The family is of truly ancient lineage (fossils of Rhynchocephalians 220 million years old have been found), and today it contains two extraordinary species that are limited in distribution to islands off the coast of New Zealand. Both are often referred to as tuataras or by their generic name of *Sphenodon*.

Here's the surprise: They look like lizards, but they really aren't lizards. They are morphologically distinctly different. In addition, they are adapted to cool temperatures (typical night foraging temperatures are 54 to 59 degrees), are largely nocturnal, and dwell in burrows. They are brownish in color, usually with a profusion of white specking, and have a noticeable vertebral crest, four powerful legs, and eyes with dual retinas, presumably an adaptation for both day and night vision.

They're incredibly protected, and only a very few are in zoos. Next time you're in San Francisco, Dallas, or St. Louis, check out the tuatara display. If you're lucky, you'll be able to see them, but these aren't charismatic creatures, mugging for the next camera shot. They're nocturnal tunnel dwellers.

Chapter 4

Tailed or Not: The Basic Amphibian

For some reason, people don't like slimy things, but when it comes to slimy, amphibians (think frogs, salamanders, and such) have all the bases covered. Not only do they feel slimy, but for them, slime is the staff of life. It keeps their skin from drying out, and it helps ward off predators, both because the amphibian can slip right out of the predator's grasp and because the slime is noxious or even toxic.

In this chapter, you find out how salamanders, sirens, frogs, toads, and caecilians are alike and how they differ from each other. You also find out how big these creatures get (one salamander can grow to 5 feet long) and how small some of them are (some newly metamorphosed toads are only a quarter-inch from nose to vent, so mind where you put your feet). But first, the following section presents the characteristics that make amphibians amphibians. Check out the appendix for the skinny on specific amphibian species.

Now, Isn't That Special?

When it comes to color, amphibians cover all the bases. Few creatures are more beautiful than the poison-dart frogs, tiny frogs that come in several colors — green and black, blue and black, yellow and black, and red — and hop around on the ground in the rain forests of South America. Or consider the scarlet-orange red efts, the terrestrial life stage of the red-spotted newt, when they leave their ponds and wander by day or by night. Another colorful amphibian is the bat cave phase of the Yonolosee salamander, with its black-and-white spangled back clouded with a russet veil, a bit like a redux van Gogh's Starry Night in a mobile form?

In amphibians, the colors are formed by special coloring-containing cells that open up or close as temperature and mood dictate. Those cells that contain the yellow pigment are *xanthophores,* those that contain a light-reflecting pigment that can be silvery or blue are called *iridiophores,* and those that contain black cells are *melanophores.* Amphibians haven't been bred for special colors and patterns nearly as much as reptiles, but you can find some captive-bred albino salamanders and a few blue-hued frogs.

If oddball body modifications are your shtick, hang on to your hat. Amphibians are already unique in their dramatic larval versus adult body shapes, like in the case of tadpoles and frogs. But sometimes larval amphibians change their appearance within a single species. The tadpoles of the Western subspecies of spadefoot toads, *Scaphiophus hammondii,* are opportunistically carnivorous or herbivorous — in the same pond. They eat plant life, tiny insects, and each other. This dietary practice sort of evens out the food supply. There are also two forms of tiger salamander larvae. The form that switches to vertebrate prey — including in some cases, its siblings! — is morphologically different from the boring old herbivorous form. Its body shape changes on its carnivorous diet — the head widens, the mouth gets broader, another row of teeth develops, and, in some populations, the teeth become curved.

Recognizing Characteristics of Amphibians

Most amphibians live a double life, starting out as aquatic gill-bearing hatchlings and then undergoing a metamorphosis to terrestrial adults with lungs. The word amphibian is a combination of "amphi," meaning "two," and "bian," which translates as "life." Thus, the resulting word means "two lives."

All amphibians share some common characteristics, including the following:

✔ They have a scaleless skin that may be smooth or warty, but is usually smooth. The skin contains glands, both to keep the skin moist and for defense.

✔ Amphibian eggs are encased in a gelatinous envelope when laid. They must be kept moist until they hatch into gill-bearing larvae, which are different in appearance from the adult.

✔ Amphibians experience metamorphosis when they lose their tails and take on their adult form, complete with lungs.

✔ They're *ectothermic,* meaning that they depend on outside sources of heat or coolness for their own body temperatures.

As adults, *most* amphibians have the following characteristics:

✔ They have four limbs, or traces thereof (all the better to climb with, my dear).

✔ They're usually nocturnal, to avoid the higher daytime temperatures and the lower daytime humidity. They may also avoid a lot of predators by being active at night.

Most amphibians start out as herbivores but switch to being carnivores as adults, eating insects, along with earthworms, spiders, millipedes, and centipedes when available. Those amphibians that aren't herbivores as larvae are, of course, carnivorous.

Revealing the skinny on amphibian skin

The amphibians' skin protects the amphibian from drying out, protects against predators, and contains a coloration system that can light up like a Christmas tree. Their skin also contains sensory organs. Aquatic salamanders have a lateral line system, like fish, although the *neuromasts* (bundles of sensory cells that lie at the bottom of tiny pits in the skin) are arranged singly or in groups on the head and body, instead of being in a lateral line as they are in fish.

A sensory projection called the *cupula* extends from the center of each bundle of cells, above the edges of the pit. In cross-section, the neuromast and cupula look like a sprouted onion. The neuromasts sense mechanical actions, such as tiny changes in the water current. Wave your hand in the water over an aquatic salamander, and he'll know you're there and, from the size of the water displacement, how big your hand is.

Amphibian skin is permeable (the skin in the pelvic area of the frogs is especially so), so it can absorb water — it can even absorb water from the soil, a characteristic absolutely unique among vertebrates and very important to amphibians' survival. There are even special skin cells that secrete a sticky substance that helps a male frog "stick" to the female during the mating grasp, or *amplexus.* (I *knew* you wondered about that!)

Never handle your salamanders (or any amphibian or reptile) if you have recently applied an insecticide, skin cream, or any other chemical to your hands, or if you've been smoking. With amphibians, smoke doesn't get into their eyes but goes into their skin. Most of these are immediately fatal to amphibians and harmful or fatal to reptiles.

Unleashing the power of poison

Amphibians have one real defense against predation, and that's the noxious quality of their skin secretions or actual toxins (see Figure 4-1). The noxious secretions simply tell a predator to back off; the toxic secretions are fatal. Both are produced by specialized glands, called *granular glands.* These glands may be scattered across the surface of the skin, as they are in the dart frogs *(Dendrobates),* or concentrated in the parotoid glands, as in the toads, familiarly called Bufos because they're members of the genus *Bufo.*

Figure 4-1:
The skin of the Cuban treefrog exudes toxin to discourage predators.

The toxin varies from amphibian family to amphibian family. Toads tend to keep most of their noxious secretions in their parotoid glands (those swollen raised areas behind the opening of the ear) or in glands on their legs. Toads keep enemies at bay by lowering their head, elevating their hips, and butting the threatening would-be predator. This brings the oozing parotoid glands in direct contact with the predator, who usually hastily backs off. (Dogs who try to gnaw on giant toads, *Bufo marinus,* may die from ingesting the secretions from the parotoid glands.) Salamanders possess noxious skin secretions.

If an amphibian's noxious or toxic defense is not effective against a group of predators, that amphibian gets eaten or, to put it more scientifically, is removed from the gene pool permanently.

TECHNICAL STUFF

Name your poison

Toxins are named for the animal that possesses it. The toxins are effective against the amphibians' usual predators. When testing of these toxins began, it was discovered that they can be vaguely effective or extremely effective even against creatures that are not the enemy of the amphibian.

Humans measure the efficacy of toxins by what's called an LD50 dose. This is the dose required to kill half, or 50 percent, of the white lab mice it is injected into. The LD50 gives us a way to measure and compare different toxins, from botulism to snake venoms to amphibian toxins. In amphibians, the amount of toxin produced by a single animal can seem like overkill. The rough-skinned newt, *Taricha granulosum*, possesses tarichatoxin, and a single adult newt contains enough of this toxin to kill 25,000 white mice. But not all toxins kill when tested. When injected, the toxin from the *Pseudotriton* salamanders, called pseudotoxin, messes with the ability of mice to stay warm, causing severe *hypothermia* (lowering of the mice's basal temperature).

One of the best-known noxious amphibians is the Cuban treefrog. Introduced from the West Indies in the 1950s, the Cuban treefrog has made its way up the Florida peninsula. It would be singing on the Georgia border today if it weren't for the periodic winter freezes that kill off any specimens that have moved too far northward or who can't find secure enough shelter to wait out the cold. The Cuban treefrogs have a noxious skin secretion that is particularly memorable if you handle one and then rub your eyes or touch your lips without washing your hands first. Your eyes will burn and tear, and your lips will burn until the effect wears off.

The defenses that a frog or toad may possess can sometimes have unexpected results when a "non-enemy" encounters that species. The Colorado river toad (also called the Sonoran desert toad) can paralyze the dog that mouths the frog.

There are far more noxious amphibians than there are toxic amphibians. Although not every toxin or noxious secretion has been tested against every potential predator, those that have been tested are pretty effective. For instance, the toxin produced by the aquatic caecilian *Typhlonectes compressicauda* is toxic to a predatory fish that feeds on Typhlonectes.

Keeping moist: Strategies that work

Amphibians have developed a number of ways to avoid losing moisture and ways to regain moisture that's been lost (see Figure 4-2).

Figure 4-2:
The Yucatan shovel-nosed treefrog uses his bony head to plug the opening of his burrow.

They stay moist by retreating to small hiding areas during the daytime that are moister than open areas. Salamanders may retreat into burrows, either of their own making or made by other animals. They may rest in *aggregations* (groups). Subadult tiger salamanders *(Abystoma tigrium),* for example, rest in tightly packed groupings that provide less exposed surface area than an individual alone would. Those in the aggregation lose moisture at a slower rate than individual salamanders not in an aggregation.

Skin secretions help reduce moisture loss, especially in frogs. Leaf frogs, the *Phyllomedusa* frogs, secrete lipids — a waxlike substance — and use their front and hind feet to spread the lipids over the surface of the body. Once waxed up, the South American frogs sink into torpor as they rest in bushes. The lipids decrease water loss by 5 to 10 percent.

Some amphibians become dormant when conditions become too dry for survival. Dormancy also reduces the need for oxygen, sometimes to only 20 percent of what an active amphibian needs, and the lungs handle the respiration needs.

One specialized type of dormancy involves the formation of a protective cocoon around the animal. For example, the South American dwarf Budgett's frog, *(Lepidobatrachus llanensis)* burrows into mud at the bottom of a drying pond and goes into a quick-shed status. The skins form a protective cocoon, and Budgett's can form thick cocoons. Under laboratory conditions that simulate a drying pond, the dwarf Budgett's can shed daily for up to 40 days, ending up with a cocoon made of 40 shed skins. The South African bullfrog *(Pyxacephalus adspersus)* can also form a cocoon to avoid desiccation, but even with the cocoon, the frog within may lose from 20 to 50 percent of its body weight. The sirens, a group of aquatic salamanders, typically burrow into the mud at the bottom of their pond and form a cocoon to avoid drying out. The only portion that's exposed is the mouth.

Sometimes animals have a simple way to keep moisture in the body. The casque-headed frogs, *Smilisca,* have bony heads where the skin is directly fused to the skull. Evaporative loss through this surface is much less than through their body surface. They back into crevices, tree holes, or bromeliads and plug the opening with the top of their head. They not only stay moist during the day but are also hidden from predators.

Bufos in arid areas store water in their bladder, and use this water to maintain their body functions when the weather turns dry. But voiding the bladder on a predator (or an unsuspecting human) is a typical amphibian/reptile defense. For an animal in the wild, losing bladder moisture poses a risk to its survival (captive animals become accustomed to being picked up and this behavior will stop — besides, captives can replace that lost moisture via their water dish).

Frogs that are active by day live in humid areas (typical examples are the dart frogs *Dendrobates* and *Phyllobates* and most of the *Colostheus*) or where water is freely available as spray from a mountain stream (such as the *Atelopus*). Indeed, the only *Atelopus* I've found in the wild was resting on a patch of moss on the trunk of a tree, just a few feet away from the spray of a hissing mountain stream.

Toads alter their body chemistry when conditions become drier, so they lose less water. The burrowing toads of the genus *Scaphiophus* (they have a digging "claw" on each back foot, hence their common name) store urea (normally a waste product) in their body fluids during dry times. When the rains return, the urea is excreted.

Lost and found: Regaining moisture

That versatile skin allows amphibians to resorb water at an amazing rate, and they can do this on a daily basis if necessary. One of the Australian burrowing frogs, *Heleioporous eyrei,* typically loses up to 22 percent of its body mass while foraging at night. During the day, it rests in spots that allow it to rehydrate.

Salamanders

Salamanders are long-bodied, four-legged amphibians that are most common in temperate areas of the Northern Hemisphere. About 400 kinds of salamanders exist. (Compare this to the 4,000 species of frogs, which are found in more places across the world than the salamanders.)

Included within the ranks of salamanders are the following:

- Typical salamanders, such as the tiger salamander
- Giant salamanders, such as the 5-foot long Chinese salamander and the smaller hellbender
- Amphiuma, heavy-bodied aquatic salamanders with weakly developed limbs
- Water dogs, robust salamanders with well-developed limbs and gills
- Sirens, slender, small salamanders with tiny forelimbs and no hind limbs
- Newts, rough-skinned salamanders with very toxic skin secretions

Salamanders are categorized or defined by their range, coloration, and size (measured from snout to vent — the tail is not included). The presence and number of the *costal ridges* (the segment-looking ridges along the torso that make it look like the Michelin tire man) also figures in the identification process.

Common names, such as salamander and newt, can be confusing. One of the reasons behind scientific names is that common names can change from area to area and country to country. In the United States, people use the term "newt" for either the Pacific newts *(Taricha)* or the red-spotted newt *(Notophthalmus);* everything else is a "salamander." Across the ocean, in England, the term "newt" means an aquatic salamander, while the terrestrial versions are called salamanders!

Salamanders have legs, but they don't travel great distances. Some are aquatic, a few are somewhat arboreal, and a few are efficient burrowers, but all need moisture to survive. Some types have no lungs, absorbing their oxygen through their skin. Salamanders hide by day and forage and travel when the sun goes down.

If you'd like to see these animals in the wild, in the springtime, go into the woods from midnight to about 2 a.m. The best places to look are the Appalachian mountains in the east, from northern Georgia through New England, and the mountains in the Pacific Northwest. Use your flashlight to spot salamanders as they walk in the woods or as they forage in ponds.

Salamanders have tails throughout their lives. The salamander's tail serves as a place for fat storage. Terrestrial salamanders use the tail for balancing, and the aquatic species use the tail for propulsion and steering. When salamanders argue over territory, the tail is a target and sometimes is torn off, decreasing that salamander's chances of survival. It really is survival of the fittest out there in the wild.

Creating baby salamanders

The more primitive salamander families have external fertilization; the female lays the eggs, and the male then fertilizes the egg mass. Two of the more primitive salamanders are found in Asia and live in torrent-filled mountain streams. These mountain stream salamanders have slight bodies, so they won't be swept away by the water. They have reduced or no lungs at all, just like some of the mountainous salamanders in the United States, because the cool water that rushes over them is loaded with oxygen. That cool water means a cool body temperature, resulting in a reduced metabolic rate and a reduced (but not eliminated) need for food.

The more advanced families have internal fertilization. Whether the salamanders have internal or external fertilization, most salamanders return to their natal (birth) ponds or streams to lay their eggs.

Spotted salamanders of the eastern United States are pretty typical of the advanced internal fertilization group. Some spotted populations, like those in Massachusetts, each meet for a localized breeding session that may last for two to three days, and that's it for the year. This means that large breeding congregations return to their home ponds — the ponds where they were hatched — in the very early spring, with the males usually arriving before the females.

Individuals often arrive in the same order, year after year. The arrivals usually occur under cover of darkness. The males get to work first. They deposit their spermatophores (up to 40 per breeding session, in this case appearing as a gelatinous stalks topped with sperm) on the bottom of the pond and await the arrival of the females. Courtship is pretty much limited to the males nudging the females with their chin. The females move around the pond and use the lips of their cloacas to pick up a spermatophore here and a spermatophore there, picking up the contents of 15 to 20 before concluding breeding. When the breeding session is completed, the spotteds leave the pond, frequently at the same point they entered it, and retrace their pathways back to their home ranges.

Show me the way to go home

How either sex can find its natal/breeding site is still unknown. Spotteds, for example, can return to their ponds after being relocated as far as 540 yards (500 meters), although the process may take up to 11 days. Researchers have shown that spotteds can differentiate between odors from their home ponds and odors from other ponds, and they move toward their home pond odors. Olfaction seems to play a major role in the spotteds finding their way to their breeding ponds and back to their home ponds.

But something else is certainly at work. The Pacific newts, from a completely different family than the spotteds, have a remarkable homing instinct. When taken out of their breeding stream and released up to 5 miles (8 kilometers) away, Pacific newts can find their way back, even when blinded. Olfaction, celestial clues, and what is described as kinesthetic orientation (a sensation/recognition of an animal's position in relation to a site), play a role, but the most likely role is played by magnetic orientation. The fact that a blind animal can orient to celestial cues indicates that some sense other than eyesight is involved, and the pineal gland (the rudimentary light sensing organ between the eyes that does much more than sensing light or dark) appears to intricately involved.

Interestingly enough, most migrations back to the breeding pond or stream occur on rainy or overcast nights, when visual celestial orientation would not be possible. The orientation question is one of the many puzzles about amphibians.

Home, home on the range

Many salamanders have home ranges, a turf they wander in their search for food and interlopers. Factors that govern the size of a range are the size of the animal and available food and water. Some salamanders, such as the *plethodontids* (the lungless salamanders), mark the limits of their home ranges by scenting with pheromones. They may recognize the pheromones placed by neighboring salamanders and are less aggressive toward those salamanders than they are toward unfamiliar salamanders.

The home ranges can be surprisingly small, and can overlap with those of other individuals. That of the spotted salamander may vary from 4.3 yards on a side during nonbreeding season (the movement of some salamanders during the breeding season may take them out of their home range entirely) to 38 yards on a side. The range size of the ensatina salamander, *Ensatina eschscholtzii,* is determined by sex; the typical male's range averages 1,550 square yards, while a female's range averages 408 square yards. Other terrestrial plethodontids have no sexual differences in home ranges. Stream-dwelling salamanders have home ranges, limited to a lineal length and the width of their stream. The burrowing salamanders have a vertical range, determined by the size and configuration of their tunnel. The mole salamander, *Ambystoma talpoideum,* digs a burrow that may be 7 inches deep.

Other salamanders don't have home ranges, and they wander wherever they feel like going. The eastern red-spotted newt, *Notophthalmus viridescens,* which is frequently sold in pet stores, is one of these wanderers. *Notophthalmus* is also known for its compatibility in community tank settings, and its lack of a territorial urge may be one reason for this compatibility.

Stayin' alive

Salamanders have developed a number ways to avoid getting eaten by something larger than they are (see Figure 4-3). Along with cryptic coloration, secretive habits, and nocturnal movements, they may feign death if threatened. Sirens, the skinny, eyelid-less salamanders, are burrowers, preferring to hide under thick mats of sphagnum or in the root masses of floating plants. If you shake a handful of water hyacinths over a window screen placed at the water's edge, you may be surprised at what falls out.

Some salamanders can actively employ their toxins to defend themselves. For example, the European fire salamander, *Salamandra salamandra,* can actually squirt the contents of its toxin-secreting granular glands, but the salamander can't control the direction of the discharge.

Salamanders may also freeze in place and display the *unken response* (a defensive or warning pose) in which the back is arched and the brightly colored underside of the feet or tail is elevated and displayed. The red eft stage of the red-spotted newt, *Notophthalmus viridescens,* may go into an unken display if frightened. The display of *aposematic* (contrasting bright and dark colors) coloring is usually a warning that the animal possesses toxic qualities.

Other salamanders try to look bigger, a little hard to do when you're 2 inches long and the width of a pencil. The mud salamander, *Pseudotriton montanus,* curls into a circle and lashes and writhes his tail while the head is hidden under his body, a display intended to make a predator back off. The tail may be discarded as a distraction; like a dropped lizard tail, the salamander tail jerks and flips while its former owner moves quietly away.

Figure 4-3:
A fire-bellied toad, like the salamander, displays the bright soles of his feet in a warning — I'm toxic — reflex.

Another salamander, the California slender salamander, *Batrachoseps attenuatus,* coils around the neck of an attacking garter snake, making it impossible for the snake to continue swallowing. At the same time, the salamander exudes a very thick sticky substance, which adheres to the snake and everything it touches (except the salamander!).

Speaking without a voice

At least one kind of salamander, the Pacific giant salamander, *Dicamptodon ensatus,* has vocal cords. Some plethodontid salamanders can make soft squeaking sounds, and the sounds produced by other salamanders (Taricha and Ambystona, to name just two) have been defined as defense mechanisms and as an aid to orientation.

Frogs: Hoppers and Leapers

Frogs are four-legged amphibians especially adapted for jumping, with enlarged hind legs. They generally emerge from eggs as tadpoles and live in water for one week to five weeks before they metamorphose into adults. They're grouped into 27 families and are distributed worldwide in temperate and tropical areas.

Roughly 4,200 species of frogs exist, and if you want to can see the most kinds in one place, head to Manu Park in southeast Peru. In this single park, some 70 species of frogs have been identified. (Getting there is easier than you might think. You fly from Miami, land in Lima, take a connecting flight to Cusco, and board a boat for Manu.)

As adults, frogs are tailless, which is why they're called *anurans,* meaning "tailless." They have short bodies and broad flat heads with big mouths. Their vertebrae and substantial pelvic girdle absorb the impact of landing. You've heard of frog-jumping contests (bullfrogs are usually the frog of choice for such contests, simply because of availability, not for any special skill at the task). A good jumper can leap 20 times its body length, and a few species can blast off for a jump that's twice that length. Having a body adapted for jumping means that walking is clumsy. Frogs prefer making short hops over walking.

Frogs by and large eat insects and other invertebrates. What gets eaten largely depends on size — smaller animals eat smaller prey items. Frogs that are large enough will opportunistically eat hatchling birds or rodents when available.

WARNING!

I used to feed prekilled white mice to my pet horned frogs until I realized what that high-fat diet was doing to their eyes and internal organs. Fats, or *lipids*, are deposited in both areas, affecting their eyesight and obstructing organs function. Earthworms are a safe diet.

Unlike salamanders, who forage for their food, frogs are more the wait-and-pounce types, resting quietly on the forest floor (or under debris on the forest floor) or in shallow water until food comes flying, swimming, or walking by. Then the mouth opens, and the wonderfully agile tongue flips out and snags the prey. (Except for the pipid frog, the tongue of a frog is secured at the front of the mouth, not at the back like yours.) The tongue and prey are withdrawn faster than most of us can see, and the food item is quietly chewed in the frog's mouth until it's flat enough to swallow. Not all frogs gather their food in this style, however. Pipid frogs, for example, with their tongues attached at the back of their mouth, can't stick their tongue out to grab prey. They end up waiting until prey comes by, and then they greedily stuff it into their little mouths with their forefeet.

Some frogs do have teeth, and some of them have very strong jaws. A few species (such as the horned frogs) also have structures called odontoid teeth, which are bony projections from the roof of the mouth that both pierce and hold prey items.

Mating and reproducing

Frogs, as a group, are one of the voiced amphibians. They use one call as a distress call, and another as an advertising call to attract females during the breeding season (see Figure 4-4). The calls are species specific; no leopard frog, for instance, is going to be attracted to the bullfrog's call. The males themselves get excited when they call, and if a likely looking female (or, as I've observed, a cow chip of the right size) comes floating by, they'll leap aboard.

Figure 4-4:
The bullfrog's large eardrum helps him discern between calls of other male bullfrogs and frogs of other species.

Calling is usually triggered by the drop in barometric pressure that accompanies rainfall, or by a combination of warmer temperatures and rainfall. Frogs in tropical areas may breed year-round. Females are attracted by the calls, and the loudest call is the most attractive. (I'm not drawing any parallels with human courtship patterns or karaoke singing in bars.)

Some species have built-in amplifiers, called vocal sacs. These single or double outpouchings of the mouth cavity expand as the frog calls, sometimes looking like miniature water wings, swelling and then collapsing under the throat. Other frogs can use natural settings to broadcast or amplify their calls. Cundall's robber frog, *Eleutherodactylus cundalli,* calls only from limestone caves and crannies. The Borneo treefrog *(Metaphrynella sundana)* sits in water within a tree cavity. When advertising for a female ("1 inch long, nice legs, good reproductive capacity, brown eyes"), he raises and lowers the pitch of his calls until he hits the pitch that resonates within his tree cavity. The best calling gets the female — plenty enough reason to keep at the process until he gets the call right.

Once the frog has found Ms. Right, he generally positions himself behind her. Some types grasp the female from behind under her armpits or around her waist in a gesture called *amplexus.* As the female lays her eggs, the male fertilizes them. Other types have no direct contact with the female but fertilize the eggs after they've been laid.

Sometimes the eggs are expressed into a pool of water where they float or are entwined in vegetation. The eggs may be laid on land, in a moisture-retaining cavity like the trunks of bromeliads or hollowed cavities in a tree. In what is described as a trend toward terrestrial life (and I'd call a huge leap of faith), some species, such as the Asian olive frog *(Rana adenopleura),* lay their eggs out of the water and depend on seasonal flooding to trigger hatching. The tadpoles swim away to complete their development.

Frogs have demonstrated a remarkable adaptive ability to increase the probability of their eggs hatching. Some species lay eggs that possess enough yolk to nourish the tadpole once it hatches. The foam-nest builders (primarily tropical in distribution) create a foam nest above a pond on directly on the water's surface by churning body fluids and water. The eggs are laid within the foam. Once the tadpoles hatch, they wriggle out of the nest and drop into the water.

The dart frogs get gold stars when it comes to parental care. Several of the dart frogs, including *Dendrobates auratus,* the green-and-black dart frog, and *Epipidobates tricolor,* the Phantasmal dart frog, provide parental care. The females lay the eggs, and the male fertilizes them and stays with the nest until the eggs hatch. He stands over the tadpoles, and they slither onto his back. He transports them to water, where they leave him and undergo growth and metamorphosis. The females of other species of dart frog lay their eggs in the trunks of bromeliads and return at regular intervals to lay infertile eggs for the young tadpoles to consume. *Dendrobates pumilo,* the strawberry frog, and *Dendrobates historionicus,* the harlequin dart frog, are two of those dart frog species.

Experiencing growing pains: Metamorphosis

Metamorphosis is the name used to describe the body changes that turn a larvae, whether a water-breathing tadpole or salamander, into an air-breathing, carnivorous adult frog or adult salamander. Within the space of a week or so, here's what happens:

1. The legs complete development.

2. Eyelids and the mouth complete development.

3. The tail and gills are degenerated.

4. The digestive system undergoes a massive reorganization, and the intestine is shortened.

5. The lung tissues are readied to assume major respiratory function.

6. For those frogs that have toxic skin qualities, those qualities develop.

And in case you were wondering, Table 4-1 can help you tell the difference between salamander babies and tadpoles.

Table 4-1	Salamander Larvae or Tadpole?
Salamander Larvae	*Tadpole*
3 pairs of gills	2 pairs of gills
Long body, two-thirds of total length	Short body, less than half the total length
No adhesive organ on head	Adhesive organ on head
Tentacle-like balancers on underside of head	No balancers
Large mouth	Small mouth
No operculum (gill-covering skin) covers gills	Operculum folds soon cover gills
Front leg buds clearly visible throughout development	Front leg buds concealed until metamorphosis

The time a tadpole spends as a tadpole depends on the type of frog and, to some degree, on the environmental factors such as temperature and food. The spadefoot toads, *Scaphiophus,* are remarkable in their rapid tadpole development (6 to 8 days or as long as 32 days, depending on the type of spadefoot). The bullfrog, *Rana catesbeiana,* spends 14 to 16 months as a tadpole. The tadpole hatches in the spring but may not undergo metamorphosis until after the third winter.

Caecilians

Caecilians (pronounced *see sil-ians*) are amphibians that, as a group, we don't know much about. They look a bit like a cross between a snake and an earthworm. They are legless and smooth-skinned but bear annular, or ringlike, grooves around the body — sort of like a very large earthworm. There are both terrestrial and aquatic forms. They range in size from about a yard for some of the South American species, to a three-incher found in the Seychelles Islands in the South Pacific. At least two species can produce clicking sounds, but we don't know what these sounds may indicate. They have a few defensive behaviors: They can "spit" copious quantities of water, and when disturbed and handled, they exude large amounts of mucous, which makes them hard to hold on to. Large adults are capable of painful bites. Caecilians are secretive and very good at burrowing. Those found above ground have probably been driven up by heavy rains that flood their burrows. They have small eyes that are covered by skin or bone. Those few in the pet trade are aquatic, retiring, and a muddy gray.

Bearing baby caecilians

Caecilians reproduce through internal fertilization. Some caecilians are *oviparous* (meaning that they lay eggs); others are *viviparous* (they bear live young). Although courtship is unknown and only a few matings have been observed, the young are born in an advanced stage of metamorphosis — they look like miniature versions of the adults, except for the addition of gills. Those developing young, the fetuses of the viviparous species, are nourished within the body of the female as they develop, but the technique is a bit unusual. The young use specialized temporary teeth to scrape the lining of the oviduct for nutrition secreted by the cells lining the oviduct, the passage leading form the ovary through which eggs pass prior to fertilization. These teeth are shed at birth, when the young go on to nibble on tiny creatures such as bloodworms, tubifex worms, very small insects, and aquatic crustaceans, the same things the oviparous caecilians eat.

Examining some physical caecilian traits

Some species have a few scales in their annular grooves; scales are something no amphibian is supposed to have. (Admittedly, we humans selected the characteristics that separate reptiles from amphibians, so we can't be aghast that some animals don't exactly fit our profiles.) A *protrusible* (capable of being protruded) sensory tentacle is located between the eye and the nostril on each side of the head. These tentacles are used to locate and identify prey. Like a snake's tongue, as the tentacle is protruded and withdrawn, odor particles stick to the tentacle and are transported from the tentacle to the Jacobson's organ for interpretation.

Part II

Finding Your Herp and Setting Up Shop

The 5th Wave   By Rich Tennant

"I built the iguana cage myself. He seems to like the chandelier over his food bowl, but we're replacing the sconces over the fireplace with recessed mood spots."

In this part . . .

When selecting a pet that can easily live for 20 years or more, you need to make certain that you know what you're getting into. In this section, you get tips on how to locate and acquire the herp that's best for you. If you're a little hesitant to reach right in and pick that critter up, herein are tips on how to do it — and why handling it may not always be in your herp's best interest. Certainly you want to know what kind of caging is best for your herp, and that's in here as well, along with information on lighting and temperature control. If you need to move or transport your herp, you can find several tricks of the trade on how to safely get your herp from one place to another.

Chapter 5

Finding the Herp of Your Dreams

In This Chapter

▶ Looking at various sources of herps

▶ Getting a herp from far away

▶ Considering other factors before buying a herp

Deciding which herp to start with — which one is the right one for you — can be confusing. It's like deciding which flavor of ice cream is best (so many kinds, so little time, so many calories!). I don't think that there is just one right herp for anyone, but I do think that, like ice cream, starting with just one is the best approach.

This chapter helps you find out how to shop for your herp and gives you the true story on importers, dealers, professional breeders, backyard breeders, and pet shops. I've purchased from all of these venues, and the 3 percent rule runs true here. This rule says that 3 percent of the people in the world are jerks. As long as you know this and know what to watch out for, you'll be fine. I also talk about why adoption, meaning taking in an unwanted herp from a rescue agency or even from your local herp society, can be a good idea, although it's more work and may be more expensive but could end up being less costly than your other options.

The soon-to-be herp owner has choices beyond just where to *buy* a herp — you also have to decide whether you want

- ✔ Captive born or wild caught
- ✔ Male or female
- ✔ Adult or young

The information in this chapter will help you make the right choice.

Exploring Places to Purchase Your Herp

Most of us have a favorite way of doing something, and we're pretty much convinced our approach is the best. Herpers are no different. Each of us knows the best way to find the herp we're looking for. I describe the four sources I've used, and then you can decide which sounds the best to you. The source you find the absolute best one time may not be your best route the next time. But for beginners, the easiest way (and quite likely the least expensive) is to go to your local pet store (you can join a tour of Borneo and go looking at frogs later).

Before you grab your keys and blast out the door, stop. If you're going out to buy (you're not simply browsing — you're coming home with a herp), you need to have the caging set up for your animal so that when you come home, he can go into that caging. Chapter 7 tells you all you need to know about getting set up.

Suppose that you want an easy-to-care-for lizard that's personable and not too big. So you do your research and you come up with an African fat-tailed gecko, *Hemitheconyx caudicinctus.* This variety is on the large side (for a gecko), about 6 to 9 inches long. It's milk chocolate and bittersweet chocolate brown and has an irresistible velvetlike texture to its skin. It eats crickets and talks to other geckos in soft clicks. Where do you go to get one? The following sections present typical choices, whether you want a gecko or any other type of herp.

No matter where you shop for your herp, assess the appearance of the animal's caging (see Table 5-1). You want an animal that's in good condition, right? Cleanliness is usually a good indicator of the level of care the animal has received.

Table 5-1	Checking Out the Caging
Bad Signs	*Good Signs*
Messy or soiled newspaper substrate	Clean newspaper or a natural substrate
Walls of caging are soiled	Glass is spotless
Debris, such as old skin sheds, on the floor of the cage	No animal cast-offs in evidence
Water dish is empty	Water dish is clean and filled with clean water
No hidebox	Hidebox is large enough for animal

Bad Signs	Good Signs
If for reptile, no lighting	Reptile cage has "hot spot" near food area
Room in which caging kept is messy with no climate control; caging tucked away on the floor with inadequate illumination	Caging is focal point of the room

Pet stores

Pet stores are about as risk free as any other herp source if you want to purchase a fat-tailed gecko or indeed almost any herp (see Figure 5-1). They're also one of the more expensive places to purchase a herp, but you have two factors working to your advantage:

- ✔ For captive-bred animals, you pretty much know that the animal has been well fed and well housed his entire life. The captive-bred herps in pet stores are the more popular types (like White's treefrogs, corn snakes, bearded dragons, and leopard geckos). They sell readily, so they don't spend that much time in the pet store.

- ✔ For the wild-caught herps, the collection and shipping process can be very stressful. So you can be pretty sure that if they've made it as far as the pet store and they're feeding, they're basically strong and healthy.

Figure 5-1: A local pet store is a good source for a pet herp.

After an animal is in a pet shop, it's very much to the pet shop's advantage to feed it well, to provide adequate hydration, and to set the animal up in a cage that displays it to the best advantage. The store wants the animal to sell quickly, and it wants the buyer (you) to be very happy with the herp so you'll come back and buy your supplies, foods, and maybe another herp there. The pet store may not make much money off a $20 snake, but if you become a steady customer, the store is happy. And you are too, I hope.

Not all pet stores have a complete understanding of what individual herps need, so use a bit of common sense when deciding whether to buy a particular herp from a pet store. Talk to the employees and sound them out. Do the employees seem concerned about the animals or will they lie to make a sale? For example, if you ask, "Is this animal easy to keep in captivity?" and the answer is always, "Yes, very easy," whether you point to a tiger salamander or dart frogs or *Uromastyx*, you're not getting the truth. Dart frogs take a lot of care, far more than a tiger salamander or a uro. Trust your own eyes.

Importers

Reptile and amphibian importers are in or near port-of-entry cities, including San Francisco, Los Angeles, New York, Tampa, and Miami. Those importers that have retail outlets will sell you anything they import that wasn't already presold. The importers sell to your local pet store, so they can quite rightly be called wholesalers.

Here's a word of caution about animals from importers: Just because an animal is right from the importers doesn't mean he's just been plucked from his home and rushed to U.S. shores. Indeed, probably the greatest stress your herp will undergo is the period between capture and landing at the importer's. Until a herp can be placed in uncrowded caging with water and food available and without humans and loud noises around him all day, the animal is going to be stressed.

When you buy from an importer, it's hard to really know much about the health of your animal. You're certainly buying an animal that isn't used to being handled by humans and isn't accustomed to caging, particularly to glass enclosures, and the food that's provided is probably quite different in smell and taste from what the animal is used to.

The importer can't make any guarantees; all he can tell you is whether the animal is feeding or not. If the animal is one that needs to be spray-misted, the importer can tell you that the animal drinks water when misted, if he's been the one doing the misting.

A wholesaler buys from the hunters and sells to retail outlets

Those who collect herps for sale to a wholesaler can quite rightly be called hunters. In the United States, some people make a living, or part of one, by collecting native herps such as leopard frogs, bullfrogs, tiger salamanders, corn snakes, kingsnakes, anoles, and house geckos, and selling them to reptile dealers. These animals don't stay in the hunters' hands too long, because turning them into cash is as easy as driving to the wholesaler.

For herp hunters in other countries, it's another matter. The hunter may not live near the dealer, and transportation is not quick or easy. The hunter hunts and keeps the animals until he goes to the wholesaler, or until the wholesaler comes by to collect the animals. This may occur only weekly or perhaps every other week. The animals are kept temporarily in sacks or dumped into larger cages and given water until they're repacked and taken to the wholesaler. (Although you don't want to think about going a couple of days without food, remember that snakes may eat only once or twice a month and that a food supply is never guaranteed out there in the wild. The vast majority of reptiles and amphibians can go several days without food and suffer no ill effects from food deprivation.) There, the wholesaler puts the animals into larger cages and ships them out as the orders come in.

Although the animals can probably get enough water to drink, the capture and caging are still stressful for them. The more animals you have in a cage, the more quickly the cage is going to get dirty.

When the wholesaler has enough animals for his order, he packs the animals, takes them to the airport, and ships them to the stateside wholesaler. The stateside wholesaler unpacks the animals, notes any losses, and places the live animals in caging with fresh food and water. If the wholesaler has a retail outlet (not all of them do), you may want to buy your herp directly from the wholesaler. Otherwise, you need to deal with a pet store. If you buy your animal at this point from the wholesaler, you're buying an animal that is not acclimated to captivity and that has just gone through a very stressful period of crowding and quite probably inadequate food and water. If you're willing to take the risk of buying a fresh import, you'll get an animal before it enters the dealer chain.

Most importers promise only that the animal is alive and in reasonably good health at the moment of sale. After you walk out the door, any health problems are your responsibility. The animals may have internal parasites. Indeed, many wild-caught herps do have internal parasites (internal parasites, which you can read more about in Chapter 12, may be good things), but this isn't a problem unless the animal becomes debilitated by stress, lack of food, or dehydration. In that case, the herp may not be able to host the parasites — and survive.

If you're not knowledgeable about herps, when you visit the importer (or a dealer, who gets his animals from an importer), you need to rely on the employees' evaluation of the animal and their opinion on whether an animal looks good to them. This, of course, means you have to believe what they say. On one side, these folks are in the business — they deal with animals 24 hours a day, 7 days a week, so their evaluation is apt to be fairly accurate. On the other side, their goal is to make a sale.

You also have to use your own judgment in selecting the animal, no matter where you buy it. Choose one with bright eyes, an alert demeanor, and no visible injuries, and if you can see the animal eat a food item you can readily obtain, choose that one. An animal that refuses food may not be hungry, may be too stressed to eat, or may have something seriously wrong with it that you can't see.

So now that you're armed with all this information about the herp you wanted to buy, whether it's an African fat-tailed gecko or something else, should you buy your herp from an importer? Yes, this can be a good source. But if you want to minimize your risk, let your local pet store buy the lizard from the importer and make certain it's feeding, and then you can buy the gecko from the store.

Private breeders

Private breeders can be a very good source for herps. To begin with, they need to know the biology of the animal they're breeding inside and out or backwards and forwards, whichever makes the most sense. They know how to take care of the animal, and they've obviously done so because the animal has bred for them. They know what the animal eats, and they know what the young eat. Best of all, they reduce the demand for wild-caught animals by providing animals that are acclimated to captivity (see Figure 5-2).

Figure 5-2:
Captive breeding has created a demand for the brightest morphs of the bearded dragon.

The downside to private breeders is that they don't do much retail business, because you can't recoup your expenses by selling one animal here and another there, unless you're selling high-end animals, such as pink-toned Argentine boas.

Will a private breeder be interested in selling one or two herps to you? It depends on the deal he's cut with the wholesaler or store chain. Maybe he's required to sell only to the pet store chain, and it'll take every herp he produces. If he isn't under these restrictions, dealing with your tiny order may not be worth his time.

Breeders who advertise in one of the reptile magazines have pretty much admitted they want to sell to individuals as well as to pet stores and wholesalers.

Smaller private breeders, ones the professionals call the backyard breeders, are another source of herps. They have jobs other than animal raising, produce fewer animals, and tend to have a less business-like attitude about the process. Some of them breed herps for fun, and some of them have a more business-like approach. A very few are jerks (they'll cheat you if they can get away with it). I have no problems in dealing with someone who treats breeding herps like a business, tracking cash flow and inventory. Like them, I want a healthy herp. I'd also have no problem in buying a herp from someone who breeds the animals just for fun.

Before buying from a smaller breeder, however, I'd want to see the animal and meet and talk to the breeder. Talk to people you know in your local herp society, and see whether anyone has dealt with this individual. Call the local Better Business Bureau and see whether anyone has lodged any complaints against this breeder. It's still a small world out there.

So go ahead. Check out the ads in the reptile magazines or on the Web. Pick up the phone and call the breeder, or send him an e-mail about what you're looking for. I think you'll be pleased with what you get.

Expos and their advantages

A herp expo is another place to buy herps. It's also a useful way to immerse yourself, albeit briefly, in the herp subculture, to learn about animals you never dreamed existed, and to find something either very typical (like fat-tailed geckos) or very atypical (bat-eating snakes that are really cave-dwelling rat snakes). Expos are trade shows where anyone with animals or herp-related merchandise to sell can rent a table (or two, three, or more) and display his wares. You'll see reptiles and amphibians galore, books, caging, cage accessories (such as thermostats, lights, and automatic misting machines), T-shirts, and more (see Figure 5-3).

Figure 5-3:
A herp expo brings vendors of animals, supplies, and artwork together in a weekend event.

At the bigger expos, the ones that aren't run by a corporation, you have the chance to attend lectures on everything from geckos of the world to the nest-building techniques of the Burmese mountain tortoise to photographing the snakes of Madagascar. The expo may include displays of herp-related art or a reptile tattoo contest. Expos are the only place I'm comfortable walking up to a stranger in the hotel lobby at 11 p.m. and asking, "Are you a snake person or a turtle person?" No matter which animal this person likes the best, I always find out pretty quickly.

Expos can certainly offer you a wide variety of herps to select from. This is one time when you need to pay attention to the health of the herp you buy. Expo vendors tend to be just a wee bit flighty. Getting them to make good on an animal after the expo is going to be hard to do, especially when they're 3,000 miles away and suffering from jet lag on top of prolonged sleep deprivation. If you end up with an animal that's sick or that died under your care, you may simply need to forget about getting your money back.

You can always adopt

In the 1990s, when the green iguana craze was at its zenith, importers brought in lots of baby green iguanas, some 3.5 *million* of the little guys from 1991–1995. What do you suppose happened to them?

Zoos and nature centers already have all the free green iguanas they need or want. When I visited the Philadelphia Zoo reptile house a year or so ago, the reptile keepers said they got easily three calls a week from people wanting to give the zoo their green iguanas. This was more than five years after the green iguana craze! The zoo doesn't want anyone's iguanas. No zoo does. Now what?

The lucky iguanas end up in reptile adoption centers, where they wait for a home from someone who's willing to cope with a big green lizard that may be wild (see how to tame him in Chapter 6) and/or not in the best of health (see the discussion of metabolic bone disease in Chapter 12). An amazing number of kind-hearted people take in unwanted reptiles and amphibians, rehabilitate them, if needed, and adopt them out to permanent, caring homes. Animals can become unwanted for various reasons. They may get too big; they may be too expensive to feed, and so on.

This is where an interested hobbyist comes in. If you want a particular herp, no matter what it is, take the time to contact several adoption agencies and see what they have available. Try the Yellow Pages, under Pets. Sometimes your local pet shelter or the wildlife rehabbers have animals you wouldn't expect. The easiest way to find a certain animal is the Web. The network is amazing. One place may tell you that it doesn't have any bearded dragons, but someone there suggests that you check with another agency or a specific Web site. Maybe none of them have what you're looking for at the time (suppose that you're looking for a lizard, a Uromastyx), but the word goes out. In a couple days, you may get an e-mail or a call from someone you don't know who says, "I have a male uromastyx that I think you may be interested in."

Expect to answer a lot of questions when you tell the agency what you'd like to adopt. You'll have to fill out an application, provide references, and maybe even undergo a home inspection. In particular, the rescue agency wants to make certain that you know what you're getting into when you adopt an animal. The agency has already rescued this animal once; it doesn't want to do it again or — worse — have the animal die because he went to a home that didn't provide proper care.

A word of warning from a herp rescue/adoption person: Ask many questions about the animal you're interested in adopting. Some people out there consider themselves rescuers, but in reality, they're nothing more than brokers. They take in unwanted herps and adopt them out for a fee. Ask if the animal has been checked by a veterinarian if you have the slightest suspicion that you're dealing with someone who simply sells unwanted herps under the guise of being an adoption site. True rescuers have the animal's health checked and won't adopt out an animal unless he is completely healthy. Recovery may take months sometimes and costs an exorbitant amount of money. Very rarely do adoption fees cover the costs of the animal's care.

Buying a Herp Long Distance

After checking Web sites or perhaps visiting an expo and going home empty-handed or seeing an ad in a reptile magazine, you may decide that the herp of your dreams is not at your corner pet store but instead resides in a cage at a dealer hundreds of miles away. Driving that far and picking up the animal yourself is impractical. So you want the dealer to ship the animal to you. In effect, you're buying a pig in a poke — an animal that you won't see until it becomes yours. In this situation, you have to trust the dealer to select for you the best-looking animal as far as health is concerned.

Tell the dealer that you're new at buying herps, and you need a proven feeder, an animal that's in good shape. Dealers understand what it's like to be a newbie, and it's to their very real advantage to treat you right in sending you a healthy animal that's eating. If a dealer takes advantage of you, animal owners can easily spread the word that they got taken by that dealer; all they need to do is join a chat room or call the chamber of commerce or the Better Business Bureau and give a dealer a negative report. Dealers want you as a customer now and ten years down the road, when you add on an animal room and expand your collection dramatically. They'll gladly ship to you.

After you talk to the dealer and agree upon a price for your herp, you need to talk about shipping. Most distance transactions, including the cost of the animal itself and shipping charges, are generally prepaid with a credit card.

Be sure to discuss the following topics with the dealer:

- **The airport you want the animal shipped to:** Make certain that both of you are clear on which airport to use if your area has more than one airport. If you like, you can use a door-to-door service, which saves you a trip to the airport (although you'll pay for the service).

- **The shipping date:** Avoid weekends, when the shipping departments at some airports may be closed. Some dealers go to the airport only one or two days a week. Allow 24 hours for the shipping process from the shipper's airport to your airport. The process may take less time if there are direct flights. The process may take more time if the shipment has to be transferred from one airline to another.

  Be sure to get the air bill number from the dealer after the animal ships.

- **The airline you want to use:** Whenever possible, keep your shipment on one airline. With live animals, you pay for each airline involved.

Give the shipper your full name, address, and the day and night phone numbers where you can be reached.

Your shipper will want to ship only in good weather — meaning weather that avoids the extremes of heat and of cold — on both ends of the shipment. Your shipment may be delayed when the weather is too hot or too cold or during holiday travel times. In addition, shipments of U.S. Mail take priority over live animal shipments, and there may not be room for your shipment at times of heavy mail traffic.

Most airlines offer three options for shipping your animal:

- ✔ **Space-available freight:** The most frequently used method and the least expensive as well
- ✔ **Air express:** Gives you guaranteed flights
- ✔ **Small package:** The fastest level of service

You pay premium rates for either of these last two levels, but they may be required by the airline depending on the weather.

After a reasonable time, call the airline and use your airbill number to determine the status of your shipment — whether it was shipped on time, what flight the animal is on, and when the plane is expected to land. Near the expected arrival time, call and check, so you'll know when to leave to pick up your shipment.

Open the shipment at the facility, before you take the box to your car, and make sure that the animal is alive. If your animal has died en route or is not in good shape, you and the airline need to fill out what's called a discrepancy report.

You may have noticed that I talk only about shipping on airlines. The other carriers, such as FedEx or UPS, don't ship live animals or accept live animals only if the shipper is a certified shipper. Most dealers won't bother with this sort of hassle, although I do know some breeders who have gone through the bother of becoming certified.

Considering Other Factors in Selecting a Herp

You may think you don't have to make any more decisions, but you do. Some of these questions are philosophical, but the answers will tell you what you're looking for in a pet herp.

Wild caught versus captive born

Whenever possible, buy or adopt captive-born animal as opposed to those that are wild caught (see Figure 5-4 for a wild-caught animal). Those that are captive born won't affect any native populations. You aren't removing anything for any wild gene pool, and wild populations aren't affected at all.

Figure 5-4:
The majority
of African
fat-tailed
geckos are
wild-caught.

Captive-born young are already acclimated to life in captivity. Snakes, for example, that have been raised in a rack system, where each cage is as deep as a dishpan and the lighting comes through the ends of the translucent pans, not from above, are used to these surroundings. They feed and breed quite well in them.

Captive-bred animals are often much easier to feed. For snakes, they're already used to prekilled lab mice or lab rats. If the mother snake is accustomed to an odor of her food, or even if she's accustomed to the odor of a food item she won't eat, her young consume that food more readily.

Is there any other difference between wild-caught and captive-born herps? Sometimes the captive-born animals cost more. It seems odd that you can buy a ball python caught in Africa and imported into the United States for less than a captive-born ball python, but both care and money have been involved in producing that cute little USA-born baby. The U.S. breeder has paid his or her U.S. taxes and electric bill, and paid for his car. That person has also spent a lot of time coaxing his ball pythons to eat, cleaning cages, cycling the snakes so they'll breed, and incubating eggs.

Male versus female

Is there a difference between a male and a female pet herp? None that I've ever been able to see. Sometimes one gender is a different size than the other. Sometimes they may be different colors. As a general rule, however, one sex doesn't seem to make a better pet than the other. The only time that gender may make a difference is with green iguanas. The adult males can become aggressive toward their female keepers, and I'm talking "leap off a branch and repetitive biting" aggressive.

Adult versus hatchling

Buying an adult herp puts you on the fast track, in terms of maintaining that herp and possibly breeding it. The animal is adult, which means it has gotten through the mortality period of youth. (No matter where you get a herp, hatchlings have a high mortality rate. Not every one of them survives to reproduce.) Once acclimated, an adult animal can reproduce, which means that you won't spend two years or so caring for it until it's physically large enough and capable of reproducing.

Buying an adult herp doesn't mean that you won't have any problems. You have no guarantee that your adult herp will accept whatever foods you offer him. For example, our stubborn friends, the ball pythons, are one very good example of "I won't eat and you can't make me," whether adult or hatchling. You also have no promise that the animal will breed, even once you acclimate him.

If you can get your adult herp to eat, however, feeding him is easier than feeding a hatchling. For example, some hatchling snakes are so tiny that they can eat only pinkie legs or anole tails, and snipping off the legs of frozen pinkies and tails off anoles is way down on anyone's list of fun things to do. Some dart frog tadpoles eat only infertile dart frog eggs, a real challenge for even the most devoted herper. Young salamanders eat blood worms or tiny bits of pinched-apart earthworms. (There's just no other way to divide an earthworm into ⅛- or ¼-inch frog- or salamander-mouth-sized pieces other than pinching them apart with your fingernails. Earthworms are too slippery and wiggly to cut apart with a paring knife, and believe me, I've tried.)

Chapter 6

Handling Your Herp

*Y*ou're looking dubiously at a herp, be it a snake, a lizard, or a frog, and you're wondering, "Now, how do you suppose I should pick this thing up?"

The good news is that you may not have to handle the herp. Some herps don't take kindly to being handled, rather like those elaborate glass sculptures you see on the top shelves in the gift shops on Rodeo Drive in Beverly Hills. Being handled is an unnatural thing for a herp. In the wild, being touched by another species, unless you're talking about turtles piling up on a log for sunning, generally means getting eaten.

Other herps can deal with a little handling; some even seem to enjoy it. Maybe you've seen the odd dude who walks around your local flea market with an adult savannah monitor clinging to his chest, or the young woman with the ball python around her neck at your herp society meetings. Their animals are accustomed to being handled, and some of them seem to enjoy it. One of my tortoises will follow me around his pen until I stop to rub his face and neck. My rhino iguana closes his eyes and stands high on straight legs when I approach him, and he doesn't seem to mind being petted. By and large, however, an animal may tolerate holding still while being petted, but he may not actually *enjoy* that human contact. Yes, a reptile seeks out heat, and if you're warm and toasty yourself, you're just as good a source of additional warmth as a sun-warmed rock. For the most part, though, the less you actually handle most herps, the better off they are.

Of course, you have to handle your herp sometimes, such as when you clean his cage or when you want to show him to someone else. I can't tell you how many times I've opened my cage and handed a corn snake to someone who has expressed a desire to hold him (see Figure 6-1). The key is to know what you're doing.

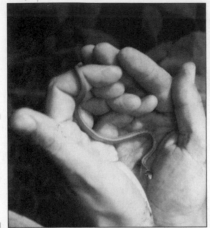

Figure 6-1:
Once lifted, you can cup a small snake in your hands.

If you've been handling food items, wash your hands before handling your herp. If you don't, some herps may mistake *you* for food. There's another reason as well, and this applies to all herps, but most especially to the amphibians. Your hands aren't clean. You've petted your dog, picked up the newspaper from a muddy puddle, laced up your shoes, moved your car keys from the dresser to the kitchen counter, and cracked and stirred eggs to make scrambled eggs. Now you want to change your tiger salamander's cage before you go to work? With *those* hands?

Before handling any herp, wash your hands, not just to remove the load of bacteria you've picked up from at least five different places but to cool them. You're operating at 98.6 degrees, remember, and your highly vascularized hands are almost that warm. Your tiger salamander is quite happy at an ambient temperature of 65 degrees. Being grabbed by hands that are 20 to 25 degrees warmer than he is no treat. Try it on yourself, if you like: Heat a spatula over a stove burner until it's 125 degrees and stick it on your arm. My, aren't you jumpy today!

Herps You Can Handle

Certain herps are safe for you to handle, but other herps are probably not. On the safe side are the small-sized nonvenomous snakes (including pythons, garters, and rat snakes), the turtles, all of the frogs (see Figure 6-2), and some lizards. All can learn to tolerate gentle handling.

Figure 6-2:
You can
certainly
handle your
horned frog,
but hold him
around his
waist.

Reptiles

You may not consider reptiles as soft and cuddly, but if you have one for a
pet, you're going to want to pick him up and handle him sometimes. In the
following sections, I tell you how to do this safely.

Snakes

The snakes that are available as pets are those that tame down well — that's
part of the reason they're in the pet market. They may not be gentle if wild
caught, but this is because they're frightened. Put yourself in their skin, so
to speak. If a monster grabbed you around the middle and held you aloft,
wouldn't you react, and quickly? Those that are captive bred are easier to
handle. They're already accustomed to the scent of humans, cages, and a
captive diet. But whether captive born or wild caught, the boas, pythons, rat
snakes, bull snakes, and kingsnakes can bite if they feel threatened. (What
else can they do? Sue you?)

So how do you handle one of these snakes? Gently and slowly. Open the cage and reach in and pick the snake up. If you need a way to slow down, count to yourself "one thousand one, one thousand two. . . ." Reach in and pick him up, almost like he's a garden hose. Grasp him up at his midbody, and lift him out of the cage, still moving slowly. Hold him firmly but not tightly. Bring your other hand near the first, to hold on to and to support the rest of his body. Your snake is not going to hurt you; he just doesn't want to be dropped. You'll notice that your snake curves his body to hang on to *you*; a 2-foot long boa constrictor can curve his body enough to hold on to one of your fingers.

And that's all there is to it. When you've finished admiring your snake, put your hands back into the cage, on the substrate. Your snake will stop clinging to you for the familiarity of his home base. Once he crawls out of your hands, close the cage. You just held your snake. How 'bout that?

Turtles

Turtles are easy to handle. Remember to move slowly but with deliberation. Cup a hatchling in one hand with your thumb on the top shell so he can't crawl through your fingers. If the turtle is larger than a hatchling but small enough to grasp in one hand, you just reach in and pick him up, with your thumb on the top shell and your fingers on the bottom shell. If he kicks hard, or if he's too big for you to pick him up with one hand, use both hands to grasp him on each side of his shell, with your fingers on the bottom and your thumb on the top. To put a tortoise or box turtle down, lower him to the floor of his cage or enclosure until his feet touch, and let go. For aquatic turtles, lower your hands until his plastron (the bottom shell) touches the water, and let go. These holding techniques work on aquatic turtles and tortoises.

Two kinds of aquatic turtles don't like being handled, and they require special care. The snapping turtles have stocky bodies and powerful jaws. Hold small ones by the rear edge of their shell or by their tail. If you hold one by his tail near your leg, keep the plastron toward your leg. Soft-shelled turtles have soft, leathery shells and long necks, and it's the long neck you must be wary of. They can easily reach sideways or backward to bite anything (or anyone) restraining them. Scoop up hatchlings and small turtles in a net or deli cup; hold adults by the back edge of the shell.

Lizards

Lizards are usually scooped up in one hand and held around the torso so they can't wriggle through. You can add your other hand as a collar around their neck so they can't go forward and they can't go backward. (This method works for tokay geckos, who are very enthusiastic biters. It's okay to wear gloves when you handle them.) You can use your fingers as a cage, with the lizard cupped between your hands, but you need to press your palms together to keep a determined lizard from diving between your fingers.

You can lift larger lizards, such as a 24-inch green iguana, by one hand, but as soon as you lift him, place your other hand under the belly, toward the front legs, as a support, while the first hand slides back to pin the scratching hind legs against the body. When held like this, most of these lizards quit kicking and lashing their tail and lie still. If he persists, pin him against your side until he feels secure and quits kicking. Delicate lizards, such as the small geckos, need to be shooed into an aquarium net or cup and held inside the container by your other hand over the top. To turn a lizard loose, lower him until he touches the floor of his cage, and let go.

WARNING! Big lizards, the carnivorous ones such as the monitors and tegus, require special precautions during handling, if only to make them feel unthreatened. These are not lizards for beginners; the way to discover how these lizards behave and how to handle them is to work with younger, smaller examples. An inexperienced hobbyist is quite likely to get hurt trying to handle a big lizard, and so is the lizard. These lizards bite if they think you're going to harm them (or if they sense food in your hands), and they're strong. Their mouths contain bacteria you wouldn't want on the outside of your skin, much less imbedded in it. If you get bitten, infection is almost a certainty. Tell the physician cleaning your bite/claw marks that you may need antibiotics against gram-negative *and* gram-positive bacteria.

To handle one of these lizards, wear a long-sleeved shirt, long pants, and gloves. Pick the lizard up by the nape of his neck and by his hips, and tuck his body between your arm and your body. Keep his hips pinned between your arm and your body so he won't feel that he's going to be dropped and he can't rake you with his hind feet. Use your hands to hold his front legs close to his body and to control the movement of his head and neck so he can't bite you. Monitors and tegus will calm down with repeated gentle handling, if this is what you want. Once the animal is tamed, he'll rest for short periods on your forearm, with his tail extending between your arm and your body, and your hand supporting his chest.

Amphibians

You can handle almost all of the amphibians, *if* you wash your hands before and after handling them, and if you handle them with wet (that is, cool) hands. That skin scratches easily, and once damaged, it's an open invitation for infection or fungus. Move slowly, open the cage, reach in, and pick up the amphibian.

Salamanders

You can hold a large-ish salamander (such as a tiger salamander) around his middle; use your other hand to support his feet if he's acting wriggly. You can hold smaller salamanders in one wet hand and gently pin them against your palm by using your wet thumb. They can be shooed into a deli cup or held in a wet aquarium net, with your other hand covering the top.

Frogs

Frogs are a bit more work to handle because they're so mobile. Pick up and hold frogs the size of leopard frogs around the waist, next to the hind legs. The more delicate frogs, such as the red-eyed treefrog, can be held for a few moments in your wet hand, but they'll heat up quickly in your grasp. Transfer them to a wet aquarium net, or to a deli cup with a wet paper towel square covering the bottom, and use your other hand to cover the top. The poison dart frogs and other tiny types are just too small to be safely (for them) handled. Shoo them into a deli cup or wet aquarium net, and snap on the cup's lid or use your hand for a cover. See the "Herps You Don't Want to Handle" section, later in this chapter.

Herps You Can Handle with Help

When is a herp too much to handle by yourself? It's primarily a factor of size and natural (to the herp, at least) behavior. Lizards, turtles, and tortoises can get big, but their natural behavior isn't aggressive. Crocodilians do get big, and some types are aggressive, but they aren't pet species. Amphibians don't get big, except for the very protected Chinese salamander, and no amphibian is dangerously aggressive. That pretty much rules out everything except snakes.

Some snakes get *really* big. These are the Burmese python, 14 feet; the African rock python, 15 feet; the green anaconda, 20 feet; and the reticulated python, 22 feet. Green anacondas, rock pythons, and reticulated pythons are known for their unpredictability and volatile dispositions. These big snakes have big mouths and big teeth; the bites alone are dangerous. These snakes are powerful constrictors. When any of these snakes get over 8 feet long, they are formidable opponents.

If you're an experienced keeper, you still need to take special precautions. When you work with your "biggie," have another experienced herper with you. He can distract the snake if it bites you and can pull the snake off you if it grabs you and constricts, things you can't do for yourself. Follow these basic rules for handling big snakes:

- ✔ It takes two people. The other person may save your life.

- ✔ If possible, feed these snakes in a separate, latchable container so they won't associate the opening of their cage door with the tossing in of prekilled food. Move the snake to the container (this may take two people — big snakes are heavy!), add the prekilled food, and close and latch the container. Check in a half hour later to see whether he has eaten, and add more food if he has. When he's finished eating, both of you should wash your hands to remove any vestige of food scent before you move the snake back into his cage.

✔ Move the snake to another container — not the food container — when his cage needs cleaning. You may be concentrating on scrubbing out the corner of the cage; your snake may see you making jerky motions that remind him of an animal in distress, and hence easy pickings. If the snake is too large to move out of the cage so you can clean the cage, have another person in the cage with you. That person can keep an eye on the snake and use a broom to push him away from the area where you're working.

If a large snake constricts you (which is instinctive behavior, triggered by a response to odor, your warmth, and the movement of your chest), you're probably not going to be able to unwind it by yourself. Like the song says, "with every breath you take and every move you make" (every exhalation, actually), the snake tightens up his coils until you can no longer inhale. The constrictors don't crush their prey; they cause it to suffocate.

Herps You Don't Want to Handle

If you want to handle a tiny herp, be careful. As a general rule, the smaller the reptile (see Figure 6-3), the greater the chance of your damaging it when you hold it, because you're just so much larger than he is.

Figure 6-3:
A peacock day gecko is best handled in a net or by shooing it into a small cup.

Mishandling geckos takes the skin off their backs

Day geckos are thin-skinned lizards that have an unusual escape mechanism: Their skin tears when they're restrained, and suddenly you're holding an animal whose skin has split right down his back. Put him down immediately, right back in his cage. The skin will heal, almost invisibly, except for a gray line marking the original split. Instead of picking this lizard up, shoo him into a small aquarium net or into a small container, and pick *that* up.

You especially don't want to handle the tiny dart frogs, such as the dendrobatids. It's not that they can harm you (the toxic quality of their skin disappears when they've been on a captive diet for a few months). It's just that they're too small and delicate for your great big (and too warm) hands. When you need to move one of these colorful little jewels, shoo him into an aquarium fish net and then cover the net with your free hand when you move it. If you don't have a fish net, shoo him into a small container, and cover it with your other hand before moving it.

Don't handle venomous snakes — the rattlesnakes, the pit vipers, the tree vipers, the coral snakes, and the sea snakes — ever. If you work with venomous herps, it isn't a matter of *if* you'll get bitten — it's *when* you'll get bitten. You get careless. Your reaction times slow as you get older. A snake (or lizard for that matter) can be nervous, and you may not pick up on it. Even very experienced venomous snake handlers get bitten. Some of them die, despite very advanced and expensive medical care, and you don't need to join that crowd.

Dealing with Bites

What happens if your herp bites you? Here are a few things you need to always remember about bites:

- They generally hurt, both during the bite and afterward, although you could call some just pinches rather than bites (a green anole can't bite you *that* hard).

- You can bleed. It will seem like a lot, because it's your blood, but these are only skin lacerations, so stop sniveling, unless . . . (read on).

- If you're bitten by something big, like a 12-foot python, the snake is going to do some damage to you. The bite can be serious for you, either because of where you get bitten, or because an infection sets in, or both if your karma was very bad that day.

You'd sort of expect a big snake to bite, but snakes aren't the only herps with teeth. Several years ago, a very pretty young woman walked past her boyfriend's uncaged male iguana. Spurred by a male iguana's response to whatever scents motivate him, the iguana leapt off his cage top and bit her across the bridge of her nose. Of course this meant a trip to the emergency room, and plastic surgery (better written as pla$tic $urgery). The young woman looks fine today, but no one needs this sort of trauma. The iguana was euthanized, which made the bite more than serious for him.

✔ The bites can mess up the herp's mouth, because you pull away from the bite and pull out his teeth or grab him to pull him off (and break his jaw in the process, you brute). Snakes have recurved teeth, designed for holding onto prey, and those snakes that eat birds have extra-long recurved teeth, the better to bite through all those feathers. They can't just open up a little and let you slide out. They have to open a lot, and unhook those teeth, as they pop out of your flesh before you can go your way and let the snake go his. Teeth that are yanked out of a snake's mouth can set him up for infection (see Chapter 12 on how to deal with jaw infections).

✔ Mouth infections don't occur nearly as much when you're bitten by a turtle or tortoise, because the turtle has sharp-edged mandibles instead of lots of bacteria-laden teeth, and he doesn't eat carrion (well, not as much as the snake). That sharp-edged mouth means that if you pull away before he opens up to let you go, what's inside his mouth stays there (ouch!).

✔ People will laugh. Everyone loves a joke, especially when it's on some-one else. You can become an urban legend in a matter of weeks when you do something particularly stupid in herp handling and get bitten as a result.

Snake bite story gets two thumbs up

Here's a snake bite story that probably became an urban legend very quickly. A man was bitten on the thumb by a kingsnake, but the man thought he was equal to the occasion. He used his other hand to peel the snake's lips back so he could extract his thumb. Kingsnakes are adept at moving the sides of their jaws independently of each other, however, so within moments, Joel was standing in the field, both thumbs inside the kingsnake's mouth, sort of a new twist on Chinese handcuffs. Fortunately, he was not by himself in the field, a good rule to follow even if his field companions did laugh before they rescued him.

Taking care of a nonvenomous bite

If you do get bitten by your herp, here's what to do:

1. **Relax. A dog bite is generally far worse.**

2. **Do not look at the animal.**

   Eye-to-eye contact is considered a challenge. In case you have a tokay gecko hanging onto your hand, you don't really want to see how his eyes bulge out when he tightens his grip. I looked when my tokay bit me, and I can assure you that the sight is most distressing.

3. **Make it easy for the animal to let go, if he's still hanging on to you.**

   Don't jerk your hand away. (If another part of your anatomy is the object of the bite, maybe you shouldn't have tempted the creature.) If you're outdoors, put the herp on the ground and release your hold. He doesn't like you any better than you like him (and you smell terrible!).

   If you're inside, darken the lights in the room and put your hand and the animal back in its cage so he can back off and will feel safe. Relax and recite some narrative poetry to yourself. Some phrases about despair in Coleridge's *The Rime of the Ancient Mariner* are particularly appropriate.

4. **When he does let go, take your bitten hand out of the cage, cover the cage, and examine your hand.**

   Pick out any teeth left in your hand. Walk over to a sink and wash your hand with water and soap. Your hand may bleed copiously. This helps wash out the wound, but soap and water are still a necessity. I know that the new waterless cleaners are considered better germ removers than just soap and water, but because they're alcohol based, I'd stick to soap and water.

5. **Put a bandage on your hand and elevate it for a few minutes or until it stops bleeding.**

   A bit of pressure atop the bandage from your free hand should speed up the clotting process.

6. **Keep your hand dry for at least a day so the healing can begin.**

   Wear a rubber glove when you do dishes or bathe, and be careful to keep the hand dry.

7. **Watch the area to make sure that infection doesn't set in.**

   Warning signs are redness, red streaks, swelling, discharge, and soreness that increases instead of lessens. If your tetanus shot isn't up to date, this is a very good time to have a booster.

If your snake was wild caught, I promise you that he has eaten a variety of carrion, some of which remains between his teeth. If you've been bitten by a water snake, you get the double bonus of carrion-laced teeth and a saliva that causes swelling. Some people are very sensitive to this saliva, and for them, the saliva is actually toxic!

How foolish of me! Venomous bites

Suppose that you're bitten by a venomous snake. Once you get to the hospital, you'll be the center of a lot of attention that you really don't want. You'll be asked repeatedly if you're certain that you know the identity of the snake that bit you. Each group of venomous snakes, from sea snakes to the coral snakes to the rattlesnakes, has its own antivenom. Hospitals have to call in for bite-specific antivenom, and it may be literally across the country (for native snakes) or in another country (for the venomous snakes found there).

Every doctor, nurse, and hospital employee in the building will find an excuse to wander into your room and look at your bite. Officials from several city, state, and federal agencies will make it their business to drop in on you, just to find out for themselves what you were messing with and why. Do not expect them to be friendly, especially if you didn't legally procure or keep the snake.

You'll probably get dosed with antivenom because the hospital doesn't want to be accused of waiting too long to treat you. (This may be ten vials or more, at $450 a vial.) The antivenom is certainly one of the treatments for envenomation, but the serum sickness that follows is in many cases worse than the bite. Here are the symptoms of an allergic reaction to antivenom:

- You have generalized muscular aches.

- Your face and neck may swell.

- You may get hives, from the soles of your feet to your eyelids and maybe in your throat. Those on the outside of your skin itch badly, and those in your throat cause your throat to swell. You may get these several times as you recover.

- The site of injection (the arm in which the intravenous line was inserted) swells and is painful.

- You may develop arthritis in the large joints of your body.

You may have to go back to the hospital, maybe more than once, for antihistamines and steroids to quell this allergic reaction. Until your body can form antibodies to destroy the foreign horse serum, you'll continue to deal with these symptoms. As with any strong allergic reaction, your reactions to any repeated dose of horse serum will be more severe than the first reaction.

An alternative treatment is to wait and see how sick you get from the bite, and to treat symptoms as they appear. For example, you may receive blood transfusions to replace blood destroyed by the venom or dialysis (venom is really hard on the kidneys).

Chapter 7

Indoor Caging Basics

. . . .

In This Chapter

▶ Finding out about the different kinds of caging

▶ Considering different substrates

▶ Re-creating your herp's natural habitat

▶ Adding furnishings to the cage

▶ Measuring humidity and temperature

▶ Keeping your herp's home clean

. . . .

*B*ecause the right kind of caging provides the right environment, lighting, humidity, and temperature for your herp, the caging you provide will affect, to a great extent, how long your herp will live. (To use as an extreme example, a frog wouldn't last long in a desert environment.)

Caging can be as simple as a box, but you have some choices when choosing exactly what kind of box you set up for your herp. You need to decide what sort of environment your pet needs: woodland, savanna, and so on. Beyond these decisions, you also have decorating decisions to make. You need to know about substrate and cage furniture, including hideboxes, branches, and water dishes. Controlling the heat and humidity of the cage and keeping it clean are important to your herp's happiness — and survival.

Looking at Caging Structures

Think of caging as a box, and yes, I'm asking you to think *within* the box for this chapter. The basic shell of the cage is the easy part. Putting together the correct "insides" is a bit more work.

The basic aquarium

Far and away, the easiest herp caging is an aquarium. Aquariums aren't expensive, are available in all sizes with snug-fitting tops, and provide excellent visibility. Accessories sized just for aquariums are also easy to find. Aquariums also work for all formats — wet, semiwet, forest, or desert.

An aquarium is a glass box. If it's in the sun, it heats up, which can be fatal to the inhabitants who can't escape the heat. So if you go the aquarium route, keep it out of the sun.

The wooden cage

The second easiest choice is the wooden cage — easy to make and not that expensive. The wooden cage opens from the top. This type of structure works for all environments except the aquatic. To make a wooden cage, just make a box with a solid bottom, back, and two sides. Use a piece of glass for the front.

Because the glass doesn't need to slide, installing it is fairly easy. You can secure the glass into the box frame with plastic channeling from a home improvement store, or you can frame the glass in with front-and-back quarter-round on all four sides. If you're skilled with a table saw, you can cut a channel for the glass into the wooden side and bottom. The top is a hinged frame with an inset of quarter-inch hardware cloth, which is a heavy sort of window screening with a bigger mesh. Hardware cloth comes in several mesh sizes, but use the ⅛ to ¼ inch size. Provide ventilation either by drilling holes into the sides and back or by cutting out a 2-inch square in each side and the back and covering the holes with more hardware cloth.

The wire mesh cage

The wire mesh cage is basically a wooden framework of 2-x-2s or 2-x-4s (depending on how big you want it), with ½-inch or ¼-inch mesh hardware cloth stapled around it. If you want to be able to tote this cage easily, keep it relatively small — two cubic feet is about my carrying capacity.

If you want a larger cage, build it with a solid bottom and put it on casters. Keep it narrow enough to wheel through the doors in your house, and you have a cage you can push anywhere. Wood and wire caging seems to work best when it's vertically formatted. The vertical format means the cage either has a small enough footprint to fit on top of a table or (once on casters) it's easy to move where you want it. Because this cage is well ventilated, it's great for animals that need a gentle air current through their enclosure or that like to climb. This is a good cage for chameleons, larger lizards, or arboreal snakes.

The commercial cages

Plastic commercial cages are molded one-piece cages that open from the front and come in multicage racks, or single larger cages you can use alone or stack (see Figure 7-1). Because they're molded plastic, they're a snap to clean. Most have built-in lighting fixtures. The larger cages are good for the larger snakes. The smaller ones are good for the snakes less than 4 feet long or for smaller lizards.

Figure 7-1: Breeders use rack systems to successfully maintain and breed large numbers of snakes and lizards.

Plastic shoeboxes

Plastic shoeboxes work for caging for smaller animals. Make certain that the lids snap on securely; you can drill ventilation holes yourself. These boxes work for hatchling snakes, small terrestrial lizards such as leopard geckos, or frogs or salamanders that do well in dampened sphagnum, such as the horned frogs or tiger salamanders in their terrestrial stage.

Getting to the Bottom of It: Substrates

Substrate is what you put on the floor of a herp cage. One purpose of substrate is to sop up moisture, whether from urine and feces, spilled water, or your own blood when you stick your hand into your tegu's cage and he takes umbrage (see Chapter 6 for what to do if you're bitten).

In the days when hobbyists who kept snakes and lizards were considered weird and no pet supply manufacturers had yet sniffed out the sweet scent of a growing market, you had two choices: newspaper or cypress mulch. Today, you can pick and choose what substrate you want, and they're roughly divided into groups: natural and unnatural. (Or you can classify them as those that clump when damp and those that don't.)

If you're worried about odor control, you may want to try odor-absorbing substrate underliners. These underliners go on the floor of the cage, under your substrate. One manufacturer makes a disposable activated carbon liner that works to absorb odors. The outside covering is plastic. One firm makes a recycled cardboard cage liner that's more absorbent than newspaper or cardboard and can be used as undersubstrate or as a stand-alone flooring.

Newspaper

Newspaper is readily available, often free (from kind neighbors or office colleagues), and is quick to clean up and quick to put down. Those are the good points. But don't forget that newspaper has its drawbacks. It's not very absorbent and not very attractive, either. It does nothing to make a cage look like a bit of nature.

Cypress mulch

Cypress mulch (or any type of mulch as long as it isn't cedar or melaleuca) is readily available, either from your pet store or from any store that sells gardening supplies. It's not very expensive; a 20-pound bag may cost you $4. It is absorbent, smells rather foresty and fresh, and does help a cage look good. Misted lightly with a hand-held mister, mulch sticks together a bit and affords burrowing opportunities for burrowing lizards, snakes, and turtles or tortoises that like to sleep mostly buried in loose substrate. The downside? It's dusty, with gobs of minute ground particles that cling to everything nearby if you open the bag and simply shake its contents into an enclosure. It's also bulky and unflushable, but you *can* take mulch out of your herp cage and toss it around the plants in your yard if the mulch isn't too stained or toss it into your trash, knowing that it's thoroughly biodegradable.

Sand

Sand is another choice for a substrate. It is readily available, comes in a variety of natural or dyed colors, and is easily washed. Just put it in a bucket and stick a hose down through it. Let the water run and swish the sand around until the water runs fairly clear. Smooth desert sand is inexpensive, so discarding it when it's soiled will give you no cause for regret. Sand heats evenly and will store up warmth from a UV or heat lamp, and it's soft to dig into. For the real sand dwellers, such as the leopard lizards, sand skinks, racerunners and western hognose snakes, sand is as familiar a part of their landscape as a paved road is to yours.

You may hear glum tales about herps getting impacted intestinal tracts from ingesting almost any type of substrate. Sand seems to be the worst culprit, with literally dozens of books dutifully saying (or repeating), "Never use sand because of the danger of impaction." But I think with a few precautions, you can use sand as a substrate and afford your animals a slightly more natural habitat than they'd get otherwise.

To avoid impaction (or to avoid the *spectre* of impaction), offer food on a flat stone or in a flat dish. Put mulch down over the sand in part of the cage and put the food in that corner. You can also move your herp to a large covered plastic trash can and feed the animal in that. Finally, make sure that your herp is well hydrated and well fed. That way, if he does swallow some sand, it will slosh along through the digestive system along with everything else.

Sphagnum moss

Sphagnum moss, moistened, is a very good choice for amphibians. It is particularly good for those terrestrial types, such as adult tiger or spotted salamanders and horned frogs, and it creates moist refuges in the cages of dart frogs. Sphagnum is readily available in pet and garden stores. You can wash the moss by swishing the sphagnum around in a bucket of water with your hands and repeatedly squishing it in your hands to help clean it or replace it. It's nonabrasive, an important feature for amphibians who wear their lungs on their skin (see Chapter 4 for more about the incredible qualities of amphibian skin). It's great for burrowing — just check out the expression on your tiger salamander's face when he burrows through his sphagnum and comes up with a particularly fat juicy earthworm.

What are the downsides of sphagnum moss? You can't use it for everything; it's only for moisture-loving herps. It will sour if you let it get dirty and don't change it, which is very bad news for the herp living in it.

Wooden shavings

Wooden shavings are another good substrate choice for some herps. Shavings are inexpensive and available at your pet store or local feed store. Shavings offer a soft, fairly absorbent surface for land dwellers such as tortoises, lizards, and larger snakes. You can choose pine or aspen shavings. The pine shavings have a faint piney odor that I hardly notice. The aspen shavings are said to be odorless. If you're worried about forcing your reptiles to live with any scent at all, use aspen.

Although shavings don't hold up to washing, you can use the soiled shavings in your garden for mulch, toss 'em onto your compost pile, or throw them away. They work well for non-moisture-loving herps. They aren't good for amphibians, though, because they aren't moist enough and they're too scratchy.

WARNING!

Never use cedar shavings for your herp's substrate. Their pleasant odor designed to conceal odor comes from the phenol or oils in the shaved wood. Phenols of any type are deadly to reptiles.

If you decide to use either pine or aspen shavings, follow the same feeding precautions as you would with a sand substrate. And if your herp shows any signs of respiratory irritation or inflammation — wheezing or liquid dripping from the nose — change the substrate and monitor his condition until you identify and eliminate the cause of the problem.

Pellets

Pelleted substrates work well for some reptiles. Pellets of rabbit feed — those pellets of ground-up alfalfa — work well for tortoises because they provide good traction for those tiny feet, and if the tortoise ingests them, they're good for the tortoise. (I never saw any of my tortoises willingly eat rabbit pellets, but yours might.) Other pelleted substrate choices are made from compressed aspen or pine sawdust. All three of these pellets fall apart the moment they get damp, which enables you to scoop out (and flush, another good point) the damaged area. If you don't clean up the wet spots that very day, they tend to turn sour and mold, so scoop out any damp areas as soon as you notice them.

Grasses and barks

Wheat grass is another substrate possibility. Originally designed for use with large lizards and their large deposits, the wheat grass is absorbent, light-weight, and flushable. Although it won't hold the shape of a tunnel, burrowing reptiles such as sand boas, sand skinks, and colubrids seem to enjoy rooting through it.

Coconut bark fiber is another resilient substrate. It can be used either dampened or dry. A block the size of a brick fluffs up enough to provide substrate for a 40-gallon tank. Like shavings, it creates a good environment for burrowing reptiles and allows the tunnels to hold their shape.

Replicating Your Herp's Natural Environment

If you want your herp to be happy and feel at home in his new surroundings (and live longer, as well), you'll want to do your best to re-create his natural habitat. Setting up a terrarium (basically a glass container, or aquarium, enclosing a bit of natural flora and fauna) is one of the easiest ways to do this (see Figure 7-2). Each type of environment works for a different type of herp, but sometimes a herp can do well in more than one type of setup. The big difference among the types is water. See the following sections to find out about the specific water requirements for each type of environment.

Figure 7-2: A small terrarium can be set up as the ideal habitat for a number of small herps.

The woodland/rain forest setup

Woodland and rain forest both refer to terrariums that are heavily planted but lack a swimming area. The woodland tank is better suited for terrestrial herps from temperate areas, such as the seasonally active salamanders, frogs, lizards from northern climes, brown and red-bellied snakes, and smooth green snakes. Rainforest terrariums contain lush plantings and higher humidity than the woodland tank, making them a good place for many of the herps typically offered in the pet trade, such as the dart frogs and some of the chameleons.

Gathering supplies

For both the woodland and the rain forest terrarium you'll need the following:

- Terrarium
- Cage light and top
- Potting soil and mulch (not cypress) or leaves for the substrate
- River rocks or gravel, deep enough for a two-inch layer on the bottom of the tank
- Water dish
- A piece of plastic screening, twice the size the floor of your tank
- Cage furniture, such as rocks, driftwood, short log sections, and climbing limbs

For a uniquely woodland setup, in addition to the previous list, you'll need the following:

- Pea-sized gravel for bottom-most layer
- Low-growing seasonal plants, from a woodland or native plant nursery

For a rain forest terrarium, you need to add tropical or greenhouse plants from a nursery to the list of basics.

Creating a woodland/rain forest terrarium

Whether you're creating a woodland or a rain forest environment, directions for setting up the terrarium start out the same.

1. **Pour the river rock into the tank and smooth it out so it forms an even layer.**

   This will be your "drain field" for your tank, storing any excess water so the substrate won't be soggy.

2. **Double the screening and put it on top of the river rock or the gravel.**

3. **Place all heavy cage furniture — the rocks, the logs, and any big pieces of driftwood — on top of the screening.**

4. **Pour in the substrate, smoothing it out or contouring it as you pour it in.**

   Some people use a 1-inch depth in the front and a 2-inch depth in the back, but this isn't a hard and fast rule. Add the contours where you want them.

5. **Plant the plants directly into the substrate.**

   See the list of plant suggestions after Step 6. You can keep the plants in their original pots and bury the pots in the substrate (this technique makes it much easier to change out the plants if you need to).

6. **Add the light and the cage top.**

   See Chapter 9 to find out what kind of lighting your herp needs. The kind of cage top depends on where you live. If you live in a dry area, you'll need to keep more humidity in the cage, so you'll want a solid top. If you live where the ambient humidity is higher, you'll want a screen top to allow for more air circulation. You can place the fluorescent light atop the screen top, but you may want to put the combined heat/UV light closer to the basking surface (a distance of a foot is about right).

   Depending on the type of animal you have, you may not need a cage top, other than to keep other animals out of the cage or prevent your dropping things into the cage. Turtles and tortoises can't climb out of a cage (with exception of the big headed turtle who will walk into a corner and use his long tail as a prop to help him scramble, if he can, out of the tank), and you can largely skip covering the tank.

Here are some suitable plants for your woodland or rain forest terrarium:

Woodland Terrarium	*Rain Forest Terrarium*
Spotted wintergreen	Philodendrons
Pipsissewa	Pothos
Showy orchis	Spathyphyllum
Hepatica	Prayer plants
Violets	Fittonia
Native ferns	Dwarf sansevierias
Native mosses	

The savanna terrarium

The savanna terrarium is one of transition. This tank isn't quite forest, but it isn't desert, either. During the wet season, savannas themselves are rolling green glades with grasses and thorn scrub. In the dry season, savannas are sparsely vegetated areas. This transitional element makes duplicating the savanna a challenge. You can find savanna plants in some nurseries, and an amazing variety is available online, but you can make do very well by using dried grasses. To keep the humidity within the cage low (or at least no higher than the ambient humidity in your house), you need a screen top and a small water dish. Generally speaking, the larger the tank, the easier it is to re-create a savanna.

Gathering supplies

For the savanna tank, you need the following:

- Terrarium
- Cage light and screen top
- Aquarium sealant for affixing rocks and climbing limbs
- Two-inch thick Styrofoam insert, as long as the tank but of variable width
- Dried plants
- Potted drought-tolerant plants
- Rocks, climbing limbs, and cholla cactus sections
- Water dish
- Smooth sand for the substrate
- River rocks or gravel, deep enough for a 2-inch layer on the bottom of the tank
- A piece of air conditioning filter, roughly the same size as the floor of your tank
- Hot rock, if desired
- Cage furniture, such as rocks and climbing limbs

Setting up a savanna tank

Because a savanna tank isn't a lush tank, setting one up is fairly simple. Good plant choices are those with small or no leaves.

1. **Position the tank and stand in its final spot.**

   It will be too heavy to move when it's fully set up.

2. **Cut the Styrofoam insert to the desired shape, and position it in the tank.**

   A piece that's one-quarter to one-third of the tank's width and the same length as the tank works well.

3. **Cover the areas not covered by the insert with a 2-inch layer of pea gravel.**

4. **Position and use the aquarium sealant to secure heavy cage furniture such as stacked rocks or climbing limbs.**

   Let the sealant cure, which may take 24 hours.

5. **Add sand to the tank, covering the Styrofoam insert and the gravel.**

6. **Place potted plants where desired, partially nestling them down in the gravel and covering the plants to their rims with the sand.**

   Here are some plants to use:

   - Bermuda grass (originally from African savannas, this grass came to the United States via — you guessed it — Bermuda)

   - Snake plant, also known as mother-in-law's tongue (sansevieria)

   - Star plants (Haworthia)

   - Purslane (Portulaca)

7. **Position the hot rock at one end of the tank to create a temperature gradient.**

   Doing this is easier if the heat source is at one end rather than in the middle.

8. **Use a pencil or a screwdriver to poke holes in the Styrofoam for the dried grass and dried plant stems.**

9. **Insert the grasses and the plant stems into the holes and carefully fill around them with sand.**

10. **Use more sand to fill the tank to the desired depth (one to two inches of sand, usually) until the tank looks like a sandy area dotted with dried plants, and to fill around the hot rock.**

11. **Add the water dish in the end of the tank away from the hot rock.**

12. **Add the screen top and position the light over the basking area, adjacent to but not over the area heated by the hot rock.**

Plug in the hot rock and the light. Wait an hour or so and check the temperatures of the tank in the cool end, at the warm end, and under the basking light.

You'll need to monitor the temperatures in your herp's savanna tank. For the summer season, daytime temperatures should be 85 degrees or cooler at the cool end, 90 degrees or so atop the sand next to the hot rock, and 105 to 120 degrees under the basking light. Turn off the heating devices at night. For the winter season, temperatures at the cool end of the tank should be 70 degrees and 80 degrees at the hot end. The temperature under the basking light should be 90 to 100 degrees. At night, if the room temperature will stay from 55 to 70 degrees, turn off all the lights and heating devices. Leave the hot rock on if the room gets cooler than 55 degrees at night.

The desert terrarium

Deserts are basically savannas that don't get enough rain. Plants in the desert have even less leaf area than the savanna plants. Because trees are infrequent and stunted in the desert, the creatures that live in the desert are ground dwellers or live near and upon, under, or between rocks.

Desert terrariums are simple to put together (see Figure 7-3 for an example).

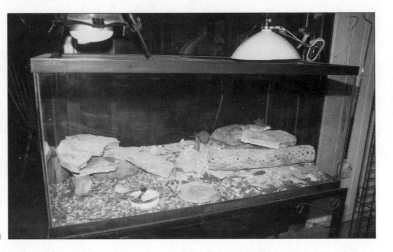

Figure 7-3:
A desert terrarium needs little beyond sand, rocks, a plant or two, and a small dish of water.

Gathering supplies

For the desert terrarium, you need the following:

- A terrarium as large as your budget and space will allow
- Screen cage top

✔ Cage light

✔ Sand for the substrate

✔ Small water dish

✔ A piece of PVC piping, 1 inch in diameter and 4 to 6 inches long, to push through the sand in one corner of the tank

✔ Drought-resistant plants, such as cacti or succulents

✔ Cage furniture, including rocks, driftwood, cork bark pieces or sections, and hideboxes

✔ Aquarium sealant for affixing rocks and climbing limbs

✔ Ventilation fan (optional)

Creating a desert terrarium

Before you place any substrate, first position and seal into place all stacked rocks and other heavy cage furniture. Many desert animals burrow, and unless the heavy objects are sealed into place, they can shift and crush your cage inhabitants. Allow 24 hours for the sealant to cure. Then you can start building your desert.

1. **Add enough sand to form a layer of 1 to 5 inches.**

2. **Nestle the plants in their original pots down into the sand.**

   If there's enough sand at that spot, hide the rim of the pot with the sand. Appropriate plants include the following:

   - Cacti

   - Euphorbias (the Old World counterpart of the New World cacti)

   - Star plants (Haworthia)

   - Snake plant, also known as mother-in-law's tongue (sansevieria)

   - Agaves

   - Desert verbenas

   - Grass palm

   - Tree beargrass *(Nolina)*

3. **Add the cork bark pieces and the hideboxes at the halfway point between the end of the tank where the light will be and the end without the light.**

4. **Push the piece of PVC piping down through the sand in one of the cool corners of the tank.**

   You'll pour water through this pipe to moisten the under layers of sand while keeping the top layer dry. Your tank may need as little as ½ cup (for a terrarium of 15 gallons or less) to 1 cup (for a tank of 44 gallons or so) once a week or every other week.

5. **Put the water dish near the cool end of the tank.**

6. **Add the screen top and position the lighting so you can heat a basking area at one end. If you're adding a ventilation fan, position it toward the cool end of the tank.**

Plug in your light to make sure that your setup is working properly. Wait an hour or so and check the temperatures of the tank in the cool end, at the warm end, and under the basking light. For the summer season, daytime temperatures should be 85 degrees or cooler at the cool end and 90 to 100 degrees or so atop the sand under the basking light. Turn off the light at night. For the winter season, temperatures at the cool end of the tank should be 70 degrees; the hot end should be 80 degrees. The temperature under the basking light should be 90 to 100 degrees. At night, if the room temperature stays from 55 to 70 degrees, turn off the lights and heating devices. Leave the undertank heater on if the room gets cooler than 55 degrees at night.

The aquatic/semiaquatic terrarium

In a way, the aquatic and semiaquatic tanks are two of the easier to set up and maintain because if you do it right (oh, with those words, I can hear my third grade teacher explaining how easy long division was), the filter takes care of a lot of the work. The downside, if there is one, is that you still need to clean the filter at least twice a week. To clean it, you remove the sponge and squish it out in running water until the junk is all rinsed out. You also need to do at least a partial water change every two weeks. Maintenance on an aquatic or semiaquatic tank is much easier if you set the tank near a window, so you can easily drain it to the outdoors.

The difference between the aquatic and the semiaquatic tank is just the amount of water in the tank. The aquatic tank is for those wholly or essentially wholly aquatic herps that dwell in water for most of their lives — most frogs, toads, and salamanders during the aquatic stage of their lives, as well as caecilians and sirens. These animals need only a haulout area (a piece of driftwood, a lily pad, or any floating object that's stable enough for the herp to climb on) as a place where they can dry off or sun themselves or get a temporary respite. The semiaquatic tank is filled only one-half to two-thirds of the tank height, and it has a larger haulout for its residents, which may include aquatic lizards, tadpoles metamorphosing into frogs, salamanders moving from their aquatic stage to their terrestrial stage, and some turtles, especially those who are weak swimmers. Both tanks are filtered, using a submersible filterhead with a foam filter.

Gathering supplies

Supplies you'll need for an aquatic or semiaquatic tank include the following:

- Tank
- Light (a fluorescent light for the aquatic amphibians and a UV/heat light for light-loving herps)
- Substrate (such as aquarium gravel that has been rinsed well to remove dust)
- Water dechlorinator
- Submersible pump with a foam filter
- Aquarium heater
- Aquarium thermometer (one that sticks on the outside of the tank is acceptable)
- Decorative rocks or driftwood
- Aquatic plants, floating and/or rooted
- A haulout surface (a small one for the aquatic tank and larger one for the semiaquatic tank)
- Tank top with fluorescent light

Setting up an aquatic/semiaquatic terrarium

After you've decided where to put your tank, put the stand and tank in place — after you add the water, it'll be too heavy to move — and then create your terrarium:

1. **Pour the rinsed gravel into the tank and smooth it out, layering it deeper toward the rear of the tank and perhaps deeper on the sides.**

2. **Put a saucer or a piece of typing paper on top of the gravel (to keep the gravel in place as you pour) and begin pouring the water into the tank.**

3. **When the water is near the halfway mark, stop adding water and put in your decorative pieces — the large rocks, the submerged driftwood, and the plants.**

   Place the rooted plants in the substrate, to the level of the plants' crowns, and push the loose gravel around the base of the plants to help hold them in place. Simply place the floating plants in the water. Here are some plants to include:

- Aquatic plants

- Elodea

- Amazon sword

- Arrowhead

- Eel grass (requires intense light)

- Duckweed (a fast-growing weed that many smaller turtles eat)

4. **Remove the saucer or the typing paper and continue to slowly pour in the water.**

   Add water until it reaches the correct levels: one-half to two-thirds of the way up the sides for a semiaquatic tank or within 2 inches of the top for the aquatic tank. If you're using tap water instead of water from your garden hose, you can regulate the temperature of the water you're using, and end up with a standing water temperature in the mid-70s, which decreases considerably your wait for your heater to warm up the tank to the desired temperature.

5. **Add the dechlorinator and give it a few minutes to disperse.**

   Most dechlorinators work against chlorine and chloramine, two disinfectants used to sanitize water. Your local water company can tell you what chemicals are in your water, in addition to chlorine, if you're interested.

6. **Add the filter powerhead, the aquarium heater, and the thermometer.**

   For a stick-on thermometer, place it against the glass near the bottom of the tank.

7. **Add the necessary haulouts.**

   Use smaller haulouts for aquatic tanks, and bigger ones for semiaquatic tanks.

8. **Put the tank top with the light in place.**

Make certain that the tank inhabitants can't escape through narrow gaps or removed fittings. Amphibians, with their slick, mucus-covered skin, can sneak through very small areas.

Before adding your herp, plug in the filter and heater, and give the tank at least three to four hours for temperature stabilization, depending on the size of your tank. The bigger the tank, the longer this will take, up to 12 hours for a tank of 100 gallons or more. Using the adjustment knob on the heater, increase or decrease the temperature as needed, waiting at least two hours between adjustments. (Remember not to take the heater out of the water when you're altering the setting, or anytime the heater is plugged in.) Your goal is a water temperature of 74 to 78 degrees.

Decorating with Cage Furniture

Cage furniture is any sort of decoration, usually functional, that you add to the caging to make the caging more useful for your herp. Cage furniture pretty much falls into three categories (climbing objects, areas for seclusion, and water features), although you'll be able to see that there's some overlap. You can add cage furniture to make the cage look better to your eyes, but only if these additions don't work to the detriment of your pets. For instance, elaborate climbing branches added to the cage of a wholly terrestrial lizard won't do a thing for him and may make it harder to warm up under his hot spot, harder for him to chase his crickets, harder to dash about, or harder for him to bury himself in the sand when the mood strikes him.

Cage decorations shouldn't adversely affect the humidity level in the cage. Sand boas, for instance, like desert surroundings, lying buried up to their beady little eyeballs in the sand, and added humidity from leafy plants isn't good for them.

Climbing objects

Climbing objects include tree limbs, vines heavy enough to climb upon, or even leafy plants for the lightweight day geckos. If the climbing objects are inert or dead, position them near the heat source so the herp can climb up and thermoregulate. If the climbing object is a live plant, place it far enough away from the light so the leaves won't get burned. Climbing objects can be as low to the floor of the cage as four inches, or they can go from the bottom of the cage to close to the top of the cage, just far enough away so the animal won't get caught by the cage door when you close the cage.

Climbing objects have to be strong enough to bear the weight of the animal. If you have any doubts, then secure the climbing objects at both ends to provide stability. You can buy pieces of driftwood that are secured to a flat base, or you can position a piece of wood, wedging the lower end in place so it won't budge when the herp climbs on it. A plant with vining branches or sturdy swordlike leaves (like a sansevieria) could provide some good hiding areas, if it's heavy enough so it won't tip over. Other lightweight herps may use Bio-Vine, a natural-looking yet artificial vine that can be bent to provide perching areas or flat areas where feeding cups can be secured.

Areas of seclusion/hideboxes

Hiding is a very typical behavior for a herp. Being exposed is a good way to get eaten. Vining plants, such as pothos, create wonderful areas of seclusion for smaller herps. When selecting a plant, look for one that is strong enough to hold the weight of the animal and one that can live with whatever lighting level is in the cage.

Hideboxes are another way for herps to feel safe. They serve as miniature caves. Snakes in particular like to sleep in hideboxes (maybe not having eyelids makes a dark place to sleep important). You can use any type of small box you have on hand, from a bank check box up to a shoe box; just add a hole in the side. You can buy hideboxes that are made of plastic and are easy to keep clean. You also can create hiding places from curved slabs of cork bark or from an overturned terra cotta flower pot or the saucer from one of these pots. You can nip a hole out of the flower pot or saucer with the help of a pair of pliers.

Your animal is going to spend a very long time in the caging you provide. Providing an area of seclusion helps your herp feel secure and makes his environment a little bit interesting.

Water features

You need to add a water dish to your herp's cage. Generally, you can fill a straight-sided bowl or dish with water and place it in a corner of the cage (so it won't get pushed around or over by the herp).

But not all herps use water dishes. Frogs and salamanders don't drink from water dishes, but they certainly sit in them to replenish their lost moisture. Their water dishes need to be big enough for them to clamber into and sit. In Chapter 11, I give you the lowdown on watering and feeding basics, but the following sections give you habitat-specific information about water.

Quenching the thirst of woodland/rain forest herps

You can use a pretty large water dish for woodland herps or rain forest herps. Just make certain that the dish is buried deep enough in the substrate so that the inhabitants can reach the water. If you can find two shallow dishes that nest inside each other, you may be able to bury one to its rim in the substrate, slip in the second dish, and fill it. When the time comes to clean the water dish, you just remove the top dish, clean it, replace it, and refill it. Your "place" in the substrate is held by the buried dish.

Offering water to desert creatures

Keeping a water dish in a desert terrarium may increase the humidity in the cage too much. Put the water dish in the cage overnight (for nocturnal creatures) or during the day (for diurnal herps) three times a week, and remove it in 12 hours.

You can add water to the lower levels of the sand in a desert terrarium by putting a stand pipe, a section of plastic pipe that "stands" in the corner of the tank (actually, the pipe is pushed through the layers of sand until it touches the bottom of the tank.) You add moisture to the bottommost layer of sand by dribbling water into the pipe once or twice a week. Don't add much — ½ cup is enough for a 15-gallon tank.

Satisfying water needs of arboreal herps

Herps that spend most of their time in the trees may not recognize water in a dish. In their natural habitat, they encounter water dripping off pendulous leaves or trickling down the trunk of a shrub or tree. Some arboreal snakes, such as emerald boas, satisfy their water needs by drinking dew droplets off their own coils. Here are a couple tips for watering these babies:

- ✔ Use a hand mister daily to gently mist your terrarium until droplets form on the leaves of the plants and the sides of the glass tank. If you're dealing with a desert species, mist the rocks in the enclosure and try pointing the mister upward so the mist falls lightly on the animal himself. Your herp may drink from what has condensed on his body.

- ✔ Secure a small water dish on the side of the tank, at the level of a climbing branch or at the intersection of two climbing limbs. Sometimes the water is more "visible" if it's moving, so try adding an aquarium air stone, powered by a small air pump.

Providing bathing pools

The larger herps, such as the pythons and boa, and the larger lizards, such as the iguanas, tegus, water dragons, and some of the monitors, enjoy using a bathing pool. Providing a bathing pool is easy if you have outdoor caging (see Chapter 8). Indoors, it's a bit more work.

You need a cage large enough for the snake or lizard and the water pool. About the largest pool you can easily move in and out is one of those under-bed storage bins that's about 18 x 36 inches and maybe 6 inches deep. Once or twice a week, put the pool in one corner of the cage and fill it halfway with water that's about 80 degrees. Of course, the water will cool down as it sits, but it will be easier for your herp to start swimming if the water is close to the temperature your herp would encounter in the wild.

Your pet will displace its own volume when it goes into the pool, and any type of activity is bound to splash even more water out of the pool. After an hour or so of swimming, open the cage door and bail most of the pool water into a carrying bucket. You'll need to change the substrate if it got wet. You can lift the pool once it's essentially emptied, but because these are flexible containers, you can easily dump water onto your floor if you aren't careful.

Don't be surprised if your lizard defecates while he's swimming — that's a very normal behavior. Just clean the pool thoroughly before you put it away.

Monitoring Humidity and Temperature

With manipulation of caging items such as water dish size, plantings, hot rocks, and lights, you can alter the humidity and temperature within your herp's cage. But how do you check temperatures and the humidity? Inexpensive humidity gauges are available from your local pet store. Some are combined with a thermometer.

If you're interested only in temperature, you have several choices. The easiest is the stick-on thermometer that goes on the outside of a tank, although that only gives you the temperature of the glass at one end. Small thermometers with dial faces, about 1½ inches in diameter, are available to put inside the cage, either on the cool end or on the hot end. An infrared gun is a good way to spot-check temperatures: It can give you a temperature read-out on whatever you point it toward, whether it's the coils of a python incubating her eggs (they actually shiver to raise their body temperature for incubation!), eggs in your own incubator, or the temperature of a cage's hot spot. But if you want to quickly check temperatures in several cages, add a thermometer to each one.

Advanced herpers may need to monitor their cages more closely, and equipment is available for that purpose. One company produces only thermostats, monitoring devices that control the power delivered to a heater. These thermostats also can provide for a nighttime cool-down and turn cage lights on and off. One unit will trigger other devices when the temperatures exceed a preset range; if it's too hot, the device will turn on a fan or the air conditioner, and if it's too cool, the unit will turn on an auxiliary heater. The unit can dial up to three preprogrammed phone numbers. These units can take a lot of work out of monitoring cage temperatures.

When the electricity goes off

What if you live in an area that experiences cold temperatures and the power goes off? Herp owners who live in cold climates quickly learn coping skills for powerless days. The tower-style kerosene heaters make adding heat to a room easy (and safe, if you read and follow the instructions). Many families buy natural gas heaters and have gas installed so that when the power goes off they aren't trooping off to sleep at a friend's house. In a pinch, the chemical hand warmers that sports stores sell can be used in a Styrofoam container with bagged animals (see Chapter 10 for information on putting your herps in muslin bags) to keep temperatures warm enough for survival until the power goes back on.

Cleaning Herp Cages

Nothing keeps your herp's home shipshape like routine maintenance. In this case, I'm talking about keeping herp cages clean with a minimum of effort. You do need to establish a regular schedule of checking the tank to see what needs doing, and cleaning spots and spills promptly.

Tidying up land-based cages

Cage cleaning isn't a lot of work after you've set your caging up. On a daily basis, check the water bowl. If the water bowl is dirty, toss out the water, clean the bowl, refill it, and put it back into the cage.

Once or twice a week, scoop out or blot up any deposited feces or puddled *urates* (the white part of feces). If you use newspaper or a paper cage liner, change the paper.

Once every two or three weeks, empty the cage. (You can put your herp in temporary quarters, such as a securely covered trash can of the appropriate size). Wash the walls and floor of the tank with misted water, or a solution of 3 parts bleach to 97 parts water. Dry the cage or let it air dry, and give it the sniff test to make sure that no lingering odors remain. Change the substrate and put the hidebox, water dish, and any plants back into the cage. Replace your herp and snap the cage top back into place.

Freshening aquatic and semiaquatic cages

With semiaquatic and aquatic cages, the water quality is largely maintained by the filtration system. The filtration system is maintained by . . . you (ever notice how it's always *you* who does all the work in taking care of a herp?).

Once a week, clean the filter for your "wet" (aquatic or semiaquatic) tank. The power head pumps with the sponge filters are easy to clean, and the sponges take only a few minutes to rinse under a running faucet. If you use the kitchen sink for this chore, wash and disinfect the sink every single time you clean your filter.

Every two to three weeks, do a partial to complete water change for your wet tank. You need to do a change sooner than this if the water turns cloudy in the tank. Cloudy water means you've put too much food in the tank or that something big has died. Cleaning means siphoning out the water that's in the tank and replacing it with fresh dechlorinated water. If you've placed your tank near a window, running a garden hose through the window makes emptying and filling the tank almost mess-free. You can use one hose to siphon the water out, while you're running new water into the tank with a second hose. This sort of rinsing action flushes a lot of the debris out of the tank. Then when you pull the siphon, it takes only a few minutes to fill the tank to the desired level.

You can do almost the same thing if you buy hose attachments that you can screw onto your kitchen sink or utility sink so you can attach your hose directly to the water from the sink. Emptying the tank may need to be done with a siphon and a series of buckets, but rinsing and filling it are easiest if you can use a hose.

Chapter 8

Giving Your Herp a Home in the Great Outdoors

Can reptiles and amphibians live outdoors, either in a wire mesh and wooden frame cage or in an open pen? Well, certainly all reptiles and amphibians have lived in the outdoors — somewhere — and with less formal accommodations.

Outdoor caging is especially relevant for the larger lizards, turtles, and tortoises, but it gives all herps what you wish you could give them inside: room to roam around and exposure to sunlight (see Figure 8-1). Providing outdoor caging for smaller herps is more work, but most of them do equally well outdoors.

Outdoor caging is easy — keeping it clean is a snap. Fecal matter drops to the ground and bacterial action reduces it to compost, and uneaten food items are easy to pick up. A monthly raking tidies up the floor of the cage. For lizards, a monthly hosing will clean perches and feeding trays.

I prefer outdoor caging for many lizards, turtles, and tortoises, but not for snakes. Snakes are better escape artists than the other herps, and they have the persistence to keep trying every nook and cranny with their noses until they find a gap they can wriggle through (and it doesn't take much of a gap). Snakes don't need access to ultraviolet lighting to keep their bones healthy; they get the calcium they need from their diet.

Figure 8-1:
A perm-
anent
outdoor
cage gives
your pet
access to
the sun
during the
warmer
months.

This chapter deals with the different types of outdoor caging, most of which are do-it-yourself projects. You don't have to be particularly talented to construct these cages; you simply need to be willing to spend some time outdoors during beautiful weather for the benefit of your herps. If you'd prefer, you can build these set-ups inside when it's wretched outside, but leave the herps inside until the skies clear and the temperature goes above 70 degrees. This chapter also alerts you to one downside of outdoor caging — predation by other animals — but I tell you what to watch out for and how to protect your herps against it.

Coping with Your Climate

The temperature range in your area is a huge factor in considering the feasibility of building and using outdoor herp caging. If your animals are indoors and it's cold outside, you can keep them warm by turning on the furnace. Or when your animals are inside and it's hot outside, you can turn on the air conditioner or a swamp cooler. But if your animals are outdoors, they and the cages must be able to withstand the vagaries of the weather, including both the seasonal changes and sudden, unexpected shifts in weather. Normally, cages usually heat up with the rising sun and cool down when it sets. On a dreary day, however, cage temperatures may remain cool all day, unless you have taken steps to overcome the problem.

Before you decide to put your animal outdoors, think about what kind of herp you have. If you live in arid southern Arizona and you want to keep white-lipped treefrogs or Chinese crocodile lizards outdoors, you'll have to go to some extremes to give your pets the amount of coolness, humidity, and moisture they need to survive. But, if you want to keep chuckwallas or Centralian blue-tongued skinks in your Arizona backyard, outdoor caging is easy to provide, for both animals are heat-loving and aridland species.

Conversely, if you live in a fog belt in California or in subtropical southern Florida, you have to think about the much higher rainfall and humidity. In those areas, although you may have to figure out how to add heat during cold spells for any herp, you'd certainly have to address the issues of humidity, wet caging and substrate, *and* temperature for desert dwellers.

In the southern tier of states, you can use outdoor cages for about half the year without creating problems for the animals. With minimal additional preparation, you can use them for another month and a half. In these states, even year-round use is a real possibility, with the use of plastic sheeting, heat lamps, and closeable, heated hideboxes.

The smaller tropical herps (such *Corytrophanes*, called the helmeted iguanas) are much less tolerant of cold weather. They don't have enough body bulk to store up heat. Any year-round outdoor caging for them would take more work to ensure better temperature control — by adding plastic sheeting or Plexiglas panels or installing a space heater; in effect, you need to re-create an indoor atmosphere in an outdoor setting, which doesn't make much sense. Smaller stuff I think is better kept inside.

In cooler places, such as central New England, the open-to-the-elements outdoor cages are usable for only about four months of the year. By enclosing them and using heating bulbs and elements, you could squeeze another two months of use out of them for iguanas and tortoises. But even with that, I still feel it to be worth the time, effort, and expense because there's less cage cleaning than if they are inside, they have more room to move around in, and they have ready access to UV light.

Free-standing outdoor caging

Different animals require different types of cages.

Cages for iguanas and other large lizards

My first iguana cage was 8 feet high and 10 feet square. Using treated lumber and wire mesh, I built it (with some help) one wall at a time, levering the walls upright and fastening them together, adding a top, and making it escape-proof. You can build your own with just a few supplies:

- ✔ Pressure-treated lumber (2-x-4s, each 8 feet long) for the frame and a door

- ✔ 134 running feet of 12-gauge 1-inch-x-½-inch wire mesh

- ✔ Three hinges

- ✔ One hook-and-eye latch

- ✔ A piece of 4-foot-x-8-foot aluminum sheeting to put over one end for shade

- ✔ Two pounds of 16D nails

- ✔ Twelve metal fastening plates

- ✔ Two packages of J-clips and a J-clip plier

- ✔ Two pounds of fencing staples

- ✔ Wire cutters to cut the wire mesh

Before you start, decide exactly where you want to place your cage. Although you can move it later, it's much easier to put it in the right spot to start with. Try to locate the cage near a power source. If you don't have a nearby power source, an electrician can dig a trench and bring an outdoor terminal to the cage. Because the door is placed in a short side, decide how to orient the cage so you can easily access the door.

To build the walls:

1. **Build the frame for one of the short walls first, just to get started. Place four 2-x-4s on the ground to form a hollow square. The narrow sides of the 2-x-4s should be uppermost. Fasten together at the corners with 2 nails (you could use screws). Add two more 2-x-4s, evenly spaced, inside the box and parallel to the sides. These 2-x-4s should lie flat on the ground with their wide side uppermost. Fasten them in place with the nails or screws.**

2. **Flip the wall frame over, so that the side that was facing down is now uppermost. Unroll some wire mesh and lay it across the frame sideways, starting at the top. Cut the mesh off the roll so that it's flush with the frame's sides. Secure the mesh in place with fencing staples, stapling it at 8-inch intervals along the top, sides, and the center 2-x-4s.**

3. **Add a second length of wire mesh, directly adjacent to the first. Position the second length as carefully as you did the first, making certain the mesh squares line up with each other. Use the J-clips and the J-pliers to fasten the edge of the first length of mesh to the next. Staple the second length of wire mesh to the 2-x-4s.**

4. **Add the third length of wire mesh, to completely cover the section with mesh. You'll notice that a foot of the mesh extends over the bottom 2-x-4; once the third mesh length is fastened in place, you'll bend that section of mesh at a right angle to the side.**

Once the cage is put together, this mesh will "line" the bottom edge of the caging all the way around and prevent any attempt to dig out.

5. **For the second short side of the cage, turn one of the central 2-x-4s so its narrow side faces up before you nail or screw it into place. This will be part of the doorway into the cage. Add one of the 30-inch crosspieces for the doorway, one foot above the bottom of the wall; add the second 73 inches above the bottom of the wall. Repeat Steps 2, 3, and 4, but don't cover the doorway opening with mesh; leave that open.**

6. **Build the door itself from the 29-inch and 60-inch lengths of 2-x-4, making sure the long sides are capped by the short pieces top and bottom. Cover the door with mesh, stapling it into place along all four sides.**

Build the two larger walls next, just as you did the first two, with four 2-x-4s parallel to each other (and the center two lying flat, rather than being on edge). Add the mesh just as you did in Steps 2, 3, and 4 above, bending the bottom edge up.

Here's how to assemble the cage (which is much easier and safer if you have two or three people):

1. **Put a 16D nail in the end of the brace, so you can stick the nail into the mesh of the side you're working with as you lever the side into place.**

2. **Move one of the short sides into place at the cage-raising site. Stand the short side upright and brace it temporarily with the 2-x-4-x-10. The side covered by the mesh should face toward the inside of the cage. Move one of the long sides into place and stand it upright, at right angles to the short side. Again, the mesh should face toward the inside of the cage. Use the metal plates to fasten the two sides together from the bottom to the top of the cage; I spaced mine at 24-inch intervals.**

3. **Add the other two sides, one at a time, securing one before adding the second. The long sides should be flush with the outside edges of the short sides. Once the pieces are fastened together, go inside the cage and make sure the bottom mesh lies flat on the ground, in effect lining the bottom edge of the cage.**

Here's how to make the roof, which really requires two or three people to help:

1. **Double-check the outside measurements of your cage, and build a box out of 2-x-4s that has those interior measurements, plus an inch or so to allow easy maneuvering when you fit the roof down over the side walls of the cage (think of a shoe box with a lid). Position the 2-x-4s vertically, with the shorter pieces inside the larger pieces.**

2. **Attach the aluminum sheeting and the mesh to the roof assembly. Staple the sheeting to cover one end of the roof to provide shelter from sun and rain over that part of the cage. Position it so that you can bend some sheeting over the edge of the roof to provide a baffle against blowing rain. Add the wire mesh over the rest of the roof, keeping the edges flush with the frame and using the J-clips to fasten the edges of the mesh together.**

3. **Slide the roof into place over the cage. Secure it in place with nails.**

Finally, hang the door in the door frame with the hinges so that the door will open outward. Add the hook-and-eye latch on the side opposite the hinges. On the inside of the cage, add the 1-x-3 baffles to the door opening, on the top and latch side. This gives the door something to rest against when you close the door, and the hinges will last longer.

This sort of cage design is easy to adapt to your location — feel free to make it bigger or smaller — or even to disassemble and take it with you when you move.

 Wrapping your enclosure with plastic sheeting (about the thickness of a heavy garbage bag) can be a viable way to keep your big lizards outside for just a few extra weeks — perhaps enough to get through the coldest part of (a Florida) winter.

Cages for smaller lizards

You can construct an open-topped round lizard pen that can house several species of blue-tongued skinks, Cunningham's skinks, gidgee skinks, and Storr's monitors. You use a single length of 3-foot-wide aluminum joined end to end to form a ring that is buried 1 foot deep into the ground. A length of about 27 feet yields a ring that's 8 feet across with a 1-foot overlap that can be wired or riveted together.

The round shape prevents any of the lizards from getting trapped in a corner by an aggressive cage mate. Inside the pen, you provide a central hiding/resting area under a pile of rocks that the lizards will use for daytime sunning. Lizards will retreat to the hiding area at night. (See the steps on building a pen later in this section). On cool, cloudy days, the lizards stay in their hiding area until the sun comes out and warms things up.

Here are the materials you need to build your cage ring:

- ✔ Sheet aluminum, also sold in rolls that are 3 feet wide
- ✔ Three to four short machine screws with bolts and a drill
- ✔ A stake and twine or nylon cord
- ✔ A posthole digger

Building the cage rings is simple:

1. **Drive a stake into the ground where the center of each ring should be.**

2. **Attach a length of twine, equal to the radius of your circle, to the stake.**

3. **Tie the free end of the cord to one handle of a posthole digger.**

4. **Quickly dig the trench for the bottom foot of the ring by holding the posthole digger exactly vertical and keeping the cord taut.**

5. **Make the trench about a foot deep, making your "fence" about 2 feet high, low enough to step over.**

6. **Remove the central stake.**

7. **Bury the lower edge of the aluminum in the trench.**

8. **Let the two ends overlap a foot or so as you scoop the dirt back into the trench, securing the aluminum upright in the shape of a ring.**

9. **Water the trench and tamp it down.**

10. **Use the drill to drill through the overlapped ends of the aluminum.**

    Space the holes about a foot apart. Put the machine bolts into the holes and screw the nuts on.

11. **In the center or near the center of the ring, bury two to three layers of half-thickness cinder blocks (available at home improvement stores), their openings parallel to the ground surface.**

12. **Add access to the cinder blocks with slanted terra cotta pipe (3-inch diameter) runways.**

13. **Pile climbing rocks in the center of the ring, over the hiding areas and pipes.**

    If the climbing rocks are in the center, away from the edge, the lizards can't clamber out and escape. Rocks with rougher surfaces allow even the clumsiest lizards to ascend to the top to avail themselves of every minute of available sunlight.

14. **Bury an easily removable and clean shallow water dish, 8 inches or so in diameter, up to its rim in the cage bottom.**

    Keep it filled with clean water.

You can build a perfectly serviceable lizard or tortoise ring (skip the climbing rocks and add a hidebox for tortoises) in only a few hours. These rings are not lovely, but they are functional. You can add netting over the top to prevent predation by crows, birds of prey, or cats; I recommend using the type you put over fruit trees. This netting is available at garden shops and home improvement stores that have a garden department. See the section "Protecting Your Herps from Predators," later in this chapter.

These ring cages are ideal for skinks and some monitors, but they're unsuitable for some other lizard species. If you live in an area where excessive rain and humidity are possible, you must choose species carefully for any given type of outdoor cage in any given location. But sometimes even carefully researched projects don't end well.

After succeeding with the skinks, I decided that I could add a few small, compatible lizards. Because I like the various green lacertas, I added some of them. All went well during the dry months of spring, but as soon as the rainy season began, the excessive moisture caused the lacertas to develop skin lesions, small roughened areas that looked like blisters. The lizards were removed to drier indoor caging, the blisters dried up, and the lizards were fine.

Cages for tortoises

My tortoises have a big (20-x-40 foot) outside pen complete with heated winter house. They usually return each evening to their sleeping house, even during the summer.

The pen is surrounded by a 2-foot fence. I've made turtle pens by using rolls of 1-inch-x-2-inch wire mesh fencing, stapled to 2-foot treated fence posts, and I've used 1-inch-x-12-inch-x-8-foot boards nailed to posts made from treated 2-x-4s. The wire mesh lets through sun and breezes; the board fence cuts breezes and some of the sun. The only criteria for the fence is that it must be of a small enough mesh size and close enough to the ground that tortoises (babies as well) can't wedge their way through it or under it.

I added a tortoise house made of ⅝-inch marine-grade plywood. I used one 4-foot square for the top and three pieces measuring 2 x 4 feet to form the sides and back. I cut a 15-inch-square entrance hole in one of the sides, and made a door from the piece I cut out. That heavy door, hinged to the door opening at the top, was kept out of the way with a hook and eye installed on the roof of the house, but it could be released to flap down and close the house in cold weather. A red spotlight, installed in the back of the house, provided heat.

At times in the winter, such as when a northerly wind comes blowing in at midday and drops temperatures 15 or 20 degrees in a half hour, some of the more-tropical tortoises simply drop to the ground and pull in their limbs and head. During sudden temperature drops, I check the tortoise pen each evening for those caught off guard by the cold, and put them in their house.

The more cold-tolerant highveld leopard tortoises (from cooler, savanna-type areas) seldom get caught by a rapid temperature drop, voluntarily returning to their house at night. You'll need to check your tortoises every night that the temperature drops below 50. Pick up any that are lingering outside and place them inside their house.

If you build a "front porch" to place in front of the entrance to your tortoise house, you can hang a heat lamp over the porch. This enables you to keep your tortoises in their outdoor pen for a few weeks longer, if you live where overnight freezes are common in the winter. If you live where winter freezes are unknown, a porch enables you to keep your tortoises in their outdoor pen until the latest cold front passes. The front porch is a three-sided barrier, built from 1-x-12-inch lumber. You can cut an 8-foot length into two 24-inch lengths and one 48-inch length and nail the pieces together in a flat U shape. A hook and eye at each end can tie the front porch to your tortoise house. Once the heat lamp is installed over the porch, your tortoises can walk and feed on their front porch and bask under the lamp on 40- to 50-degree days.

In colder areas, such as New England, you can build an open-topped 8-x-8-foot daytime enclosure made of 2-foot-high, shiny, heat reflecting aluminum sheets, which provide tortoises with a suitably warm daytime basking spot even in very cold temperatures. On still, sunny days, the temperature in such an enclosure will hover in the 70s or 80s, and even with snowbanks still on the outside of the pen, the tortoises can revel in the reflected heat and light. Put your tortoises outside after the sun is well up, and take them inside in the late afternoon.

Cages for amphibians

Not all outside cages have to be large or intricate. You can provide a very simple, open-bottomed cage in a well-shaded area that works well during the warmer months for some terrestrial frogs (toads, horned frogs, and others).

Here are the materials you need to build an amphibian cage like mine:

- Large aquarium with a snap-on top. The smallest feasible size is a 40-gallon tank.
- Water dish or tray about a foot square
- Hidebox
- Piece of welded wire the same size as the bottom of your tank. The 1-inch by ½-inch mesh size is best.
- Stack of newspapers
- Hammer
- Trash can
- Broom and dustpan
- Gloves and safety glasses or goggles
- A pair of pliers

1. Open several newspapers to make a bed of newspapers, at least five sheets thick, and bigger than the footprint of your tank.

2. Put your tank on the newspapers, and put folded sheets of newspaper inside the tank, covering the bottom with several layers. You want no bits of broken glass to sneak past the newspaper.

3. Use the hammer to gently but firmly break the glass in the bottom of the tank. After a few hits, peel back the newspapers to see how your impact-level is working. Replace the newspaper to re-cover the bottom. Continue tapping and inspecting until you can lift the tank and leave both layers of newspaper, with the glass sandwiched in-between, on the ground. Add another couple layers of newspapers if the ones you first put in are getting tattered.

4. Use the pliers to remove any pieces of glass still caught in the adhesive in the bottom. Put the tank aside and very carefully roll up the broken glass inside the newspaper layers and throw them away.

5. Replace the glass with the ½-x-1-inch mesh welded wire.

6. Dig a hole under the shade tree you selected just wide enough for the aquarium to sit in and about 12 inches deep. Save the dirt you scoop out.

7. Set the wire-bottomed aquarium into the hole, level it, and replace the dirt you removed when you dug the hole.

   This step gives you a sunken cage partially filled with soil.

8. Plant a vining philodendron.

9. Sink the water dish almost up to its rim into the earth, and add a hidebox.

10. Water the entire setup copiously.

After your cage is done, place a half dozen compatible frogs in the enclosure and snap on the lid. From that point on, except for feeding the frogs, replacing the water in the dish, and occasionally watering the entire cage, almost everything else is up to Mother Nature.

In my frog cage, when the rains fall, the frogs emerge at night, eat, sit at the edge of the water receptacle, trill or bleat as is their nature, occasionally breed, and are burrowed in again by daylight. I chose species that could readily withstand the vagaries of weather in our area, and the amphibians thrived in their enclosure.

This type of cage is acceptable for many newts and other salamanders, many frogs/toads, box turtles, and some lizards. Depending on the animal, the dimensions of the water container may need to be larger or smaller. If your soil is more clay than soil, or if the soil tamps down, you may need to loosen the soil by mixing in some sphagnum or peat. Be sure the mesh used on the top and the bottom is small enough to retain the creatures being housed.

 Place this caging (or any other caging that is in contact with the earth) in a pesticide-free area, water it with chemical-free water, and always consider the seasonal track of the sun. Direct sun is a killer for animals in a glass house, even if most of the house is buried.

The window cage

A window cage is a cage that is both outdoors and indoors — it protrudes from a window into the great outdoors, but is accessible from the inside. Another variation of this caging is a wire cage placed in front of an open window, in the path of sunlight. Because of the real danger of overheating (or cooking) your herp, you can't use a glass tank.

The window cage is designed to extend outward from an open window for a distance of a foot or two (more if possible). A south or west exposure is best. The cage should be of wood and wire mesh or all wire mesh construction (not glass!). Covering the mesh sides with window screening prevents any feeder insects from escaping, a good thing to remember when you're buying crickets at 12 for a dollar. Covering one end of the window cage with a solid surface affords some shelter against rain or bright sunlight.

The cage should rest firmly on the windowsill and may be braced by adding L-brackets to the bottom of the cage, with the other leg of the bracket resting against the side of the house. This cage can be an ideal summertime home for many sun-loving lizards and small tortoises and allow the entry of summer rain, humidity, and a natural photoperiod (natural day/night length — one without artificial lighting) as well.

You can make wood and wire cages in either of two ways:

- ✔ You may make each side and end as a separate entity, and hold all together with screw-on corner brackets or hooks and eyes. This style of cage allows easy disassembly, removal, and storage at the end of each usable season.

- ✔ You can simply nail or screw the frame together as a cube, wrap the four sides in a single piece of wire, and use a separate piece of wire for the outer end.

In either case, you have to make a latchable door of some sort on the inner end to facilitate the entry and removal of the reptile as well as the cleaning of the cage.

Provide plants or other visual barriers and make sure one end of the cage is shaded. A dish (or other watering system) providing fresh water must always be available.

Movable outdoor caging

Movable cages can never be as large as stationary ones, but they may be your best (and only) choice. They can be *relatively* large. Many of the wood and wire mesh movable cages that I use for day geckos, chameleons, and rat snakes have a footprint of 4 feet by 4 feet and are 6 feet tall. These cages are intended to remain outdoors year round, but because they have large (4-inch diameter) bottom casters, they require only that you have a smooth, hard surface (such as a patio or a deck) so that you can move them at will. See Figure 8-2.

Figure 8-2:
Wire mesh and wooden caging is more useful on casters.

If you construct your wood and wire mesh caging so it's narrow enough to fit through doorways (24 inches wide — the cage can be 48 inches long if you like) and low enough to go through doorways once large casters are added to the bottom (total 72 inches top to bottom), the cage can go indoors or outdoors as weather permits.

During the dog days of summer, you can keep the cages largely in the shade (if shade is available). During cool weather, you can move the cages into the sun or into a sheltered spot away from the wind.

Once the weather cools, you can extend the useful life of the cage by wrapping it with plastic sheeting on the top and on three sides. Keep the side with the door accessible by stapling another piece of plastic from the top so it hangs like a flap over that side of the cage.

Add several days to several weeks to the cage's usefulness by hanging a heat lamp or two inside. Use the proper type of electrical wiring and sockets for the bulbs and place them where they can't overheat and burn any items such as plants, perches, animals, or the cage itself!

If you have only one or two small lizards, a White's treefrog, or a small snake (one less than 6 feet long), you may want to make an even smaller, simpler, and lighter moveable cage measuring 3 x 3 x 4 feet. You can make one by using precut panels of wire (of suitable mesh size) and holding them together with J-clamps. J-clamp hinges can hold the door in place. Secure the door with spring latches you buy from a feed store, or use at least two of the snap latches like those found on dog leashes, which you can find at most hardware stores. Such a cage is easy to lift, and you can hang it by a wire from each upper corner from a limb or simply place it on a table.

You can buy ready-made mesh cages. These are made from a PVC frame that's covered with a zippered mesh shell, and they come in several sizes, ranging from 14 x 14 x 25 inches to 29 x 29 x 72 inches. They readily house herps such as tree boas, tree pythons, small monitors, chameleons, and other popular herps.

The ready-made mesh cages come apart for easy storage, and they're easy to reassemble. Their zippered design permits easy access, and the cage is so lightweight that moving it takes just a moment. The mesh permits excellent air circulation but does impede visibility of the interior somewhat. The mesh covering seems relatively impervious to the chewing of crickets and is long lasting. These cages are available at many pet stores, as well as at herp expos and on the Web at www.bigappleherp.com/Pages/Product/106200.html.

Cleaning the Outdoor Cage

Outdoor cages are quite easy to maintain, but don't assume that you can ignore yours just because the cage is outdoors. Keep all cages clean, whether they're for amphibians or reptiles.

If your herp's cage has an earthen floor, rake and remove debris such as uneaten food, feces, fallen leaves, and whatever else is accumulating. Periodically spray the cage floor heavily, allowing the water to carry impurities far away from the surface of the substrate. Some hobbyists choose to periodically remove and then replace the top two or three inches with fresh soil.

If the cage has a wooden or wire floor, periodically remove any large pieces of debris. Occasionally spray the entire cage thoroughly with a water jet. About once every two weeks, remove the herps and scrub the cage floor with a weak bleach solution (10 percent bleach to 90 percent water). Afterward, rinse the cage thoroughly with fresh water. Rinse amphibian cages especially well; delicate amphibian skin soaks up everything it comes into contact with.

Splish Splash! The Outdoor Pond

Nothing brings a feeling of peace and well being to outdoor herpetological endeavors like a garden pool (see Figure 8-3). A pool is an ideal summer home (and sometimes a year-round home) for turtles and other herps.

Figure 8-3:
An outdoor pond is easy to set up and provides a naturalistic setting for turtles.

You may not have to stock the pond, at least not by going out and getting herps and moving them in. They may move in on their own volition. Many native herps (especially turtles, frogs, toads, and treefrogs) are drawn to a newly installed pond like metal filings to a magnet. Within a few days of installation, many pools, even those in urban areas, take on a life of their own. See the section "Welcoming the locals: Native herps move in," later in this chapter, for more on enticing the natives to your pool.

Many communities have regulations pertaining to pools, whether they're for swimming or for frogs. Among the more common restrictions is the need for a childproof fence surrounding the pool or pond. Check and comply with regulations when considering the construction of your pool. It might be in your best interest to post a keep out sign because you know how some people are.

Location, location, location

As with other outdoor setups, exactly what species of herps you can keep successfully in an outdoor garden pool largely depends on where you live and what type of pool you install.

In the far northern United States, water temperatures may be so low even in the summer that you can keep only the most cold-tolerant temperate species. In the southern states, although the water in in-ground pools may never freeze, their water temperatures can easily drop into the 40s in midwinter.

Pools stocked with tropical species can be used only from late spring until mid-autumn. In the cooler weather, you must carefully watch even temperate species for signs of distress (see Chapter 9 for the effects of cold). A cold herp has trouble moving and will drown if he's in the water. His digestion is stopped, which leaves any food sitting in his stomach.

In Florida and southern Texas, where both ground and water temperatures are more moderate, you can keep a greater diversity of species outside for a longer period of time. In southern Florida and the Lower Rio Grande Valley, many species, including tropical forms, can safely stay outside year-round.

In the north, you'll probably want to place your garden pool in a sunny area. In the Deep South, you may need to choose a partially shaded location.

You can rather easily drain and reposition an above-ground pool — even a large one — after initial setup. Moving even a small in-ground pool is more difficult. Choose the location carefully. Keep in mind those small pools both heat up and cool down much faster than large ones and that above-ground pools usually heat up and cool down faster than an in-ground pool.

Although you need to be careful no matter what size pool you install, a larger pool is more forgiving of oversights and omissions. If you accidentally put in too much food, the larger water volume means more dissipation of the food and more friendly bacteria to break down that food. If you forget to turn on the pool heater, a larger pool takes longer to reach chilling temperatures.

When situating the pool, take into consideration the seasonally variable hours of direct sunlight caused by the changing angle of the sun. Create sunning areas for the turtles by positioning logs and/or smooth rocks in the center of the pond, and add the water via a garden hose. Always dechlorinate, dechloramine, or age pool water before you add any herps, to remove chemicals. It just seems unfair to prepare a gorgeous site for herps and then plunk them into water that they can't tolerate.

Selecting your pond type

You can choose from many styles (and prices) of garden pools. They run the gamut from huge, free-form, concrete-lined showpieces to preformed garden pools to small kiddie wading pools.

In selecting your garden pool style, take stock of the following important aspects:

- ✔ **Monetary outlay:** The bigger the pond, the more it will cost.

- ✔ **Space available:** A small pool is going to look pretty dinky in the center of your big yard; conversely, it's pointless to buy a pool too large for its designated spot.

- ✔ **Geographic location:** If you live in Michigan's Upper Peninsula, you may have only a few months out of the year you can use a pond. If you live in a condo on Miami Beach, is there room for a pool of any size?

- ✔ **What species of herps you want to keep:** The water dragons are gorgeous active lizards that are one step faster then the cartoon road-runner. They aren't going to stay in a pond, unless there's screen around the pond, and even then, they'll smash their noses against the screen, trying to get out. Fall in love with a herp who'll think the new pond is just dandy, thank you, and won't budge out of the pool except to dry off and dive back in. Think about a slider or a cooter, both attractive turtles who like ponds, the sun, and eating.

Choosing an above-ground pool

A few baby semiaquatic turtles can do quite well in something as simple as a kiddie wading pool or a small 50- to 100-gallon free-form rigid plastic pool. Such simple setups can be placed on a porch, deck, or in the yard, and you can set up a haul-out area (an area where the turtle can get out of the water to dry off and warm up) in the center of the pool. Keep the water level high enough so that the inhabitants can totally submerge themselves, but not so deep they can haul their heavy bodies up over the edge and escape.

If you choose a kiddie wading pool, choose one that has no ramp leading to its rim. If yours is ramped, enclose the pool securely either within a surrounding fence or with a top to prevent the escape of your animals.

I've used galvanized stock-watering tanks (available at feed stores) for pools, and they worked well. The pools were 8 feet in diameter, 30 inches high, and surrounded by a deck. The deck was built to flow around the ponds, and the ponds' rims were a few inches above the deck surface. Vertical planks of weathered cypress concealed the exposed metal. The pools were partially filled with 22 inches of water, and each was home to a few turtles and hardy fish. Large pieces of easily accessed driftwood haulouts protruded from the center of each tank and angled, and partially submerged logs provided additional basking haulouts.

One pool housed basically nonherbivorous map turtles, some huge siren (large, two-legged, aquatic salamanders), hardy water lilies, and potted emergent vegetation such as dwarf papyrus and cattails, permitting us to enjoy both the activities of the turtles and the beauty of the plants. The other pool contained herbivorous sliders and a hearty supply of native aquatic plants (such as hydrilla and hyacinths) that were replenished weekly from a pond in a nearby golf course.

Although these pools will usually serve admirably for several years, the galvanized tanks will eventually rust. When this happens, drain and empty the pond. Let the tank dry thoroughly and add a coat of fiberglass to the inside surfaces. (You can buy a fiberglass paint at home improvement stores.) You can also line the tank with a flexible pond liner of appropriate size; these will last for several years.

If you hope to breed your reptiles, this type of setup does have drawbacks because, although many of the creatures breed in the water, turtles must nest on land. An in-ground pool is better for these projects.

Digging an in-ground pool

In-ground ponds are largely permanent ponds, but they're also the most natural looking. The simplest are made from pool liners, heavy vinyl-type plastic sold by the square yard. You can buy liners that are up to 12 feet wide in garden centers for ponds larger than this, and your best source is a catfish farm supplier. Explicit directions for making these pools are available in the same garden shops where the liners are sold.

Choose your pond site carefully. If you have a septic tank, don't try to install a pond on top of the drain field.

In some areas of the United States, a water-impervious, easily worked clay called bentonite is available that you can use to line the depression that will become your pool. Pools of these types can be variably tiered and decorated in the deeper parts with potted lilies and spatterdock, or with submerged plants. On the tiers you can use potted emergents, such as St. John's wort, cattails, and blue flags. These plants are the most natural, but not necessarily the best because they grow very fast and may become a pest.

If you're particularly artistic, you may choose to install a truly elaborate cement pool or pond. One of the best I saw was about 20 feet long and 12 feet wide, and was spanned by a functional bridge that was maybe a foot above the surface of the water, and a large elevated deck at the far end of the bridge overlooked the entire pond area. The depth of the pond varied from about 18 inches at the deepest point to 12 inches at the shallow end. The pool was made of cement reinforced with hog wire, and was troweled to a smooth finish to assure that the turtles didn't abrade their bottom shells while entering or leaving the water. I sat for a long time, watching the turtles paddle about in the shallow water.

Once your in-ground pond is installed, add a low fence (with a several inch overhang) about 3 feet from the rim of the pond. Plant shrubbery and other types of cover in the enclosure, especially if you're in the southern or southwestern United States and if the pond receives more than a couple hours of direct sun each day. You want to provide the pond's residents with choices in temperature selection.

Should a female turtle be carrying eggs, she can select a spot to dig and bury her eggs. Unlike the reptiles, most amphibians that are routinely kept in pool areas (frogs, toads, treefrogs, and aquatic salamanders) lay their eggs in the water. Many amphibians can successfully breed with no land area available.

Cleaning the pool

If you have a small pond in direct sunlight that houses many resident turtles that get fed everyday, you may need to clean it once every two or three days. If you have a larger pond with adequate filtration and you carefully monitor the feeding, you may need to clean the pond only once every month or so.

When cleaning the pond, here's what to do:

1. **Drain or siphon out as much water as possible.**

2. **Hose off the algae or wipe the pond down as part of the cleaning process.**

3. **Partially refill and then re-siphon out that water.**

4. **Refill the pond for the final time.**

5. **Let the pond sit for 24 hours before adding any animals, or add your dechlorinator. Don't add any sort of chemicals to kill or inhibit the algae. These chemicals are often toxic to herps.**

Gauge the amount you feed your herps carefully. Uneaten food quickly causes bacterial buildup in the pool (especially in a small pond) and may necessitate a water change.

Adding filtering and lighting systems to your pond

Although filtration is optional for all garden ponds, providing filtration helps maintain water quality and almost certainly will improve water clarity.

Pond filters are readily available online, at many larger pet stores, and at the garden shop areas of home improvement stores. The pumps run on electricity, so you need to install or have installed an outdoor-type outlet. The pump draws the water — some of them are capable of moving hundreds of gallons an hour — through the filter medium, removing particulate matter (but not ammonia or nitrites) from the water along the way.

The same pump can activate a small waterfall or other decorative water feature. Waterfall additions and other items such as pond-to-pond waterslides are also available. Underwater or other pool lighting is also readily available. Entrust the installation of these items to a qualified electrician.

Nighttime lighting, also optional, can add to the hours that you can enjoy your pool. During the winter months, even in the Deep South, night may fall before a hobbyist returns home from work. A pond with nighttime lighting takes on almost a magical quality.

Welcoming the locals: Native herps move in

It has never seemed to matter where I've lived: If I had an outdoor pond, local herps (and insects) took up residency in and around it.

Within weeks after installing an in-ground backyard pond in western Massachusetts, I found worm snakes, ring-necked snakes, and red-bellied snakes beneath the surrounding flagstones. American toads trilled in season from the shallows and deposited long strings of eggs that produced thousands of tadpoles. When those that survived metamorphosed, my yard would literally seethe for days with the tiny toadlets as they dispersed into the neighborhood. Green frogs and pickerel frogs moved in from the natural pond across the street, and an occasional painted turtle visited and basked before returning to more natural surroundings.

In north central Florida, in-ground ponds and their environs draw southern toads and green treefrogs. Yellow-bellied sliders visit and often stay for weeks. A 6-foot long alligator stopped by for a visit, but thinking it a little much for such a small facility, it was relocated to a nearby swamp. Garter snakes prey on the treefrogs and baby toads, while crowned snakes and pinewoods snakes are under stones and vegetation at pond's edge. Green anoles bask and forage on the cattail leaves, and broad-headed skinks are common visitors.

It was in central Florida that I was most surprised by the local animals that moved in. There, in a very urban setting, I would have thought reptiles and amphibians to be rarities. Within days after the in-ground pond was installed and landscaped, however, southern leopard frogs, narrow-mouthed toads, and southern toads came from out of nowhere. A black racer made a hurried visit, and green treefrogs and squirrel treefrogs were abundant.

The nicest part about hosting these locals is that they all seemed perfectly able to care for themselves. I didn't have to clean them, and I didn't have to feed them. I only had to enjoy their presence.

As you can see, the species of herps that take up residence at your garden pool depend on where you live. Sometimes you may get a newt or three. Sometimes native frogs and toads may move in. And sometimes creatures you hadn't considered may drop in.

A friend in the Lower Rio Grande Valley of Texas has in his yard one of the most viable colonies of the rare (in the United States) Mexican treefrog, and near the environs of the pools, Brahminy blind snakes (an Asiatic species), Rio Grande chirping frogs, and black-striped snakes are also common.

A friend in central Arizona gets visits from many species of local herps at her tiny pond, but rabbits, countless birds, foxes, and herds of javelinas (collared peccaries) also regularly stop and drink.

A friend on the Pacific Coast hosts Pacific treefrogs and red-legged frogs.

If you're in tune with the natural world that surrounds you, a garden pond or pool, either in ground or above ground, can be a wonderfully attractive addition, even if you don't keep exotic herps as pets.

Protecting Your Herps from Predators

You must protect the herps you keep outside, whether in a cage or a pool, from predators. Some predators, such as cats or raccoons, can be fairly easily controlled. The control of other critters, such as crows, moles, shrews, and fire ants, can be more challenging.

Sometimes predation comes from unexpected sources. Mice and rats may opportunistically feed on lizards and amphibians, and if they gain access to a cage by burrowing, their tunnels may serve as escape routes for your exotic herps.

Prevention is, unquestionably, the best solution to ingress by rodents or other potential predators. Keep cages secure. Having bottoms in the cages or vertical metal barriers a foot or so in height buried in the ground at cage perimeter will prevent casual visits by rodents. But if they do gain entry, eradicate them as quickly as possible.

You may also find that shrews and moles visit your outdoor cages, but discourage these visitors, too. Shrews readily eat small herps, and moles may eat or injure herps buried into the substrate or any clutches of eggs they happen across. Vertical cage-edge barriers may discourage moles, but these little mammals may simply dig deeper than the barriers — and are certainly easily able to do so. Collapse mole burrows that are near your cages as soon as you find them.

Raccoons may be the single greatest scourge to any outdoor herp collection. These masked bandits are now found in rural, urban, and suburban areas. They're immensely powerful for their size, frighteningly dexterous, and tremendously determined. Physical removal of raccoons by any means available to you is necessary to protect your animals.

Visits by opossums and foxes often occur, but neither of these creatures display the persistence and tenacity of a raccoon. Secure cages and fencing often quickly discourage these predators.

Because in their snuffling quest for insects and other buried culinary treats, armadillos can quickly destroy a landscaping project, do all you can to thwart them, too. They will eat any buried reptile eggs they may find. Scarlet snakes and kingsnakes are also fond of reptile eggs, but many herpers would be so pleased by a visit by one of these beautiful serpents that some indiscretions would be overlooked. Physically removing and relocating armadillos and the visiting snakes is a simple matter: Just pick up the armadillo (they don't bite), put him in a box and turn him loose elsewhere, or you can chase him out of your yard with the spray from a garden hose. See Chapter 9 for tips on moving snakes.

Feral and free-roaming pet cats may be one of your most persistent problems. If pleading with the cat's owner doesn't work, then you may need to resort to humane trapping and taking the felines to a shelter or city pound.

Predatory birds such as raptors and wading birds can wreak havoc on stock in open cages or pools. Make sure that all cages are covered, and physically drive wading birds away. Crows can also be a problem — I've had crows watch my tortoise lay eggs and then call other crows to join in the feast. As unfair as it may seem, these birds are protected by federal law. Be innovative but firm in your efforts to discourage them. If you discover something that works well, you can sell the idea to farmers and become rich.

Wandering dogs — even your own — may be tempted to remove and injure or kill an easily accessible reptile or amphibian. Water-loving dogs may consider the pool their very own swimming pool, happily clambering into the water at the most inopportune times. Dogs that would never bother any reptile indoors may view herps kept outdoors as fair game. Keep cages closed and know what your dog is doing while he is outside.

Native garter snakes, ribbon snakes, and water snakes (and rarely, a cottonmouth, if you live in the country) may settle into the backyard pond and prey on the available frogs and toads. If you don't want to have them in residence, physically remove them or call a pest removal service.

Remember that cottonmouths are venomous! Don't handle them unless you're experienced. Check with a local museum, college biology department, or herpetological club to find a qualified venomous snake handler. Cottonmouths have heavy bodies, and only the Florida subspecies retains the characteristic light-bordered dark cheek streak. Don't take chances on trying to identify a cottonmonth in your home pond. Call an expert.

I can't overemphasize the importance of keeping fire ants out of any and all facilities where you keep reptiles or amphibians. These aggressive, toxic, non-native ants are able to swarm and overcome many animals, reptiles, amphibians, birds, and mammals.

If the hill of fire ants is outside of your caged area, you may use a fire ant bait and poison. If the hill is in the facility, pour a little dish soap and boiling water into the nest. You may take several applications, but the ants usually quickly move their colony to an area where traditional baits and poisons can be used.

Perhaps the most disappointing predators of all are uncontrolled children and dishonest adults. Herp theft is not uncommon. You and the appropriate authorities must deal with this problem on an individual basis. As a general approach, even though you're probably proud of your herp setup, you may not want to show off the residents of your outdoor caging or pond to every person who rings your doorbell.

Do not use garden pesticides in your yard. It's hard to control exactly where a spray goes; even a small breeze can pick up a mist and deposit the mist on your pond or in an outdoor cage. Rain washes the pesticides off the plants, and some of the run-off trickles into an outdoor cage or your pond.

Monitoring Behavior and Health

Monitoring the health of animals is more difficult when the animals are kept outdoors. Your creatures can be more difficult to find and observe in quasi-natural conditions than they are in a relatively stark indoor terrarium or cage.

Yet the importance of monitoring the health of your herps doesn't diminish with a simple change of venue. If you observe your herps carefully, you'll find that their body language can tell you whether they're well or sick.

Noticing the effect of sunlight

It becomes more important than ever to understand the subtle body language of reptiles and amphibians. They can't tell you if they feel ill or if they feel positively terrific. Expect a few changes when your herp goes into outdoor caging and receives natural sunlight, perhaps for the first time in a long time.

- ✔ Your herp may seem aggressive toward you, perhaps acting a little "wild." For example, he may respond to your presence by evading you, hissing, curling the body when you reach toward him, or even making a fast dash to the far side of the enclosure.

- ✔ Your herp may look at another herp and love blooms. Suddenly your red-bellied turtle is swimming crazily alongside the female, poking his face into her face and fanning her face with the long claws on his front feet.

- ✔ Your herp's appetite may increase. A lizard that normally picks at his mealworms perks up and wolfs down his mealworms.

Feeding your outdoor herp

Feeding arrangements don't really differ much between indoor and outdoor settings, but herps you keep outside need careful observation. Be especially observant after any significant and unexpected periods of cold. If your herp shows any sign of nasal discharge or any other unexpected behavior, bring it indoors where you can readily observe him and consult a veterinarian.

Chapter 9

Let There Be Light — and Heat

*H*erps around the world depend on sunlight and the seasonal variation in day-night cycles to warm up their lives and to regulate their breeding cycles. The strength of the sunlight is determined by the latitude, with the effects being the strongest near the equator. Once you head away from the equator, temperatures drop, and seasonal variations become more pronounced.

The single most important factor that determines the distribution of reptiles and amphibians is temperature. Temperature determines how far north or south a herp may be found. Temperature affects herps on two levels: It determines how well the animal can function and the hatching time of the eggs, regardless of whether those eggs are retained or deposited into the ground or leaf litter. The young must emerge early enough in the warm season so they have enough time to eat and store energy before the winter cool-down.

Temperatures that are too warm also limit where herps are found, especially for specialized herps. One example is the lungless salamanders, the plethodontids. They do very well in temperate areas; many of them inhabit mountain streams where the cooler water is loaded with oxygen. They can't live in warm environments because warm water can't carry as much oxygen as cool water.

Temperature: Herps Like a Little Change

In the wild, reptiles and amphibians deal with day and night temperature fluctuations as part of the change of seasons and the changes in day length. The day/night changes are a part of the annual cycling process that readies an animal for reproduction. In the Amazon, nighttime and daytime temperatures differ. Day-to-night temperatures — up to 40 degrees — are even more distinct in a desert.

Herps thrive best when you provide a bit of nighttime cool-down for them and offer a natural day-night length. Providing this kind of environment may be as simple as turning off the lights and all sources of heat in the early evening.

Amphibians, creatures that don't really need any strong lighting or any heat beyond the ambient levels in your house, get their evening cool-down as the temperatures in your house cool with the evening. For reptiles, if temperatures in your house go below 60 degrees at night, you may want to leave a heating pad or hot rock on during the night. Because the heating pad or hot rock covers only a portion of the cage flooring, if a reptile doesn't want any heat, he can easily move away from it.

 Providing a natural temperature range and day length for your herp is easier than you might expect, thanks to the inexpensive timers that turn your lights on and off according to a preset time. You can turn your lights on and off yourself, or you can buy a couple of timers and save yourself a lot of bother.

For wild-caught captives, you have two choices in cycling: You can replicate the day-night cycle in their native habitat, or you can switch the herps over to your day-night cycle. To duplicate the photoperiod found in your herp's native haunt, go online for the sunrise and sunset times for your herp's area of origin. Try http://aa.usno.navy.mil/data/docs/RS_OneDay.html or www.auslig.gov.au/geodesy/astro/sunrise.htm, or call your local librarian for these times if you don't have a computer or access to one. You can switch your animals over to the day-night cycle where you live, by checking your local paper for sunrise and sunset times and changing the timers accordingly. (See the section "Imitating Mother Nature," later in this chapter, to find out how to set things up for your herp.)

Getting It Light the First Time

Lighting is so much more than turning on a light switch. For reptiles and a few amphibians, lighting is the primary source of warmth and a source of ultraviolet light. So you can understand what wavelengths of ultraviolet light are the most useful, ultraviolet (UV) light is in turn divided (arbitrarily, I'll admit) into three types of lighting, UVA, UVB, and UVC. Only the first two are produced by herp lighting.

UVA and UVB: Knowing the difference

UV light is the very short wavelength end of the lighting spectrum, wave lengths too short for the human eye to perceive. Although you can't see UV lighting, it has a powerful effect on plants and animals. You've probably heard about holes in the ozone layer of the earth's atmosphere, and the harmful effects of too much UV. UV light can be broadly described as an exciter — it stimulates the body (in this case, herps, primarily reptiles) into producing vitamin D and a whole host of other natural behaviors.

There are three types of ultraviolet (UV) lighting, defined by wavelength. All can be damaging. As you progress from UVA through UVC, the energy in that wavelength gets greater. I discuss only UVA and UVB here because pet lighting doesn't produce UVC.

- **Ultraviolet A:** UVA has a wavelength of 320 to 400 nanometers. It is unaffected by the ozone layer. In humans, this invisible wavelength causes wrinkles. For reptiles, this *visible* wavelength makes things look "normal," from food to the surroundings to potential mates. Normal behavior is the result. Without UVA, everything is colored just a bit "off" for reptiles, rather like having your own world subtly tinged blue. We do not know what function UVA serves in amphibians.

- **Ultraviolet B:** UVB has a wavelength of 280 to 320 nanometers. This is the UV wavelength that is normally filtered by the ozone layer, but holes in the ozone means UVB streams through. In humans, this is the wavelength that causes sunburns, immune suppression, and skin cancer. In reptiles, exposure to UVB triggers the formation of vitamin D3, which is used to metabolize calcium, necessary for avoiding bone disease.

Lights that produce UVB produce UVA as well, in much higher quantities than UVB. The fluorescent UVA/UVB bulbs produce UV lighting, but little heat. Typical brands are Big Apple's White and UltraBlue 7.0 Fluorescent, Vita-Lite Plus Fluorescent (manufactured by Duro-Test), DayCycle (Tetra Terrafauna), Iguana Light and Reptile Light (Zoo Med), and Repti-B Glo and Sun-Glo (both manufactured by Hagen).

A newer light, the mercury-vapor light, has really caught on with herp keepers. Active UV heat is one brand. The mercury vapor lights churn out not only UVA and UVB but substantial heat as well. You only need one light in your terrarium, instead of the usual UV-fluorescent and the incandescent bulb for heat.

Pet stores stock a wide variety of lights; be certain you read the label and know what you're buying. You can also order them online.

Reptile requirements

Most reptiles are *heliotropic,* meaning that they're sun-loving creatures that become active when in the sun or when their cage is brightly lit (see Figure 9-1). They're also *poikilothermic,* dependent on outside sources of heat to regulate their own body temperature. In nature, heat and sunlight pretty much come packaged as a unit. Nocturnal reptiles (such as the geckos) and reptiles from the rain forest depend on conducted and atmospheric heat to keep them active.

Figure 9-1:
The heliotropic green iguana is active when the sun shines and passive when it's cloudy.

A reptile that's too cool has trouble moving, or if he's cold, he literally can't move. Both the voluntary and involuntary muscles are affected by the cold. Extremely cold conditions result in shallow respiration that often leads to pneumonia. Reptiles that are too cold won't eat and can't digest their food or eliminate waste. They need both light and heat to stay well.

So what happens when you don't light up a lizard's cage? Years ago, I was in a pet store in New England that had a wonderful array of herps, all kept toasty warm with hot rocks, but with no lighting atop their cages. All they had was the ambient lighting in the store. In one sad cage was a black-and-white tegu, lying listlessly on his hot rock. An employee of the store noted that the lizard just didn't want to eat. My husband, Dick, suggested that they add bright light over his cage. Five minutes after the addition of light, the tegu wolfed down a thawed mouse. He had been warm enough to feed, but without light, there was no spur for activity. (Oh, if only we could control our *own* appetites by dimming the lights . . .)

Why reptiles in particular need UVB lighting

Your reptile (and most particularly your herbivorous or insectivorous lizard and tortoise) needs three things from his light:

- ✔ Heat (so he and his body can move and function).
- ✔ The visible portions of light (so he can see where he is and what's around him).

✔ The ultraviolet portions (so his body can turn the D3 precursor into gen-
uine D3 and stop pulling calcium out of his bones). Herps that eat warm-
blooded creatures such as mice and birds get the calcium they need
from their diet, already processed, so to speak.

UVB enters the skin of the reptile and triggers the skin to transform provitamin D3 (7-dehydrocholesterol or 7-DHC) into previtamin D3. In chickens, at
least, more provitamin D3 is in areas exposed to the sun (such as the legs)
than areas that are covered with feathers and don't get much sun (such as
the back of the chicken). It would be logical to guess that a reptile's back has
higher levels of provitamin D3 than the belly skin, but I am just guessing.

Previtamin D3 changes to vitamin D3. But if the sunlight is too weak, the vitamin D3 that had already been made is degraded into inert compounds. Weak
sunlight packs a double whammy. The higher-energy photons needed to crank
up vitamin D3 production are absorbed by the atmosphere; the lower the sun
is in the sky, the more atmosphere the sun's rays must pass through before
they reach the earth. So almost no high-energy photons reach the earth, so the
reptile's skin doesn't get "excited" to produce the provitamin D. The lower-
energy photos are absorbed by the vitamin D3 in the skin, and the photons
break the vitamin apart. During several months in the winter, the light is at a
low angle — and may have no high-energy photons —so no previtamin D3 is
produced in the skin.

Vitamin D3 is carried by the bloodstream into the liver and then to the kidney.
It's altered in both areas to become the active form of D3, which serves as a
hormone to regulate calcium metabolism. You can supply D3 through dietary
supplements for some species, but this doesn't work for all species. You do
need to supply the calcium through the diet. The body can't make calcium.

Without D3 and calcium, bones are weakened, because the body actually
pulls calcium from the bones to supply the necessary level of calcium in the
blood. Metabolic bone disease (MBD) begins, and this is an awful thing to
happen to a lizard, turtle, or frog. The longer that the animal goes without
sunlight/D3/calcium, the weaker the bones (and the shell, for turtles) get,
until they won't bear the weight of the animal in normal activity (see Chapter
12 for more on MBD). The bones break very easily under normal day-to-day
activities.

The addition of UVB, either by sunlight or artificially, is crucial for reptiles
(see Figure 9-2) and some frogs. Two studies on humans have shown that
artificial UVB will double the amount of circulating D3 *one day* after exposure,
but circulating D3 was back to the baseline levels after 7 days, and below
baseline after 15 days. Of course humans aren't herps, poor things, but we're
all vertebrates. Because herps use the D3 to metabolize calcium, it seems logical that herps need an ongoing supply to replace what is used up.

Figure 9-2: Sunlight is free. In warmer weather, a simple outdoor pen for baby tortoises gives them exposure to the sun.

Meeting your reptile's lighting needs

The pet industry has responded to the marketplace (and the needs of her-pers) by producing a variety of lighting products. You'll see basking lights, bright lights, full spectrum lights, heat spot lights, sunlight lamps, UV fluorescents, UV full spectrums, reptile lamps, day lights, and night lights.

All of these lights emit some type of heat or lighting, and a few of them emit UVA and UVB. The UV bulbs emit different amounts of UVA and UVB, because not all herps need the same amounts. Some bulbs are very good, some are ho-hum, and some are produced (it looks to me, at least) just so the supplier has something different to offer.

Most of the packaging copy and the ad copy seem to promise a lot, so you need to be a little cynical. If the label says it's full spectrum, that's all you get — just the manufacturer's version of what full-spectrum lighting is (which won't include UV light). If the label says the product is a basking light, "basking" is warmth and light, not necessarily UV. Read and re-read those labels and ask a few questions to make certain that you know what you're buying. See the section "Imitating Mother Nature," later in this chapter.

TECHNICAL STUFF

Spring: When a young frog's fancy turns to love

Circadian rhythm is that great day-to-night and winter-spring-summer-fall cycle that tells you when to go to sleep, when to wake up, when to slow down for winter, and when to look about and find a mate. (And you thought it was coincidence that put Valentine's Day just before spring, didn't you?) Humans aren't the only ones whose interest in the opposite sex surges in the spring.

As the days lengthen in early spring, the internal action of reptiles and amphibians consists of readying the body for reproduction. The gonads enlarge, and production of ova and sperm is stepped up. The gonads feed hormones back to the brain and pituitary and urge behavioral changes.

What you see are the visual, overt changes. The hormonal rushes cause color changes in lizards such as green iguanas and cause behavioral changes in snakes, turtles, green iguanas, and almost all other reptiles and amphibians.

My male iguana, caged outside, begins to display for the female iguanas (and any human within view) in early February. His dewlap darkens to black, his jowls begin to widen, he holds his crest fully erect, and he shakes his head from side to side to display these attractive characteristics. Male chameleons climb to the highest portion of

their cage and look around for females (good) and males (bad). The males display their breeding colors and hope that the females will respond with their breeding colors. (Females that have already bred or that aren't interested in breeding flash a distinctive color pattern that tells the male "not interested," so the males won't waste their time displaying to them.)

Here are some other springtime animal behaviors:

- Frogs start calling from flooded pastures.
- Male broad-headed skinks get wide red heads.
- Green anoles bob like animated jackhammers.
- Spotted salamanders migrate to breeding ponds, where the males deposit spermatophores for the females to pick up. (No this isn't very sexy as sex goes, but it's all they've got.)
- Male box turtles trail after attractive females and bang their shells against them.

These herp behaviors are external evidence of internal action, all aimed toward the final goal: sperm transfer.

Amphibian requirements

Amphibians aren't dependent on the sun the way reptiles are. Amphibians can function quite well at temperatures that would stop a reptile, and they limit their activity to "safe" times — when the lower ambient temperatures mean less moisture lost through the skin, and when the humidity is high enough to reduce moisture lost through the skin.

Amphibians differ from reptiles in many ways. By and large, amphibians are nocturnal and don't need direct UV lighting. They have that breathing, permeable skin that mustn't dry out. They don't need much warmth, another benefit of adaptation to nocturnality. (The tree frogs that sit in direct sunlight secrete lipids to protect themselves from the effects of the sun. They use their feet to deliberately disperse the lipids all over their bodies, rather like someone thoughtfully soaping up in a bathtub before bursting into song.) Amphibian caging needs illumination for your benefit, not for the animals within. For them, an ordinary fluorescent light works fine.

Imitating Mother Nature

You can provide light and heat a cage for your pet in many ways. This section is aimed at reptiles; amphibians are largely nocturnal, and they don't need (or like) heat or extra lighting.

Heating with lighting

You can supply the heat and light with an incandescent bulb (no UV) or with one of the new mercury vapor lights (plenty of UV) (see Figure 9-3). Ordinary incandescent light bulbs are a good heat source; the higher the wattage, the more heat is churned out. If you'd like to spend more money than you need to, you can purchase reptile basking bulbs, which are a high-end incandescent.

Figure 9-3:
A mercury vapor light provides UVB year-round, and reptiles enjoy the light and the warmth.

Put the incandescent bulb in a metal reflector hood, the kind you can buy in any hardware store or any pet store, to direct the light and warmth down toward the cage floor and your reptile. Position the bulb toward the substrate so that it creates a hot spot in one area of your cage. Secure the light and hood so they can't fall into the cage. (Don't put them directly on top of a plastic screen cage top, or they'll melt their way through.) Once the light has been on for an hour or so, use a thermometer to see whether the bulb and reflector will keep the cage warm enough. If the hot spot is 90 degrees or above, that will allow the reptile to select the warmth he likes the best. (See Chapter 7 for more information on cage temperatures.)

For reptiles, you may be able to get away with using a heat source such as a hot rock or an undertank heating pad (like a human heating pad, except it's smaller and has only one heat setting, which is "on"), along with a regular fluorescent fixture or a lower-wattage light bulb. But remember that the position of these devices is important. At least one researcher has shown that spatially separating the heating element and the lighting elements — putting them at opposite ends of the cage, for instance — alters normal thermoregulatory behavior. No matter what bulb you use, make sure it provides a bright light and that the light is focused near any other heat source, such as a hot rock.

You may elect to use two lights: one for heat and light and the other one for UV light. In this case, use an incandescent bulb for heat and light, and one of the UV-emitting fluorescents for the UV light. The incandescent/fluorescent combo costs less for the initial set-up, but you need to replace the UV fluorescent every six months. (The UV-emitting portion slows and quits altogether long before the light itself burns out.) You can choose from a wide variety of fluorescent bulbs. Read the label to make certain that you're buying something with the UVB output your animal needs.

You can supply light and UV with one of the new mercury vapor lights, which take the place of the incandescent bulb and the fluorescent bulb. These bulbs seem expensive — somewhere between $55 and $70 each, depending on the wattage and the supplier. (I can see you sticking your fingers in your hair and whispering, "Whaaaat?") These bulbs, however, churn out heat, visible light, and UVB and UVA light all at once, and they last for some 2,000 hours. Unlike the reptile fluorescent UV bulbs, the UV-emitting ability of the mercury vapor lights doesn't quit after six months; their efficiency and usefulness last until the bulb burns out. Because these bulbs put out so much heat, use only ceramic light sockets in the metal reflectors.

Some very knowledgeable reptile keepers are very firm in limiting the amount of time a herp should spend under the very bright mercury lights, citing eye and other possible damage. I've used a bank of these lights over my aquatic monitor cage and my indoor-wintertime-tank-for-turtles daily for three years and noticed no problems. Both of these tanks have shaded areas where the inhabitants can get away from the lighting. If you use these bright lights or any bright lights, be sure to provide a shaded area.

You can use one of the new halide lights, if you like. These are sold as "task lights" in home improvement stores, and they do give off a very bright light. Read the label. Unless the label says that a light gives off UVA or UVB, and what the percentage of such rays is, the light doesn't give off either one of the UV rays. Bright light and a good coloring index (how true to sunlight in terms of revealing actual colors of object illuminated) do fulfill your herps' need for bright light, but you still have to provide UVB (and probably UVA, as well) if you're keeping a herbivorous or insectivorous lizard or turtle. Position this light to create a hot spot in one end of the cage, and check the temperatures in both ends of the cage to make sure that the caging is warm enough.

Heating without lighting

You can supply heat without lighting in individual cages year-round via the following items, which all require electricity:

- **Heating pads:** These go under a glass tank. Like the name implies, they give off a steady heat to the bottom of the tank. These can't be used with plastic tanks.

- **Hot rocks:** Hot rocks are three-dimensional heating pads that go inside a tank. They're molded to look a bit like a lump of sandstone. The animal rests on top of the hot rock and gains heat through his belly. They give off more heat than the under-tank heating pads. In the past, these have caused severe burns to the bellies of lizards and snakes that have rested on top of the rocks. The newer models seem to have better thermostats.

- **Heat emitters:** These screw into a standard light bulb socket and give off heat. Shield these emitters from herps because herps can sustain severe burns from them, if they can get to them.

Place the heating pad, the hot rock, or the heat emitter in one corner of the cage. You want to provide a thermal gradient, so your herp can move toward or away from the heat source. Most herpers partially bury their hot rocks in sand or the caging substrate to help diffuse the heat. Use a thermometer or a heat-sensing thermal device, a small, battery-operated heat sensor, to check the daytime temperatures at the warm and cool ends of the caging. You point this device at the object and press a button, and the read-out tells you the temperature of the object. Radio Shack is one manufacturer.

To use a ceramic heater or the kerosene heater to warm up an entire room of cages, place it near but not in contact with your caging units. Put a thermometer on top of one of the cages so that you can check to see how well the heating system works.

Positioning the lights

Place incandescent lights over the spot you've designated as the basking spot, anywhere from 24 inches to a foot away. These bulbs light up and warm the basking area. Check the temperature of the basking spot; it should be between 90 and 110 degrees.

The UV fluorescent light can go over the entire cage, or just one end of it. The longer the bulb, the better the UV-emitting ability. In all cases, the UV-emitting light should overlap the reptile's basking spot. You want the animal to bask, to get warm, and to want to eat and make D3 so he can use the calcium in his diet (for more information on good diets, see Chapter 11). In order for the UV fluorescent light to do any good, it must be 12 inches or less from the floor of the cage. In a tall cage, you need to drop the fluorescent bulb down into the cage or provide an elevated basking spot.

Suspend the mercury vapor light, which replaces the basking light *and* the UV fluorescent light, over the basking spot. Depending on the wattage (100, 160, and 275 watts were available as of 2003) and the focus (floodlight is better than spotlight), position the light so that it's about 12 inches above the basking area for a 100-watt bulb or 18 inches for a 275-watt bulb. Check the temperature of the basking spot; it should be between 90 and 110 degrees.

Understanding the bulb label

Read the labels on any bulb you're thinking about buying. As you do, think of real estate ads and personal ads; both use a curious sort of double-speak that you have to admire for creativity. With reptile cage lighting labels, you need to look for what the labels *don't* say.

Unless the label says the bulb provides UVB, it doesn't.

"Full spectrum" on the label merely means that the light contains all the *visible* colors, like a rainbow, and your animals will look very pretty under the light. That light bulb may not actually provide anything your animal needs, other than illumination.

Bulbs that use clear glass or have blue glass provide less protection for your eyes and the eyes of your reptile (but read the copy on the packaging if you'd like to see creativity at work).

Figuring out when to replace the bulb

Replace UV fluorescent bulbs every six months — even if they're not burned out. You can reuse them above your own bathroom sink, in your workshop, or in your utility room. They're still okay to use as fluorescent lights; they just no longer provide the UV light that your animal needs.

Replace incandescent bulbs when they burn out. Keep a couple spare bulbs of different wattages on hand, but you probably do this anyway, right?

Always keep at least one spare mercury vapor light on hand. Mercury vapor lights are so popular that the manufacturers sell them like hotcakes, and sometimes they do run out of stock. If you have to mail-order these, you're looking at a wait of at least a week while a new bulb is sent to you. A week is too long for your herp to go without proper lighting. These bulbs are expensive, but it's just easier to bite the bullet and buy two or three at once and be done with the agony of spending $50 or more per bulb.

Chapter 10

Do the Locomotion

In This Chapter

▶ Moving your herp

▶ Taking your herp on a trip with you

▶ Leaving your pets with a sitter

*O*ne of these days, you're going to need to move your herp, even if he's one of those types that doesn't take kindly to being touched, such as the day geckos or the dart frogs. Maybe your breeding efforts have paid off, and you're headed to an expo (see Chapter 5 for more on expos) with 60 strawberry dart frogs or your new banded morph corn snakes. Maybe you're getting married, and you're moving to your new home and taking your herps along.

Moving or traveling with herps or even shipping them can be stress-free for you and the animals. You simply need to know how to keep your herps feeling secure during the process, what packing materials to use, and how to work with transport companies.

Packing Up Your Herp

You have two goals in packing up your herp. You want him to arrive at his destination in good shape and unstressed, and the same for the transport company. You have several choices when it comes to items to use for transporting herps.

Cloth snake bags — not just for snakes

A snake bag is a long cloth bag that's open at the short end. It's used for transporting reptiles, not for housing them, and it's always used inside out — with the seam of the bag exposed. This keeps the inside of the bag the smooth side. Snake bags are made from a lightweight fabric such as muslin (the classic snake bag) or bed sheet fabric (the prints make for an aesthetically pleasing bag). The fabric has to be lightweight enough for the herp to breathe through, but closely enough woven so he can't get his feet caught in the fabric or scratch his way to freedom through the sides of the bag.

Snake bags generally are only used for reptiles, not for amphibians, because of amphibians' need for moisture and their easily damaged skin. You can use cloth bags for amphibians, as long as you remember that the amphibians will dry out very quickly in a cloth bag because the fabric wicks away moisture. In addition, the fabric will abrade the amphibian's delicate skin. For amphibians, deli cups or plastic bags are much safer.

But for collecting and transporting snakes, lizards, turtles, and tortoises, the best and most convenient way to go is the snake bag.

You can buy snake bags from any reptile dealer or online, but many people find it's just easier to make the bags. The proportions are all-important. The length should be at least three to four times the width so that you have room for the herp and still have enough free space in the bag to tie a knot in the neck.

Don't use a snake bag with a frayed spot, and always check the seams to make certain that no threads are broken. I borrowed a ball python to use in a photo session from a dealer about ten miles from me. Of course, I felt confident that the bag was secure — this guy's a dealer, for golly's sake, and he *knows* what trouble a snake bag with a hole can be. Well, apparently he didn't know because pretty soon the ball python crawled right out of that bag into the dashboard of my car. I caught his tail as the rest of him was disappearing. After some protracted pulling while I tried to be very gentle but firm, the snake unwound himself from whatever he had curled himself around in dashboard never-never land, and slithered out backwards. I held him in my hands and said sternly, "You shouldn't do that," as if it was his fault.

Getting your reptile in the bag

You can put multiple animals of the same kind in a snake bag, but don't put in more than two or three. Also, never put a kingsnake in a bag with another snake because kingsnakes eat other snakes. If the herp is big, like a snake over 5 feet or a turtle longer than 12 inches, put only one in a bag.

"Bagging" a herp is as easy as it sounds. You open the mouth of the bag, and hold the bag in one hand. Then you grasp your herp — a turtle, maybe — and put him inside the bag. Don't drop the animal. Hold on to him until you touch the bottom of the bag. With wiggly things, such as snakes and glass lizards, you can put the creature's head into the opening of the bag and relax your grip on him a bit. Sensing that you've loosened up and wishing to get away from you, the snake or glass lizard will usually continue on into the bag.

After the herp is inside the bag, tie the neck of the bag into a knot about halfway down the bag, to secure the animals within the bag. You don't want to pin the herp in place so that he can't move, but you also don't want the herp to get lost in the excess fabric of the bag. Tie only a single knot so that the bag will be easy enough to loosen with your hands.

Don't use your teeth to untie a reptile bag, if someone has really pulled the fabric taut. You don't know where that bag has been or what it held before you got it.

Just because a herp is inside a bag doesn't mean he won't bite you through the bag. A herp will bite through a snake bag if he's frightened, uncomfortable, tired of it, or in a bad mood. Don't be surprised when your herp tries it. Snapping turtles are known for this behavior. They don't like you, don't like the bag, and will readily bite any soft yielding surface they feel against the bag, just because they feel like it. Do not sling the bag over your shoulder to carry it, okay? A venomous snake is especially likely to try to bite. (Of course, you have too much sense to work with venomous snakes without direct one-on-one guidance from a professional herpetologist or herpetoculturist.)

Don't use string ties to close a snake bag, although some people do try. Snakes, for instance, are persistent creatures, and they'll brace themselves in a bag and push, then relax, and then push against a part that feels different from the rest of the bag or has less resistance to their pushing. By working in this way, they can loosen a set of ties that you thought too snug to loosen. Turtles and tortoises can become miniature earth-moving machines, although in this case they're pushing against the end of the snake bag. Lizards have noses that can fit into and push against amazingly tight areas (at least, you thought those areas were tight!). After all, reptiles don't have much else to do when they're inside a snake bag. You can use a plastic cable tie to secure the end of the bag, if you fold that end over again and use a second cable tie. You'll need a knife to cut the cable ties.

Lift a snake bag by the tied knot at the upper edge of the bag to move the bag. An alternate and safe spot to grasp the bag is by the edge. Because snake bags are used inside out, with the seam exposed, you can grasp the bag by that cloth edge. (People who handle bagged venomous snakes use a pair of tongs to touch or move the bag.) Gently grab a corner of the bag and lift the bag so that the animal inside slides down to the bottom of the bag. Landing in a heap inside a bag isn't all that comfortable for a snake, lizard, or turtle, so lay the bag down as soon as you finish moving it.

Remember that a snake, upset by being jostled in a bag, can sense where you are in relation to him, and is perfectly capable of coiling up inside the bag and striking toward you, as far as the bag will allow him.

Letting him out

After you untie the knot, hold the bag by its open end, open the edges carefully, and peer inside. You should already know what's inside the bag, because you put the animal in there yourself, someone told you what you were transporting, or you've gently touched the bag to feel the contours of the animal within. You need to be particularly cautious when you open the bag because snakes that are especially irritated about being confined are smart enough to brace themselves against the bottom of the bag and to lunge toward freedom (or strike at your face) as you open the bag. Some lizards (skinks in particular) can scramble up the sides of the bag when you open it and they see light up above. If you see the animal heading out toward the mouth of the bag as you open it, put your hands together quickly and clutch the bag in one hand to prevent the escape.

Making your own bag

Snake bags are made fairly long and skinny so that you can easily tie the neck of the bag closed once the herp is inside. They're not turned after the bottom and side have been sewn, so the inside is a smooth surface, and the raw edges of the bag are on the outside. Some people turn the bag and then restitch it so that the raw edges are caught within a second seam (a technique called French seaming). If you're careful to snip out any loose threads, a French-seamed bag is the best type of snake bag to use. French-seaming gives you a nice double-thick edge of the bag to grab and lift, in case you're moving something like a snake with long teeth or a snapping turtle.

Always be careful with loose threads, whether the bag is French seamed or not. Here are some potential dangers of loose threads inside a bag:

- ✔ They can entangle a snake and strangle him.

- ✔ They can restrict circulation in a turtle or tortoise's leg and cut it as well.

- ✔ A snake or lizard can partially swallow loose threads and choke to death or end up with a hard-to-diagnose intestinal obstruction, which is usually fatal.

Be hypercareful with loose threads.

Plastic bags

Plastic bags are one of the standard ways to transport amphibians. They're fine for temporary storage, but not for permanent housing.

You can use two types of plastic bags:

- **Long, skinny bags like the ones used in aquarium stores to bag your fish:** You can purchase these bags from your local pet store, or by the hundred-lot from a plastic supplier. They're harder to open and close than the zipper-style bags. You have to tie and untie a knot to close or open the bag, and they don't hold up well to repeated use.

- **Plastic bags with a sliding plastic zipper:** Smaller reptiles, such as small snakes or lizards, can be transported inside a plastic bag, but their higher oxygen requirements mean that you must limit their bag time to maybe 30 minutes or so. The bags with the press-together zippers are too flimsy to stay closed, so don't use them.

  The zipper style bags are easier to find — every grocery store sells them — and you really can open and close them with one hand, if you need to. You can use them multiple times if you're careful to wash them out between amphibian residents (use soap and water and rinse twice).

Plastic bags are useful for several reasons:

- You can see inside them, so you know what you have without opening the bag.

- They're water tight, so damp things stay damp and the amphibian inside won't dry up and die.

- They're inexpensive, so you won't get cheap and double up on bagging amphibians. (You must keep amphibians in separate bags because of their skin toxins.) Add some dampened sphagnum moss or live aquarium plants to provide moisture and something for amphibians to hang on to.

- Because you trap air inside when you seal the bag, a protective cushion forms, preventing the amphibian from getting crushed when you put several sealed plastic bags inside a box or a larger cloth bag. The air cushion, however, does not protect the animal if you drop the bag.

Plastic bags do have disadvantages:

- You can overheat and kill an amphibian or a reptile kept inside a plastic bag even if the bag isn't in the sun.

- If you reuse a bag and don't wash it before reusing, the skin toxins left inside the bag can kill the next animal you put in.

- That bit of air trapped inside isn't enough of a cushion to save the animal if you drop the bag; he'll be on the bottom of the bag and hit the ground first.

Deli cups

Plastic deli cups, the disposable cups with the flimsy snap-on lids, are the gold standard for shipping amphibians and some of the tiniest herps (see Figure 10-1), such as hatchling snakes or the smaller day geckos. They're fine for temporary storage, but not for permanent housing. Some advantages include the following:

✔ They're water-tight when the lids are snapped on.

✔ They're easy to ventilate — simply punch a few holes with a single-hole punch.

✔ They're easy to clean.

✔ You can keep the inhabitant moist by adding a moistened paper towel to the bottom of the cup. The towel also gives the animal something to hunker down in when the cup is moved or handled.

✔ Those with clear tops let you look at the animal without opening the cup.

Figure 10-1: Horned frog babies are placed in individual containers before they're transported.

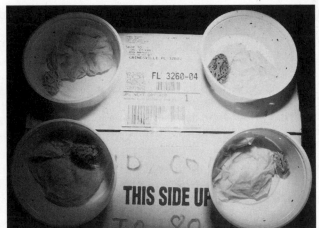

You can buy deli cups from a deli, wholesale clubs, and restaurant supply houses.

If you don't want to buy deli cups, reuse bait cups from a bait store or 16-ounce butter tubs, although they don't have clear tops. Just be sure to thoroughly wash these containers before putting your herp in.

The advantages of the deli cups are the same as the ones that apply to plastic bags. They do prevent an animal from being crushed, and you can stack the cups if you have limited space. They're easy to clean when the herp defecates in them. For amphibians, you can add cushioning in the form of dampened sphagnum moss, short lengths of aquatic plants, or a folded, dampened paper towel. For reptiles, use a folded, dry paper towel. Wash the cup if you're going to reuse it (putting plastics in a landfill is environmentally irresponsible, so you're doing a good deed).

You can overheat and kill an amphibian or a reptile in the cup if you leave the cup in a car or place it in even a moderately warm spot. If you drop a cup, the animal inside is dead, even if you have a wet paper towel inside the cup.

Rolled newspaper tubes

Rolled newspaper tubes are a quick way to temporarily house and locally transport lizards. The tubes must go inside a larger holding box (a cardboard carton will work) with a closely fitting lid, but the tubes do provide a quick and effective way to move lizards from one house to another or from your house to a pet store.

Making the tubes

1. **Arrange four to five full sheets of newspaper in a stack on a table or clean flat surface.**

2. **Beginning at one corner, roll the sheets into a tube about 2 to 3 inches in diameter.**

3. **Tape the loose corner against the side of the tube.**

4. **Fold over one end to close that end and tape it in place.**

Call it a wrap!

After you make your tube, hold the tube in a horizontal position and slide the lizard into the open end of the tube. Add a crumpled paper towel so he'll have something to hold onto once the tube is closed. Fold over the open end of the tube and tape it into place. Keep the tube horizontal and place it in the holding box.

These tubes are easy to make, and the newspaper is recyclable. They aren't strong, so they won't work for a lizard with strong claws, such as a monitor. They aren't large, so you can't use them for a lizard much larger than 12 inches long. They are strong enough to stack two or three deep if you use four to five sheets of newspaper for each tube and don't compress them in the holding box. Because it's dark inside the tube, the lizards will lie quietly.

Free at last!

When you reach your destination and you're ready to put your lizard in his new home, here's what to do:

1. **Move the holding box next to the lizard's opened cage.**

2. **Lift the tubes, one at a time, out of the holding box, keeping each tube horizontal as you lift it.**

3. **Hold the tube near the cage and tilt it up slightly as you open the tape at the raised end.**

4. **Gently unfold the end and hold it open by squeezing the tube a bit at the fold.**

5. **Reverse the tube's direction and carefully slide the lizard out of the tube into his new home.**

Shipping Your Packaged Pal

When you ship herps, they go by air transport, and you use layered containers. Cargo services have strict rules for safe shipment of animals, and they have rules on how to pack herps. Do check with individual airlines for any updates on acceptance deadlines or other changes. Some carriers, such FedEx, leave acceptance of live reptile or amphibians shipments to the discretion of the local office, but this section gives you the basic packing guidelines. These guidelines have two main purposes:

- ✔ To ensure that the animal can't escape
- ✔ To make sure that the animal reaches his destination safely and in good health

The basic holders for the herps (tied snake bags or deli cups with the snap-on lids) go inside an insulated box, and shredded paper is liberally added for cushioning. The insulated box is sealed with packing tape (see Figure 10-2). You can use an ordinary cardboard box, lined with sheets of Styrofoam, sized and placed so they brace each other, or you can use a Styrofoam shipping box, the very thick shipping boxes used to ship tropical fish. Pet stores get their weekly fish shipments in Styrofoam boxes, and you can quite probably pick one up there.

The inside containers are placed inside the shipping box, on top of and amidst crumpled or shredded newsprint (added as padding). A copy of the packing list goes on top of the bags or cups, and the lid is placed and the shipping container is sealed and addressed (and a copy of the packing slip is in a clear envelope on the outside of the package, too). The shipping box has enough air for the herps for about 24 to 48 hours, which is longer than transport time. Add one of the chemical hand warmers sold in hunting supply shops if you're shipping during cold weather or if you're shipping to a cold area.

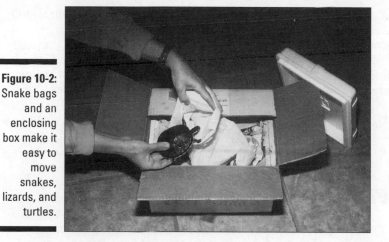

Figure 10-2: Snake bags and an enclosing box make it easy to move snakes, lizards, and turtles.

Traveling with Your Pet

Sometimes you just need or want to take your herp with you when you take a trip. Maybe you're a college student going home for the holidays, and you have no one to tend your pet while you're gone. Maybe you've moving.

When you're driving in your car, you can bag up your herps, tuck your lizards in a newspaper tube or put your amphibians in deli cups, and then put those containers in cardboard boxes in you car. Add crumpled paper for padding, and close the top of the box. Don't put the box where it will get direct sun. Coolers, with hot water bottles or freeze packs, where necessary, take a lot out of the worry in moving your herps. Put a thermometer in the cooler and check the temperature inside the cooler when you stop for meals.

A throw tossed over the top of the box or cooler helps deflect the heat if the top of the box or cooler gets the sun during part of your drive.

If you're traveling in a car with amphibians, clean their containers every night while you're on the road or at your final stop. Although reptiles can easily go up to three days without water, when you take them out of their traveling containers and put them into proper caging at your destination, be sure to offer them water and food. The one exception to reptiles not needing water every day is chameleons. Each evening, take them out of their containers, let them hang onto a cloth surface over the tub or in the shower (I put my shirt on a hanger and put the chameleons on the shirt), mist them, and watch them drink.

If your animal is flying with you, pack your animals according to airline regulations and ship them as you would if you were shipping them to a friend. The airlines work to ensure that your precious pet stays on your flights and arrives on the same flight as you do, but the U.S. mail always comes first when it comes to deciding what gets the available cargo space in an airline. (See the section "Shipping Your Packaged Pal," earlier in this chapter.)

Don't even think of trying to take your herps in the cabin with you. It's not allowed, and no one wants to aggravate an airline on purpose these days.

Using a Herp Sitter

Surely the best thing to happen to herp fanciers, other than good lighting and better caging, is the pet sitter. A pet sitter is someone who comes to your house to take care of your animals when you're gone. This person makes it easy for you to be gone for a day or for a month, knowing that your pets are taken care of.

Although pet sitters are primarily known for taking care of dogs and cats, the savvy ones realize that many households have a dog and a cat, and a bearded dragon and a couple of turtles (I won't go on — you already know what I mean). As a result, they have adjusted their thinking and their services accordingly.

Most people go into pet sitting not for the money, but because they like animals. (The money is nice, but pet sitters spend all their holidays taking care of other people's animals and thus have no life of their own on those special occasions.) And who better to care for your own animals than someone who likes animals?

Finding a pet sitter

Your best bet in finding a pet sitter is word of mouth. You're better off using a sitter recommended by someone you know. Ask your friends, your veterinarian, and local pet stores. You'll be surprised how many people use pet sitters. Your pet sitter should be bonded, insured, and locally licensed, if your area requires all businesses to have a license (do check on this), but if that someone somehow fails to show up at your house, your pets are in trouble. So that's why a referral from someone who uses a reliable pet sitter is important, too.

National associations of pet sitters have certification processes, mission statements, and guidelines. You can contact Pet Sitters International (www.petsit.com) or the National Association of Professional Pet Sitters (www.petsitters.org). Perhaps you'd feel better if your pet sitter was part of a national group. None of my sitters were members of a national group, but all of my sitters were spouses of workplace friends, friends, or employees of my veterinarian — people I knew I could trust with my pets and my house.

Going over the ground rules

Make an instruction sheet for your pet sitter so he or she will know what to needs to be done twice daily, once daily, or once every three days. Include on the sheet contact information for your veterinarian and for a trusted friend who can help if something unforeseen happens, and give a number where you can be reached while you're traveling. Ask the sitter to come over once or twice to take care of your animals while you're there so you can answer questions or discover any instructions you forgot to include (and yes, you pay the sitter for these visits). Discuss the following topics with the sitter:

- ✔ Fees
- ✔ How many visits the sitter needs to make to care for your pets (twice daily? twice a week?)
- ✔ How much money you need to leave for food purchases while you're gone

Before your trip, arrange for your sitter to meet your neighbor or friend who's serving as an emergency contact, perhaps during one of your instruction sessions. The sitter may find it easier to ask for help if she already knows the person she's asking. If your sitter has an auto accident and breaks a bone in her foot, she may need some help for a day or two, and your neighbor or friend can be prepared to help. You also need your neighbor or friend to keep an eye on your place for the first day or so just to make certain that your sitter shows up. I've never had a sitter fink out on me — indeed, sitters have become my good, dependable friends — but it pays to err on the side of caution.

When you return from your trip, call your sitter and thank her for her work. If she hasn't left an invoice, ask for the total and pay it the next day. She has earned the money, so don't make her wait for it. Tipping your sitter if you're pleased with her work is polite, but it isn't required.

Part III
Open Wide!
Feeding, Hydration, and Health

The 5th Wave   By Rich Tennant

"I'm sorry, Mr. Mathews. Your turtle is gravely ill. I don't think he's got much more than 30 years left."

In this part . . .

After you have your herp home and in a really nifty cage, you have to give him water and feed him. This part tells you what to feed and how to offer food and water, which is not the same for all herps. You can find out about normal herp behaviors and which abnormal behavior may indicate something is wrong and that your pet may need veterinary care. The chapter on longevity talks about how long your herp can live and what to do to ensure that your herps are taken care of in case of your own death.

Chapter 11

Water Me! Feed Me!

In This Chapter

▶ Ensuring that your reptiles and amphibians have clean water

▶ Providing a suitable water supply

▶ Feeding your reptiles and amphibians

You've gone and done it. You've bought a herp, who's now peering earnestly up at you from the depths of a snake bag or from a deli cup. You have his cage all set up in a quiet part of your dwelling. You're looking forward to enjoying years of companionship and to watching your pet grow and develop under your care. But hey! It's 6 p.m. and you're thirsty and hungry. You can break and head for the fridge. But how about your herp? He may be thirsty and hungry, too, but he can't get his own food and drink. He's counting on you to water him and feed him, so you'll have to forget about your own needs for a while.

The good news is that watering and feeding a herp aren't all that complex. You do have to know how to present the water (which can make a real difference to a herp) and what sort of food your herp devours in real life. It makes sense to offer only what the animal will actually eat. If you don't believe me, just think of your cat. You know that if you offer him a big bowl of sprouts, he'll look at you once and stroll insolently away. Getting your herp to feed may take some effort on your part, but I start with the basics to help make your job easier.

Recognizing the Importance of Safe Water

Amphibians meet their moisture requirements by sitting quietly in water, on wet leaves, or on rain-drenched tree trunks or even by burrowing deeply downward through desert sands until they encounter moisture. The moisture, along with any additives or impurities, is absorbed through the skin. Because the water is absorbed directly through the skin, and not the stomach, nary a trace of stomach acids or digesting nematodes is present to "filter" the water. The water source for all herps, but especially for these interesting little creatures, must be clean and pure and not something that's been sitting in a plastic dish on your porch for a week. It must be *herp potable,* which means water that is acceptable to reptiles and amphibians.

Ideally, the water you offer your herp contains no dangerous (well, dangerous to reptiles and amphibians, at least) chloramines, chlorines, or other soluble chemicals that municipalities add to your water to make it safe for you to drink, but that are potentially harmful to herps.

You can use bottled (but not distilled) water if you want to be very careful. You can also use water from your tap. Unless you want to use one of the chloramine removers that are designed for aquariums, let tap water "rest" in a bottle or a covered pitcher for 24 hours before giving it to your herp to let the chloramines and chlorines dissipate. Then you're free to offer it to your reptiles and amphibians.

Water provided by a municipality is treated to remove harmful bacteria and viruses and as many chemical contaminants as possible. Chlorine and/or chloramines are great at killing the tiny buglets that cause disease in life forms such as humans and herps (these sorts of disease-causing buglets are called *pathogens,* which you can find out more about in Chapter 12).

If you want to use well water for your herp, you'll have to pay someone to analyze your water for contaminants, but you may want to do this anyway, because you're drinking it and bathing in it, too. If you haven't watched or read *A Civil Action,* a story about chemical contaminants in water, hoo boy, you may have some surprises coming!

Because a dish of herp-potable water will draw most amphibians to it like a baby to a bottle, change the water regularly. Herps won't move out when nature calls, so that water won't stay clean for long.

You Can Lead a Herp to Water, but . . .

When you're caring for a herp, the presentation of water is just about as important as the water itself. So once you figure out what kind of water to offer your herp, the next hurdle is getting your pet to recognize it as water (see Figure 11-1).

The red-sided garter snake enjoys swimming. He will catch and eat live minnows placed in his water dish.

The candy cane corn snake is one of the brighter color morphs that have been bred from the corn snake.

Everybody's favorite, the boa constrictor, can grow to a length of 8 feet.

A snake sheds his skin at regular intervals, more frequently when young than adult. The first signs of an impending shed are dulled coloration and "blue" eyes.

A terrestrial caecilian is caught above ground. The eyes are tiny and hidden under the skin.

An Eastern painted turtle (center) joins an albino red-eared slider (upper left) and other basking turtles on an emergent snag for sunning.

The red-footed tortoise is a personable tortoise that may reach 18 to 24 inches as an adult.

The map turtles of the southeastern United States can be differentiated by the stripe patterns on their head. A Mississippi map turtle is shown here.

The water-loving and highly aquatic green basilisk is found in Central America. Males develop a high crest on the head, body, and tail.

The veiled chameleon is captive-bred in large numbers. It is remarkable for its high head casque and brilliant coloration.

The giant day gecko is found in Madagascar and is highly arboreal. Like other day geckos, its skin will tear if the animal is handled.

With more than 50,000 leopard geckos being bred in captivity annually, it's not surprising that color morphs of this popular lizard began appearing. This is a very desirable form, called a high yellow.

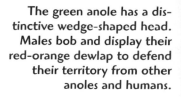

The green anole has a distinctive wedge-shaped head. Males bob and display their red-orange dewlap to defend their territory from other anoles and humans.

The bars on the body and tail of a young brown water dragon will fade as the animal matures. Originally from Australia, those in the pet market are captive-bred.

The red-eyed treefrog is found from Mexico through Central America. It lives in communal groups and is readily captive-bred.

The bright orange-red mantella is originally from Madagascar. It is full grown at a snout-vent length of one inch.

The ornate horned frog hunts by concealing itself under leaves and soil. When a prey item (an insect or smaller frog or toad) wanders by, the frog leaps out of concealment and grabs the prey in its strong jaws.

The green treefrog is highly arboreal, but captives learn to descend to the tank front at night to await delivery of crickets.

The giant monkey frog from South America is a canopy species that suns extensively. Captives need access to ultraviolet light.

The waterdog, or larval tiger salamander, boasts a notable set of bushy gills. These will be lost as the lungs develop during metamorphosis.

Lungless salamanders, like the red-backed salamander shown here, derive their moisture needs through their skin and mucous membranes.

The fire-bellied newts can live in either an aquatic or a semiaquatic tank. They eat prepared fish pellets or pieces of earthworms.

Many species of slimy salamanders exist. Genetic testing has yielded some 13 different species designations.

Figure 11-1: This decorative hiding place also drips water from one of the tree's "limbs." The top of the stump lifts off to make filling the water dispenser easy.

How, you ask, can a reptile or amphibian _not_ recognize water as being water? No animal is that dull witted, is it? Actually, some herps really can't identify a puddle of water. In the wild, they don't drink from puddles — a puddle has no relevance to them.

Although many species — those that naturally drink from puddles and seeps — seem to recognize water no matter how it's presented, other herps seldom or _never_ see a puddle on the ground. In fact, some of the tree-dwelling _(arboreal)_ species seldom even see the ground. One kind of monitor was thought to be extinct until someone discovered that it lives way up in trees and hits the ground only when it's dead. For tree dwellers (such as an emerald tree boa), rock dwellers (such as the Cordylus lizards), and the desert dwellers (such as the Molochs and the horny toads), water is a marvelous substance that drips from the tips of leaves, beads up on their own body scales, or trickles down a tree trunk or rock face. Water may also be an all-encompassing mist the herp absorbs through its skin. For these non-puddle drinkers, _their_ water is in motion or is somehow inescapable.

Ta-da! The water dish

The most common and the easiest way to present herp-potable water to your pet is to put it in a dish and put the dish on the bottom of the terrarium or cage. Then walk away and let your pet sniff out the water. Most reptiles will find the water and drink; the amphibians will find the water and sit in it. For the vast majority of pet herps, this presentation is entirely satisfactory.

Amphibians don't drink water in the normal manner. Instead, they absorb it through their skin and their *cloaca* (an internal bladder that accumulates urine and feces before they are excreted from the body but that can also absorb water). These absorption methods satisfy amphibians' need for moisture.

Setting up a drip bucket

Chameleons, day geckos, tree boas — these are tree dwellers, not ground-dwellers. How do you supply water to herps who don't usually see puddles? The easiest way is probably via a terrarium-top drip bucket. This is nothing more than a plastic bucket with a tiny hole in the bottom, set on top of the cage over foliage. It serves as a tiny, one-drip-at-a-time water source. You can buy commercial drip containers at your local pet store; these even have a tiny spigot so you can alter the drip rate. Or you can use any of the following items to rig your drip:

- A plastic souvenir cup from a fast-food restaurant
- A tall deli cup from the grocer
- A small bucket from your local hardware store

When you make the hole for the drip bucket, remember to start small. You can always make a hole larger, but you can't really make one smaller.

I find it easiest to make the hole in my drip bucket by puncturing it with a small nail that I heat by holding a lighted match over the pointed end. But ow! Hold the head of the nail with pliers before you hold a lighted match to the pointed end. Those little short nails conduct heat in an amazingly short time.

To establish your drip bucket system, follow these steps:

1. **Put a shallow *cache* (French for storage and pronounced "cash," like the money) basin in the cage.**

   A cache is basically a water dish, but you don't fill it with water. It should be big enough to hold all the water from the drip bucket, yet too shallow for an animal to drown in, in case it falls in. The basin keeps the cage from getting soggy — a no-no in herp care.

2. **Put the filled water bucket on the screen top of the cage, above the cache basin. (Use dechlorinated or rested water if you can.)**

   I've found that any screen top I use is strong enough to hold the drip bucket, since the tops have a rigid frame that clips them onto the top of the tank. You may have to move things around a bit, but what you're trying to do is to have the water drip from the bucket, hit some foliage on the way down, and end up in the cache basin. The sight, sound, and scent of the dripping leaves entice reptiles and amphibians to the water.

3. **Empty the cache basin each night.**

   You empty it daily because it won't hold more than one days' worth of drippings, and to keep the humidity level in the caging low.

4. **Repeat the process the next day.**

   This twice-a-day empty-and-set-up-the-drip-process not only provides fresh water to your herp every day, but also gives you a chance to look at the animal and the caging both morning and night, to make certain all is well.

See Chapter 7 for more information on cages.

Misting your herp

If you have an arboreal herp, or a spiny desert-dweller like a Cordylus, another way to provide water is to mist him. You can use a hand-held mister, the kind you can buy in hardware stores and in drug stores, and fill it with tepid water. You mist the foliage and furniture with safe water in the cage on a once- or twice-daily basis. Because there's no cache basin for the runoff, be careful not to soak the cage. Just mist enough to have standing beads of water on the plants and perhaps on one wall of the tank. For more information on plants in your setup, see Chapter 7.

You can also buy commercial misting units that create microscopic droplets of water, much like a fog. This type of device is especially good for creatures such as montane (mountain-dwelling) frogs and lizards that come from regions (often cloud forest) where clouds moisten the habitat and the animals daily. Some species absorb the fog-moisture through their skin, and others drink the droplets from the vegetation.

The misting units work on a timer. You set the timer, fill the unit with tap water, make sure it's plugged in and turned on, and your part is done. When the unit is on, the mist rolls out and fills the cage. The process is enchanting to watch — you hear a faint "chug-chug," and clouds begin to fill your cage. As with the hand-held mister, monitor the cage to make sure that it doesn't get soaked.

Many pet retailers stock the misting devices or will order one for you. These machines are also advertised in the reptile hobby magazines or you can order them online.

Bubbling over: Using an elevated watering system

A fourth method of providing water for your herps uses an elevated watering dish — one slightly smaller than the one you use on the floor of a cage. The smaller water dish is secured in the foliage, perhaps on a cross branch or in the pot of an elevated plant. Place water in the dish, and create a bubbling effect by adding an air stone and an air pump from an aquarium. The effect of moving water is a bit like a tiny cascading rivulet that has pooled. Tree-dwelling anoles and snakes know all about these little puddles, and they seek them out and drink from them avidly. See Chapter 3 for more info on anoles.

As with the other watering methods, you must be vigilant when using the elevated watering dish so that the cage floor doesn't become soggy.

How dry I am: The dangers of dehydration

When herps don't get the water they need, they dry out or become dehydrated. Dehydration is a problem that can happen in your terrarium, but it may also happen elsewhere. It may happen at a wholesaler's, at an exporter's, or during transportation. The animal looks listless, and the eyes may be dull. The animal may look thin. It may be unable to eat. At its best, short-term dehydration is debilitating. At its prolonged worst, well, the animal dies. That's why you need to make certain that your herp has the water it needs, in a form it can use, from the very start. (See Chapter 12 for information on correcting dehydration.)

Menu Planning: Deciding What Kind of Foods Your Herp Needs

In the wild, herps tend to be wanderers, moving about during their active time. (Some herps are active at day, some at dawn and/or at dusk, and others during the night.) Herps are pretty basic creatures; when they wander, they're either looking for a spot to thermoregulate (warm up so they can have normal body function, or more rarely, where they can cool down because they're already just a bit too warm), to procreate (if it's breeding season), or to find food.

What that food item may be depends entirely on the animal — carnivore, herbivore, or omnivore. These three commonly applied terms indicate the feeding preferences of animals and, in this case, of reptiles and amphibians.

The terms give you some basic guidelines on what to feed your pet. For more info, checkout the appendix in the back of the book.

- **Carnivores eat flesh (or meat).** Typical herp carnivores are all the snakes, tegu lizards, monitors, and crocodilians. Typical dietary items are mice, rats, birds' eggs, insects, and fish, all eaten raw of course.

- **Herbivores consume only (or primarily) plant materials.** Green iguanas and some tortoises are examples of the vegetarian herps. They eat foods such as chopped collard greens, romaine lettuce, chopped squash and bananas.

- **Omnivores consume both meat and plant material.** Bearded dragons and many aquatic turtles are examples of omnivores. Typical food items include crickets, mealworms, earthworms, chopped veggies, and romaine lettuce.

Occasionally, you see more specific terms in place of carnivore or herbivore, including the following:

- **Folivore:** An animal that eats leaves. Iguanas are good examples of folivores, and in the wild, they roam the treetops of the forest, noshing on whatever leaves look the most tempting.

- **Insectivore:** An animal that eats insects. A chameleon is a good example of an insectivore, as is the anole. Their diets consist basically of crickets and mealworms.

- **Piscivore:** An animal that eats fish. Crocodiles are piscivorous, although not exclusively. The matamata turtle, called by its original South American name, lies in wait until its fish prey swims by and then it inhales and slurps in dinner. For captive herps, bait-store minnows fill the bill — er, I mean the mouth.

Feeding Your Herp

Before you bring home a herp, you first need to think about what kind of food you're willing to feed it. For example, someone who is squeamish about feeding rabbits to a snake should not decide to purchase a Burmese python. Burmese pythons start out pretty and small and you may have to feed it mice or rats, but they don't stay small (but they do stay pretty). As they grow, they need bigger and bigger food items. A large snake needs large food.

Insectivorous herps need live insects, specifically crickets or mealworms. Most people are probably comfortable offering that menu (see Figure 11-2). Piscivorous creatures eat fish, meaning bait minnows or perhaps goldfish. Again, serving those items probably wouldn't bother most people.

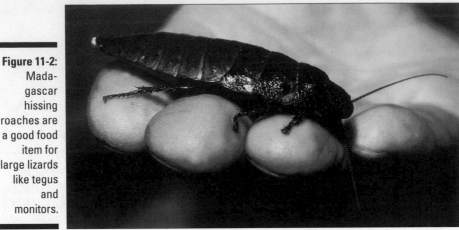

Figure 11-2:
Mada-
gascar
hissing
roaches are
a good food
item for
large lizards
like tegus
and
monitors.

Carnivorous herps need to eat meat, and for snakes this generally means rodents (or birds, to a lesser degree). But you don't have to feed your snake or other herp live food. In fact, I recommend that you don't feed live food (I never do). Tegus, snakes, turtles, and larger monitors will thrive on a diet of prekilled mammals or birds. And you don't have to do the killing.

Using prekilled prey accomplishes several things, all of them good. The vast majority of herps readily feed on prekilled prey. Using prekilled prey removes the disgust that many people feel tossing in a live creature, only to have it devoured by another creature. No one enjoys seeing an animal in terminal distress. The prekilled animals available in your pet store are humanely killed and then frozen (see Figure 11-3). They don't suffer, and neither will your herp.

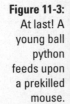

Figure 11-3:
At last! A
young ball
python
feeds upon
a prekilled
mouse.

How much should you feed your herp?

- ✔ For insectivorous herps, give as many insects as they'll consume in a half hour, repeated twice daily (for chameleons) or daily/every other day (for frogs and salamanders). The good news is that you don't have to stand there and watch your herp eat the crickets or mealworms — you can tip them in or put them in a small dish and put the dish in the cage. Of course, crickets will crawl all over the cage, but the herp will follow and slurp them up. When feeding earthworms, start with one earthworm, neatly nipped apart into head-sized pieces with your fingernails; when all of those pieces are gone, you *may* need to offer a second.

- ✔ For snakes, tegus, and other carnivorous herps, offer a prekilled mouse or food item no larger than the animal's head. If it's readily eaten, offer a second.

- ✔ For herbivorous lizards, offer a pile of chopped veggies as long as the animal's body and twice as wide, and check later that day to see how much remains. Veggies don't have a lot of protein, so your herbivorous lizard will eat a lot.

The process of offering prekilled food is pretty simple and painless:

1. **Thaw the mouse or rat (or rabbit, nutria, chicken, or quail) in warm water for half an hour or so.**

   The larger food items need longer to thaw, up to an hour with a water change every 20 minutes or so.

2. **Blot it dry.**

3. **Put it in your pet's cage.**

   You may want to wear gloves when you do this, in case your herp lunges toward the food item.

By feeding your snake/tegu/herp prekilled food, you remove the risk that your pet will be injured by its intended prey.

Why is it important *not* to offer live food? Offering a live rodent to a captive snake in a small cage can be very different from a snake or a monitor ambushing and overcoming a rodent in the wild. In the latter case, the herp is already in an active hunting mode, is probably well camouflaged, and will be the one to pace its encounter with prey. In the cage, if the prey rodent (or bird) happens to turn the tables by darting toward and startling the supposed predator, the predator will probably shy away. And, following that, if the prey and predator are left alone for any length of time, the intended prey is apt to start chewing or pecking on the snake or lizard. Every veterinarian has had an instance where an owner has brought in a grisly remnant of what had been a perfectly healthy snake or lizard that now has no eyes, displays exposed ribs, or is missing a tail. Gulp! Not a pretty sight!

Can you feed live food to your snake? The answer is yes, but only if you check the snake every 15 minutes and then remove the food item if it isn't killed and eaten within 45 minutes. But you need to examine your motives here. Why would you want to feed your snake live food when a chance of injury to your pet exists?

What are the advantages of using prekilled rodents instead of live prey animals? Prekilled rodents are often more readily available, easier to store, easier to use, acceptable to almost all (yes, a very few snakes do still insist on live food) rodent-eating herps, and sometimes cheaper.

Chapter 12

An Apple (or Mouse) a Day Keeps the Vet Away

In This Chapter

▶ Recognizing normal behavior

▶ Being alert for signs of trouble

▶ Watching for parasites

▶ Preventing accidents and trauma

▶ Considering congenital diseases

You'll need to know normal herp behavior before you can tell whether your herp is ill or just behaving abnormally. Relax; getting to know your pet really does come with time. But until then, here are a few things you should watch for so you'll know when something just isn't quite right.

There's Nothing to Be Alarmed About, Ma'am

Certain behaviors — like sleeping — are all a part of being a herp. All herps sleep. Lizards are the most fun to watch — some lie flat on the ground, their head outstretched, their limbs parallel to their body with the palms tuned upward, thoroughly zonked out. Aquatic turtles, especially the hatchlings, may sleep underwater, wedged under a submerged log or perched atop a small branch, just inches below the surface of the water. Snakes are the least interesting to watch. They look just like they do when they are awake, but when they're sleeping, they look somehow quieter. Frogs tend to hunker down, pull their limbs close to their body, and duck their head down before closing their eyes in sleep. This is all very normal behavior.

Hibernation or (gulp) the Big Sleep?

When they hibernate, herps from temperate areas sleep at least part of the winter or significantly decrease their activities. Reptiles from tropical areas tend to eat less and spend more time directly sunning. (The angle of sunlight is lower during the winter months, and fewer photons "excite" the skin into producing vitamin D3, so the animals sun themselves longer.) It's normal for herps to move around less, resting quietly in the lighted/warm part of the cage. Amphibians from tropical areas behave much as do the reptiles, but amphibians aren't much for sunning at any time.

During hibernation, herps' appetites naturally go way down. Don't worry that your snake or your gray treefrog doesn't eat with the fervor he displayed in June. This behavior is normal and will change as the days begin to lengthen again. That's when you'll long (for just a moment) for those weeks when the frozen mice stayed stockpiled in your freezer, the greens lasted more than a day, and you didn't have to make those 7:30 a.m. weekly trips to the bait store for earthworms.

A herp that's near death behaves differently from one in his wintertime slowdown. A dying herp is unresponsive, lethargic, and withdrawn. His eyes have already begun to sink back into his head, and he won't pull back when you gently pull on one of his legs. If you see those signs, it's critical that you take your pet to a veterinarian.

Achoo! Normal sneezing

Reptiles sneeze to clear their nostrils of salt-laden fluid. Many reptiles — essentially all the sea-going species, and most of the lizards — have some form of salt gland that extracts excess salt from the body. When the gland is overflowing with concentrated brine, the reptile sneezes to clear out the brine. I know it seems like the only time your lizard sneezes is when you lean over close to him to make sure that everything looks as it should. You could call the sneeze an audible health check: You get sneezed on and know that things are okay in the salt gland area.

Sneezing is why the inside of a glass tank occupied by reptiles, especially green iguanas, gets cloudy looking on the inside. That's accumulated . . . ahhh . . . salt. (No, don't try to taste it to make sure.)

Flop! Normal defecation

All herps defecate. Normally, it's two-colors: a white portion, which is urates, and a darker portion that is the byproduct of food passing through the stomach and colon.

In all herps, the cloaca serves as a general hold-all storage bin for the urates from the kidneys and the feces from the intestinal tract. (Turtles and most lizards have an added feature, a urinary bladder that stores the urates until they are excreted to the cloaca.)

Feces are usually a mix of semisolids and liquids. If the feces are mucous-laden, that should serve as a yellow flag: This generally indicates some sort of internal infection or inflammation.

The usual flora and fauna

Like you and me, reptiles and amphibians have internal and external fauna. We have *E. coli* to help digest our food (no, we don't do it by ourselves). Herps have an amazing array of external and internal "guests," including the following:

- *Saprophytes:* They live on a host but neither harm nor help the host.

- *Commensals:* The relationship helps both parties in some way, like a house guest who shares his lottery ticket winnings with you.

- *Parasites:* The intruder benefits directly from the host, and the host doesn't benefit at all.

The nonbacterial, nonviral life forms are either *protozoans* or *metazoans*. (A protozoan is a single-celled creature, like an amoeba or coccidia. A metazoan is any creature possessing differentiated body tissues and a digestive tract.) Although some are labeled some as parasites and some as "not harmful," we aren't certain, in many cases, what the details of the relationship might be. We have little exact knowledge of how these life forms interact with (and within) the herp and vice versa. For instance, 20 years ago, we thought that all intestinal parasites (note the term "parasites") were bad, and the ideal herp had zero in his system. A fecal smear shows your iguana has trematodes? Purge that creature! The truth is, trematodes are present in enormous numbers in iguanas' guts. Rather than being parasites, at least some types are commensals. They assist in digesting cellulose, something an iguana eats lots of. As these tiny worms crawl through the gut contents, their movement helps bring the digested food into contact with the gut wall so it can be absorbed.

When it comes to herp health, if parasites are present in his body, you may not have to intrude if your herp is doing well. The exception is for parasites, namely ticks and mites. These always need to be eliminated.

186

Part III: Open Wide! Feeding, Hydration, and Health

Sometimes the herp has too many visitors — the parasite load is too heavy. For example, when axolotls are kept in water that isn't cleaned regularly or are kept in crowded conditions, the ciliates that live on their skin and gills proliferate (these ciliates are little prickly things that feed on suspended organic matter). The large quantities of ciliates and their grasping adhesive disks actually damage the surface of the tissues they live on, which sloughs off, and the ciliates begin feeding on that. Because there's more food, the ciliates proliferate. You can see how the problem gets "worser and worser," so be sure to keep your herp's caging clean.

The dirty truth about salmonella

Salmonella is a ubiquitous bacteria. It's everywhere — in the soil, on the trunks of trees, between chicken's toes, on chicken eggs. It grows well in unrefrigerated mayonnaise-based salads, which is why salmonella is linked with big family picnics and summertime buffets.

Once in a while, a virulent strain of salmonella is ingested, or a person with a compromised immune system contracts salmonella. This last category includes very young children, whose immune systems aren't developed yet (which is why little kids in schools or daycare centers contract every cold that's passed around). These people can become extremely ill, and they may die. A few of those cases have been tracked to individuals who have handled or touched reptiles prior to becoming ill, and the DNA strain of salmonella was identical.

Salmonella is why you can't purchase turtles with a shell length of less than four inches. The United States Public Health Service (USPHS) decided that a turtle with a shell length of four inches was harder for a child or baby to jam into his or her mouth than a smaller turtle, so they forbade sales of small turtles. Of course you can touch a turtle of four inches or any size and then put your hands in your mouth (well, maybe not you, but a baby would), and contract salmonella, but forbidding sales of baby turtles was an action that USPHS could take. (Babies, of course, don't listen to USPHS any better than they do to their mothers.)

In response to this problem, the big turtle hatcheries in the southern United States developed techniques to produce salmonella-free hatchlings by bathing the eggs in a dilute chlorine solution. The babies are salmonella free, and they're packaged so they arrive at their destination salmonella free. But once those hatchlings get into contaminated water (water that's been in a nonsterile container or had someone's hands in it) or are handled by someone with dirty hands, they have salmonella on their shells. Keeping a salmonella-free turtle salmonella-free is extremely difficult in the real world.

If your reptile or amphibian has ever touched the bare ground with his feet, been exposed to a substrate that's been on the ground, been kept in a cage or aquatic tank with other herps, or been handled by someone who has ever touched dirt in any form, he probably has salmonella on his skin. Do not worry. Wash your hands before you feed your herp or touch him or clean his cage. Wash your hands again after feeding or handling your herp. Don't let children touch your herp unless they go through the same routine. Be zealous about this practice because the stakes — more correctly spelled "$take$" — can be very high. End of problem.

Shedding: Snack attack

Reptiles shed their skin at regular intervals, young specimens more frequently than adults. You may not even notice that your lizard is shedding, other than seeing the flaky patches on his head. Geckos actually pull off their shedding skin and eat it, a bit like eating lettuce.

Snakes are much more impressive here. Their eyes turn blue as the transparent scale that covers the eye is replicated, and the top, old eye covering is loosened. Their overall color dulls as the same thing occurs with the skin on the body. The eyes clear up, and a day or two later, the snake rubs his lips against a rock or hidebox in his cage, catches the old skin, and then crawls out of his old skin. When freshly shed, the old skin is quite pliable and actually measures longer than the snake.

Amphibians can't bear to be parted from their skin. They eat it. Because they're most active at night, you may never see this, but it is quite normal.

Recognizing Trouble Signs

In the following sections, I point out the trouble signs to watch out for. When you see any of these, observe your herp carefully. It could be time for vet care.

Raspy breath

Your herp seems quieter than usual, and he may breathe with his mouth open. Bubbles may be coming from his nose. These symptoms are typical of a respiratory infection, which can be cured if caught early, or a parasite overload. No matter what the cause turns out to be, you need to treat it.

Loss of appetite or weight

Sometimes herps decide not to eat, especially during the winter months or the short-day cycle. Not eating is not a cause for concern, unless it continues. Then it indicates that something else is wrong. Maybe the animal has an infection, or the caging is too cold, too dry, or too damp, or the animal is too stressed. For example, chameleons don't even like to *look* at each other if it isn't breeding season. Is your herp being kept where he can be dissed by others of his same kind?

Some herps just don't want to feed in captivity, or at least that's how it looks to people. Ball pythons are famous for this. Don't even think of buying a ball python without first seeing it feed. You may pay dearly for believing the word of the dealer or pet store. I don't mean to be cynical, but a dealer and a pet store are in the business to make money — even if it means selling animals they don't expect will live very long.

The problem when herps don't eat is that, if the animal is ill, he can't get better. Human burn victims need three times the number of calories a day that a healthy human needs. It takes that much energy to live and to heal (even though putting that number of calories into the human body is a real challenge).

 An amphibian needs to take in 50 percent more calories than usual if he's ill just to meet his metabolic demands. You can reasonably extrapolate that ill or stressed reptiles need the same proportional increase in calories. Take special care to provide nutritious food to a herp exhibiting signs of illness. He's already in trouble.

Lethargy

Your herp acts as if he doesn't care about anything any more. He suns like he used to, he eats some food, but he just doesn't respond to you the way he once did. If this attitude lasts more than a couple of days, chances are, your herp's in trouble. Maybe your iguana has fed upon some toxic houseplants. Maybe the apartment complex pest control man came in to spray for roaches, and your tiger salamander was exposed to the fumes. Maybe you burned up a Teflon-coated frying pan on your stove (these fumes are *extremely* toxic for birds and reptiles). Maybe your herp has a whopping respiratory infection you haven't yet noticed. Maybe that chubbiness is constipation; your herp has an impaction and can't pass his feces.

 If your herp seems lethargic, don't delay getting a veterinarian's advice. She or he can observe things about your herp that you won't notice. The better shape your herp is in when you walk through your veterinarian's door, the more likely your herp is to make it.

Stargazing

Stargazing is a disease that occurs most frequently in boas. The main symptom is the boa holding his head vertically for long periods of time, as if he's looking at something directly over him. Other maladies may be involved, so you need training and brains to find the cause of this behavior.

Stargazer's disease is caused by a retrovirus that takes up residence in the boa's nervous system. It is progressive and irreversible. The gazing is followed by tremors, disorientation, the inability to right itself once turned over, and paralysis. The disease is transmissible to the other snakes in your collection.

This disease is also called inclusion body disease, or IBD. It is diagnosed by examination of a bit of nerve tissue for the retrovirus inclusions.

Dietary problems

A number of dietary problems can affect your herp. Most are avoidable and treatable.

Metabolic bone disease (MBD)

Both reptiles and amphibians can develop metabolic bone disease (MBD). The malady is characteristic of herps that are herbivores or insectivores (carnivores get lots of calcium from their diet of plump little mice and birds).

A couple things can cause this disease — not enough sunlight and too little calcium. (Calcium carbonate can help prevent bone disease. See Figure 12-1.) Sunlight stirs the herp's body to produce vitamin D3. Vitamin D3 enables the body to metabolize calcium. That seems simple. What's really impressive is how these two factors work together, or rather what happens when this partnership is broken.

Figure 12-1: Calcium carbonate helps prevent bone disease in geckos.

When the body doesn't get enough usable calcium, it leaches calcium from the bones to support the needed levels of calcium in the blood. The bones become weaker and weaker and become distorted because the muscles that surround them actually bend them.

Symptoms of MBD are malformed upper and lower jaws, muscular tremors, generalized weakness regarding movement (the limbs are too weak to support the weight of the animal), and scoliosis (a humped backbone). The animal is too weak to move, and the effort of trying to move can break bones in the limbs and toes. An iguana with MBD looks like somebody wadded him up in a ball and threw him in a corner. The bone malformations are largely permanent, although sunlight, supplemental calcium, vitamins, and minerals will restrengthen the bones.

The problem begins with an inadequate diet. Herbivorous reptiles in the wild nibble on a bit of this and bit of that, and they sun extensively. Amphibians in the wild have a varied diet, and they encounter reflected UV radiation even if they don't actively sun. In captivity, neither has much choice in diet, and they rarely have access to sunlight. That vitamin D3-machine in the skin never gets working, and the body has trouble using whatever calcium is present in the body. Calcium is pulled from the bones to maintain the needed levels in the blood.

Treatment is supplemental oral calcium and vitamin D3 coupled with UV light. For the necessary (simulated) sunlight, position the UV bulb over the cage, about a foot away from the bottom. (See Chapter 9 for more details about lighting.)

To provide your herp with necessary calcium, you need to prepare calcium-rich food. You have a couple choices:

- ✔ You can dust the crickets you feed your herp with a vitamin/mineral supplement.

- ✔ You can gut-load the crickets; meaning you feed them nutritious food before feeding them to a herp, either with a commercial gutloading food, or one of your own making.

Gut-loading is easy. Because crickets don't live long if fed a diet that's chock-full of calcium (the little unobliging things), it's easier and more practical to feed them a diet that's good for them, such as chopped broccoli (at last a use for broccoli!), dampened chicken starter mash, shredded carrots, and dampened dog kibble, so they're kicking their little heels all the way down into your herp. In effect, you're stuffing a cherry tomato with tuna fish salad.

Dusting crickets is also easy. Use a glass jar with a screw-on top. Put ¼ teaspoon vitamin/mineral supplement in the jar, and add a half dozen crickets. Screw on the top of the jar and shake gently. The powder coats the crickets and will stay in place for about three hours. These are called "shake and bake" crickets, and they're the mainstay of any insectivorous herp's diet.

Spindly leg syndrome

Amphibians growing up sometimes develop thin, sticklike legs, a problem called spindly leg disease. This condition is a skeletomuscular underdevelopment, and if you guessed it was a vitamin "thing," you're right. It seems to occur most frequently when the young amphibians are fed a flake fish food that doesn't offer total nutrition. Those amphibians fed a good diet (the researchers used Aquarian by Wardley) don't have this problem. Make certain that any fish food diet you offer your amphibians includes the vitamin B complex. Provide live algae and aquatic vegetations as a dietary component.

Thiamine deficiency

Herps that are fed a diet of thawed frozen fish are missing thiamine in their diet. (Thiaminase, an enzyme that's a natural component of fish, destroys the thiamine already in the fish.)

If your herp has been on a diet of thawed frozen fish and begins to exhibit tremors, seizures, or muscular twitching in part of a limb (these twitches are called *fasciculations,* in case you need the term), he may need thiamine. The treatment usually starts with an instant "loading" of thiamine by injection, which requires the assistance of your veterinarian. Follow-up with dietary supplementation as long as frozen fish is a food item.

Vitamin A deficiency

If your turtle has puffy, swollen eyes that he can barely open, review his diet. Swollen eyes are typically a symptom of vitamin A deficiency. Upgrade the diet to include foods that contain vitamin A. Dark green leafy vegetables are one good source as are a few tiny bits of chicken liver.

Dehydration

When a herp doesn't get the water he needs, he dries out or becomes dehydrated. Just as in people, dehydration throws all kinds of body functions out of kilter. In herps, early dehydration is easy to overlook. As it progresses, dehydration will do the following:

✔ Cause amphibians to look dry and shriveled

✔ Cause reptiles to look gaunt and sunken-eyed

✔ Inhibit the ability of both amphibians and reptiles to drink water and to digest food

✔ Result in the herp's death

Dehydration is deadly, but in its early stages, you can overcome its effects by assuring that the herp has access to clean water or by use of a hydration chamber. For herps that are reluctant drinkers, your only choice is a hydration chamber (see Figure 12-2).

Figure 12-2:
A
dehydrated
box turtle or
tortoise can
be saved
with a
hydration
chamber, the
equivalent
of a heavy,
warm,
summer
thunder-
shower.

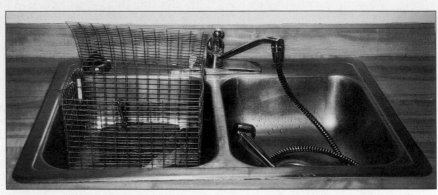

A hydration chamber is a rain chamber. You can set one up, using a wire mesh cage.

Skin peeling

Peeling skin is one of the classic signs of *hypervitaminosis A*, or too much vitamin A, and it's typically an amphibian problem. The fault may lie, in a matter of speaking, in the way amphibians' bodies work on a diet of white mice. They get too much vitamin A from the mouse, specifically the liver. No, I'm not suggesting that you excise the mouse's liver prior to feeding, à la Prometheus. I'm saying don't feed white mice to amphibians. Once in a while is okay, but not as a steady thing.

Constipation

When your herp stops eating, his belly seems to be bigger than usual, and he hasn't defecated in the last two weeks, he may be constipated. The easiest and least stressful way to deal with this is to let your herp swim in your bathtub.

Clean the tub and rinse it very well. Put down a rubber mat so your herp will have firm footing, and add maybe 5 or 6 inches of warm water to the tub. The water should be about 85 to 90 degrees for reptiles and 60 to 70 degrees for amphibians. Place your pet in the tub and watch him swim for 15 minutes or so.

If he's constipated, swimming in a warm tub is usually enough to get him to defecate. After he's defecated, or after 15 minutes, take your herp out, dry him off with towels, and put him back into his warm, dry (for reptiles) or cool (for amphibians) clean cage.

Constipation may also mean gastric blockage. Avoid having bite-sized or tiny hard items in the cage. Herps aren't terribly bright. Horned frogs have been known to lap up pea-sized gravel as if it's cinnamon sugar. Leopard geckos may swallow anything they can fit into their mouths, sort of on the "oh, well, could be food" approach. Make certain that food items are small in size. Gastric blockage is something for a veterinarian to handle, and in a best case scenario, it generally involves going down through the mouth to remove the food item.

Runny stools

Diarrhea for more than four or five days means the herp has a problem that you're going to have to fix. Short-term diarrhea may be caused by stress, a change in diet, or a change in drinking water source, from well water to city water, for instance, or from one city's water to another city's water. (I do know people who offer their iguanas only bottled water, but I don't let *my* iggies meet them.)

One cause is too heavy a parasitic load. You can't really diagnose this yourself, so take a stool specimen to your veterinarian, who can do an analysis and prescribe drugs to treat the problem.

To gather a stool specimen, you can scoop up the solid portion of the stool, using a plastic bag everted over your hand, or use a plastic spoon to scoop some into a plastic bag. The very liquid diarrhea can go into a jar with a screw lid.

You can store fecal samples in your refrigerator for up to four hours before you take them to your vet. If you store them any longer than this, the parasites (protozoans including amoebas and ciliates, or metazoans like roundworms or tapeworms) may not be identifiable.

Ingestion of poisonous plants

Herbivores may nibble on anything green or anything that may be green, especially if they've been deprived of food for any length of time. Although they generally can tell from the smell or initial taste of a plant that it's toxic, such is not always the rule. If your herbivore ingests a plant that's toxic, symptoms may be lethargy, foaming at the mouth, change in skin color, restlessness and distress, vomiting, paralysis, and convulsions. Your pet may try to rub his face against something firm, as if to rub off a sensation or taste.

This problem is out of the home treatment league entirely. Call your veterinarian immediately. If you can't reach your veterinarian, call the ASPCA National Animal Poison Control Center (NAPCC) at 888-426-4435. This number is staffed 24 hours a day, 7 days a week, by a staff of 23 veterinarians who are active in the field. At a fee of $45 per case, billed to your major credit card, it's a bargain without comparison.

Corneal lipids

Sometimes, reptiles and amphibians (particularly frogs) develop opaque spots on their corneas, a condition called corneal lipidosis. A major cause of this problem appears to be diet. When a reptile or amphibian is fed a diet that's higher in fat than what the animal would encounter in the wild, the body doesn't know what to do with the extra fat, and it gets deposited in soft tissues. This is another reason to not use rodents as a diet when you're keeping creatures that ordinarily wouldn't feed upon rodents in the wild.

Gastric overload

This condition doesn't mean that your herp is making a pig of himself, but his diet is literally too big for him. Bearded dragons go into twitches and sometimes die when given food items too big for their stomach. This also occurs in horned frogs, African bullfrogs, and maybe some other herps as well.

The distended stomach presses on the major veins in the abdomen and the lungs. The animal not only can't breathe, but his circulatory system goes into shock. The digestive system shuts down. If the animal doesn't die of shock, he runs the danger of dying from having rotting food in his stomach.

Think prevention rather than cure to prevent gastric overload. Only offer food items that the animal can swallow easily. The treatment consists of removing the food item without tearing up the stomach in the process. Regurgitation is *not* the cure. This is a job for your veterinarian.

Prolapse

Sometimes the inside comes outside. Part of the cloaca and/or the testes becomes extruded through the anus or the cloacal opening in a condition called *prolapse*. Caught in the restricted opening, the tissue quickly swells, and then it can't be pulled back into the body.

Sometimes you can moisten the tissue and gently push it back into the body, rather like pushing the finger of a rubber glove back into the hand of the glove when both are filled with water. For reptiles, you can try letting your pet swim in a few inches of warm water in your bathtub, with a cup or two of sugar added. The sugar solution pulls moisture from the engorged tissue, and maybe the reptile can pull the tissue back inside, or you can massage it back into place and it will stay.

If these techniques don't work, it's time to call your veterinarian. She/he may add a purse string suture to hold the replaced tissue in place. Amputation of the damaged extruded tissue may be the last resort.

Pathogens

Pathogens are small life forms that cause disease. Technically speaking, you could consider parasites pathogens, but usually the term means bacteria, viruses, rickettsia, or a fungus.

Abscesses

When a herp's skin is damaged and bacteria enter the lesion, sometimes the lesion closes over, and the bacteria are sealed inside. The bacteria don't mind — they go to work, eating body tissues and destroying red blood cells, and a localized infection develops and erupts at the spot. Your first indication is a swollen area that's very tender to the touch, and the abscess may get larger and can be fatal. Usually your veterinarian will use antibiotics and may surgically remove the abscess. The bad part is the abscess may recur even when it's been cleaned and treated with antibiotics.

Mouth rot

When a herp injures his mouth, from fighting with another herp or perhaps when he lunges toward freedom and hits the wall of his cage instead, the mouth may not heal right away. Damage to the tender tissue of the mouth is a problem because the tissue is thin there and easily damaged, and the jaws themselves get infected (and an infection in bone is notoriously hard to cure).

The symptoms of mouth rot are yellow crusty patches on the outside of the mouth — dried pus, to be technical. You can use a dampened cotton swab to moisten and remove the dried areas. While you're doing this, open the herp's mouth and look for bleeding areas — even just a few bloody spots are bad — or whitish area that differs in color from the rest of the mouth tissue. Either one of these signs is an indication that a visit to your veterinarian is in order. If all you see are the yellow crusty areas outside the mouth, try gently removing them for a week or so. They should go away. If not, the problem is more stubborn than cleanliness can fix. Talk to your veterinarian about a systemic or topical antibiotic.

If the problem is caused by running into the walls of his tank, you can help. Tape typing paper or newspaper over the glass sides, at least two-thirds the way up the sides. Herps don't understand glass, and they'll repeatedly run into it. If they see an actual wall, they won't make that that headlong dash. To help prevent that from happening, try not to startle them. Make some noise every time you approach your nervous herp's cage, if only to let him know that soon he'll see your face looming over the top of his tank.

Skin problems

Both reptiles and amphibians can have skin problems, but these problems are especially acute for amphibians. An amphibian with redleg or a skin fungus is like you trying to breathe with pneumonia.

Redleg

Amphibians are particularly susceptible to this bacterial infection, which may be caused by a variety of opportunistic bacteria that are always present. When an amphibian is stressed and kept in crowded conditions, redleg is the inevitable result.

The symptoms are red legs, caused by engorgement of the capillaries in the skin as the body suffuses the skin with blood in an effort to fight off an overwhelming infection. The body's action might work if the amphibian was immediately transferred to clean water, but this rarely occurs. Along with the engorgement of the capillaries comes skin lesions as the skin breaks down under the bacterial onslaught. Tiny hemorrhages begin in skeletal muscles, the kidneys, spleen, and the interior of the body.

 Redleg is highly contagious, and most treatments work only to a limited degree. Perhaps the easiest one is one of the oldest: cold. By putting the amphibian in cold conditions, just above freezing (32 to 40 degrees), the bacterial infection may be slowed enough to allow the amphibian's immune system to take control. Various antibiotics have been touted as cures, and a broad-spectrum antibiotic is certainly worth a try. Just don't hold your breath.

Fungus

Fungus infections generally appear in animals that have been stressed to the point of inhibiting the immune system. In herps, it's the amphibians who develop fungal infections, and then when housed in groups. Fungus may appear on baby soft-shell turtles when they're kept in a small tank and the water isn't clean. Not only is it easier for a fungus to spread when there are potential hosts living in contact with each other, but the stress of group living in an animal that is usually solitary tends to predispose them to problems. Fungus spores can be spread from one area to the next on the hull of a boat or rubber boots, or carried on the legs of wading birds. Some herp species can deal with and throw off fungal intrusions, but a few frog species, like the Wyoming toad, are immunologically clueless about fungus. Wyoming toads die when they encounter fungus. That's why the isolated few left in the wild are in so much trouble.

Herps are subject to two types of fungus to be concerned about. One is the type that invades your frog or salamander in captivity. Usually the infection begins with a lesion or skin damage on one herp. That enables the fungus to gain a toehold, and then it leapfrogs (sorry) to every other amphibian that's in contact with the first.

Symptoms depend on the species of fungus invading but usually involve some discoloration or the skin, if not actual visible mold growth, along with lethargy and anoxia. The water molds cause cottony growths on the skin and gills. For *Basidiobolous*, the fungus that's killing the Wyoming toad, the toad responds by sitting in water for longer and longer periods of time and by hunching his back. The skin on the back darkens. The ventral skin is sloughed off, and death occurs usually within five days.

The other fungus that causes concern is the chytrid fungus, one of the agents that's destroying frog populations worldwide. Chytrid fungus dermatitis, first described in 1996, has been isolated from a dozen different species of amphibian. It attacks keratin, one of the major components of the topmost layer of skin. It affects the digits first, if any overt signs are noted. Death occurs within two to five weeks.

When you breathe through your skin and your skin gets fungus, you don't have much time. Take your amphibian to your veterinarian, who will probably first prescribe periodic baths in a dilute fungicide.

Parasites! Maybe Not So Bad

A parasite is a creature that lives off another creature and provides no benefit to the host. Parasites feed off their host; a "successful" parasite doesn't damage its host enough to kill it.

External pests

Parasites are either amazingly or distressingly adaptive. They must either be able to find a protected hiding spot on the outside of the herp, so they can't be scraped or rubbed off, or they have to go internal. Reptiles are the hosts for external parasites.

Mites

Mites are less than pinhead-sized dots that bear eight legs and cause more grief than any other malady in most collections. Mites can infest your collection if you bring in a new herp and fail to quarantine it for 30 days. (Quarantining a new herp for 30 days gives you a chance to observe the animal for illness or other problems and to ensure that he eats on his own, before you bring the new animal in contact with your present animals.) Mites proliferate exponentially. They live on the outside of your reptile, stick their sharp little mouth parts in between the scales, and drink blood, slurp slurp slurp.

You can usually see the mites as they cruise about on your reptile, seeking new areas to sip from. They move around a lot at night. Mites especially like the areas around the eye, the armpits, or folds of the skin. They can pierce your herp's skin so much that your pet will develop crusty, oozing patches. A heavy infestation is a real health problem for your herp.

Treatment must include getting every single mite off your reptile and out of his enclosure. Mites have been implicated in the spread of IBD, the neurological disease also called stargazing (see the section "Stargazing," earlier in this chapter).

You can try the warm water soak technique for snakes or lizards. This technique uses a series of warm baths to drown some of the mites while you physically remove the others. While your herp is soaking, use a dampened cotton swab to remove the mites around the eyes. While your herp is soaking, clean his cage thoroughly with hot water and soap. Rinse the cage and dry it. Repeat this process daily for five days, and then again in a week for three more days so that you can catch the young mites that hatched in the meantime.

If your tortoise has mites, you can't soak him to rid him of mites — he'll drown. A few mite treatments are available, including Provent-a-Mite. This commercial spray is designed for use on all reptiles and their enclosures. Unlike other mite sprays in the pet market, this one is designed specifically to be used on reptiles. It's easy to use and said to be very effective. You may be able to buy this at your pet store, or you can get it directly from the manufacturer at www.pro-products.com.

Your veterinarian has access to drugs that are very effective against mites, and a variety of ways to administer them. She'll probably recommend ivermectin as a dilute spray. You spray the animal, being very careful around his eyes, and spray the cage as well.

Ticks

Ticks are ¼-inch-long, eight-legged parasites that can carry communicable diseases (see Figure 12-3). The good part is that getting rid of ticks is much easier than getting rid of mites. Ticks are easy to see and easy to remove. Simply grab them with a pair of tweezers and exert a gentle pull until they extract their mouth parts. Crush the tick in a bit of tissue, making sure that it's totally dead, and throw it away. Ticks can carry diseases that affect both people and stock animals, and you don't want to take any chances on having one of "your" ticks being part of that problem.

Figure 12-3:
A tick will lodge where it cannot be dislodged. Here, a tick feeds between the back spines of a Ctenosaur.

Internal buggers

Many wild-caught herps have internal parasites, and current thinking says that's not usually a problem. Broadly speaking, it's pointless for a parasite to kill its host, because it's going to die as well. Mites and ticks could metaphorically shrug, disengage, and go toddling off to find another host. Internal parasites are more committed. Internal parasites live in sort of a détente with their host, drinking from the well of life so to speak, but not so deeply the well runs dry.

But when the parasitic load becomes too heavy or the animal becomes debilitated or stressed, the parasites gain the upper hand. This is particularly likely when many animals are kept in close quarters, and crawl through each others' feces, sharing every parasite and pathogen. If any a wild-caught or new import doesn't seem to be doing well, have your veterinarian analyze a stool specimen. She or he can advise you on the best course of action to take.

Accidents and Trauma

You never mean for an accident to happen. Some you can head off before they occur, but some just happen. The following sections tell how to deal with some scenarios.

Falls

For most herps, a fall is a damaging thing that can have unexpected consequences. A friend of mine had a 3-foot house iguana that launched himself from the back of the sofa to the carpeted floor. He incurred permanent paralysis of the hind legs.

If the limbs have been weakened by MBD (see the section "Metabolic bone disease," earlier in this chapter), serious damage is almost impossible to avoid because bones weakened by the loss of calcium have no elasticity at all. Try to prevent this sort of damage by providing stress-free housing where distance falls are impossible. A thick layer of leaves or mulch on the floor of the cage will absorb much of the impact from a fall.

Bites

Reptiles may bite each other when excited about smell of food, when dealing with territory disputes, or during courtship. These bites are rarely serious — you're apt to incur more damage if you get caught in the middle.

You do need to place the herps in separate caging, if only to avoid future disagreements. Rinse the wound with hydrogen peroxide (you can apply one of the over-the-counter antibiotic creams to the bite areas if you wish), and put the animal in his separate quarters. Leave him alone for a couple days, only bothering him to offer water (and food, if it's a lizard), before you resume your regular regimen of checking, feeding, and cleaning.

Burns

Burns generally occur when the herp is allowed (or gains) unrestricted access to an unshielded heat source. Light bulbs are one such source; a space heater is another. Amphibians, with their built-in cool skins, don't seek out such heat sources, but reptiles do. Snakes and lizards are quite inventive when trying to get to a heat source. Then you'll be able to see, with startling clarity, how an 18-inch-long snake could crawl on top of a small wooden clamp-spot for a light, swing 12 inches away to gain the rim of a aluminum light hood, and then curl under the edge of the shade to coil around the bulb itself.

Once the animal is burned, all you can do hope the burns will not be fatal. Take your pet to your veterinarian, but be warned that he probably can't do much to help. Veterinary medicine is still light years away from skin grafts for reptiles. Your treatment may be limited to applying a prescription antibiotic ointment once a day.

Broken tail

Lizards may break their tail in fleeing an enemy or damage it when it's accidentally closed in a cage door. Once a tail is gone, it's gone. You can put some antibiotic cream on the stump, but don't worry about the bleeding; the stump stops bleeding within minutes. The tail will be regenerated, but the point of the break will always be evident, and the new tail will differ in appearance and mobility from the original.

Blister disease

Blister disease occurs when a reptile is kept too moist. The skin breaks down into small fluid-filled vesicles or "blisters." This condition can be fatal; it can be so severe that the progression is irreversible. Once the skin breaks down, other opportunistic infections will set in. The skin will continue to deteriorate until you take your herp to your veterinarian and put in clean, dry caging.

Congenital Diseases

Alas, some herps are just born with certain problems, which I discuss in the following sections.

Kinked back

Captive-bred snakes sometimes crawl out of the egg looking as if they have zigzag backbones. This is a congenital problem, caused (we think) by inbreeding. No treatment can undo the damage, but when the young are born normal but develop kinked backs later, there may be a solution. When giant monkey frog tadpoles at the National Zoo in Washington, D.C., were developing kinked backs (an awful sight), vitamin B supplement was added to the water. Future young were successfully reared. Once scoliosis occurs, it's not fixable (in tadpoles, it's progressive and terminal). If your herp has a kinked back or is developing one, double-check the diet for calcium levels and vitamin B content, check the caging for access to sunlight, and take your animal to the veterinarian.

Color-linked maladies

Captive-bred colubrids can be subject to maladies that are linked to their color morph. The maladies may be the result of inbreeding with a limited gene pool. Perhaps the best known is the blood red corn snake — a deep, intense orange red, gorgeous snake — that frequently is a poor feeder. By and large, blood-reds fail to thrive. For some, the lack of appetite decreases as the snake ages (and it turns from that gray-red baby to a solid, intense red).

Albinos of any sort have impaired vision, and their skin is prone to sunburn (the skin has no pigment to absorb the sun). Their eyes are sensitive to light, especially in full sunlight, as opposed to a cage with shaded areas. Offer your albino plenty of shade, both for his eyes and for his skin. If he has trouble locating food, make certain that he can find his food and that he eats it.

Chapter 13

How Long Can This Relationship Last?

Getting a pet reptile or amphibian used to be such a simple thing. You got the pet and kept him for a while. When you got tired of the pet, you gave him to someone else. Besides, nothing lived that long. Red-eared sliders, sold with a shallow plastic dish complete with a plastic palm tree, lived for maybe a year. True chameleons lived for maybe six months.

But the era of the disposable pet is a thing of the past. Improved husbandry (general care and feeding), a huge assortment of books with good information, ready-made commercial caging, and the development of a line of herps that flourish in captive conditions have cleared the way for long-term keeping of herps.

But with long-term animal ownership comes increased responsibility. Most of you are probably used to shorter commitments, such as 2 years for a hamster or 12 years for a cat or dog — and maybe 10 for a marriage. The thought of a pet that will live 20 years or more is a bit scary. Will herps really live longer than man's best friend? Who keeps track of this stuff, anyway?

Looking at Herp Longevity

Actually, quite a few people and organizations keep track of how long herps live in captivity. Some of these people just plain like herps, others like numbers, and some people are convinced that herps are wild creatures, not pets, and collect whatever data will support this thesis.

Demographics and herps

Longevity records are raw data, and nobody likes raw data better than demographers (unless it's the IRS, and I understand you don't want to talk about that right now). Demographers use data to identify trends and tendencies. For example, if you live in the Midwest, do you call a carbonated soft drink "soda" or "pop"? (If you're thinking of putting out a new soft drink, what you name it may make a big difference in its success.) The die-hard rock fans who think that Elvis isn't really dead — are they scattered all over or do they all live in the rural parts of the southern United States? (Thinking about having a reunion of Elvis impersonators? You may want to hold it in Mobile.) Other demographic tidbits include this info:

✔ Dieters, or rather people who watch their weight, as they'd prefer to be called, are heavily concentrated in a north-south band between the Rocky Mountains and the Mississippi River. (That's where you should market your breakfast bran!)

✔ Stick-shift drivers are more likely to live in the central western states. (They tend to be drivers for the fun of driving, and they like a car that's fun to drive.)

The earliest data trackers that I remember were the herp societies. Before any good books on herps were available, and before the people had the Internet to communicate with people all over the world, herpers joined herp societies. The bigger societies, such as the Philadelphia and Chicago herp societies, had monthly newsletters for their members. Herpers joined these far-off societies for the newsletters, which they grabbed and read as soon as they showed up in the mail. Members of the societies dutifully recorded their husbandry successes and failures, and longevity was one item well worth reporting.

One typical record set was reported by Gerry Salmon in the Chicago Herp bulletin of July 1997. This record was for the gray-banded kingsnake, a pretty and variable snake found in west Texas and long the darling of field trip adventurers and breeders alike. Gerry's point was that you can't depend on one source for longevity records. At the time, Frank Slavens's book (see the sidebar "Bicentennial spawns herp-lifespan project," later in this chapter) showed longevity of 14 years and 4 months.

Gerry quoted additional records that showed longevity of the gray-banded kingsnakes ranged from 17 years 10 months to 19 years and 11 months.

The lesson is clear. With good care, you can expect your snake to live almost 20 years, or possibly longer (see Figure 13-1). By implication, if your healthy-appearing snake keels over when you've had it for only five years, somebody has probably messed up somewhere.

Figure 13-1:
The California kingsnake can live for 33 years or more in captivity.

Bicentennial spawns herp-lifespan project

Probably the best-known accumulator of captive lifespan data is Frank Slavens, the curator of reptiles for the Woodland Park Zoological Garden in Seattle, Washington. Back in 1975, as the U.S. Bicentennial loomed, everyone came up with a project to recognize 200 years of achievement in any field. Slavens thought that maybe herpetologists should examine how well they were doing with herps. Were "postage stamp" collections (one of this, one of that) still the style for zoos? What species were being kept and which of those were in breeding programs?

He sent letters to 62 zoos, requesting their herp inventories (correspondence was a pain before computers were invented, even if letters only cost 13 cents to mail). About a third of the zoos responded, and Frank set up a tracking system, entering the data by hand. When the data was all compiled, he typed a 79-page report on mimeograph masters, and copies were run off on a mimeo machine. The sheets were bound and copies were distributed free of charge to institutions.

Frank repeated the process in 1977, and 57 zoos responded. Again the data was processed by hand. A 141-page book was compiled and photocopied, and the 35 copies were distributed the next year. Ensuing editions had the book printed by a professional printer, and then on a used printing press Frank bought to save money. (Zoo people tend to be remarkably responsible about money and expenditures.)

By 1981 the project had become an annual publication, about the same time that Frank progressed to a personal computer (with 64K! — wow!). By 1988 the book included information from 400 public and private collections; the 1998 publication was almost 400 pages.

The last edition was in 1999, and response from the public sector has been so slow that there are no plans at present for an update. Admittedly, part of the data was a recounting of which zoos held X male and Y females and Z sex unknown of every herp in their collection. In the future, Frank may be able to turn over the inventory of breeding records to ISIS (International Species Information System), which you can find on the Web at www.isis.org. He'll then be able to concentrate on breeding, longevity, and bibliographical records.

The Max Planck Institute for Demographic Research is in Rostock, Germany. It collects and disseminates information, mostly on human demographics. It has reptile and amphibian longevity records from J.R. Carey and D.S. Judge's book, *Longevity Records: Life Spans of Mammals, Birds, Amphibians, Reptiles and Fish* on its Web site (www.demogr.mpg.de/longevityrecords/0403.htm). Check out the institute's list of some 90 species and subspecies of reptiles and amphibians.

Reptile longevity

When you begin discussing reptile longevity, the figures fling themselves off the charts (see an example of such a reptile in Figure 13-2). Reptiles include the "long livers," as one wit described them, the massive creatures such as the crocodilians and the giant tortoises. Both live a long time. Records show that American alligators can live more than 70 years in captivity; the spectacled caiman, 38 years; the gharial, 27 years. The Galapagos tortoise may hold the record, though: One lived for 68 years.

Figure 13-2: The red-eared slider has been documented to live more than 44 years in captivity.

On the other side are the reptiles with short lives. Some lizards (including some lacertids and some teiids) live only one year or slightly more, no matter how much care you may lavish on them. These lizards could be termed "annuals."

When discussing the usual pet herps, the figures are even more interesting. Take a look at these records; you should be able to come close with your own herps:

- ✔ **Leopard geckos:** 25 years
- ✔ **Green iguanas:** 19 years
- ✔ **Red-eared slider:** 40 years
- ✔ **Common boa constrictor:** 20 years
- ✔ **Corn snake:** 32 years

Amphibian longevity

Amphibians don't seem to have the longevity of reptiles, but many records show that amphibians live five or more years in captivity. Some live a lot longer. Records for tiger salamanders (see Figure 13-3) range from 10 to 25 years, while records for other salamanders in that same family are just 2 to 5 years. Records for the plethodontid salamanders are between 5 and 10 years. The record for barking treefrogs is just 2½ years.

Figure 13-3:
Tiger salamanders can live 20 years in captivity.

But when you factor in popularity, the records change. Not a lot of people keep salamanders, sad to say, so in a larger sense, less accumulated data is available on salamanders compared to the more popular amphibian species. For example, take the horned frog, those fist-sized solitary frogs from South America with the big mouths. Records for the horned frogs show the frogs live just over ten years. The record for White's treefrog is 19 years, 1 month.

You also need to consider that the techniques for the care and raising of amphibians are a bit more complex than those for reptiles. There isn't a great margin for error in keeping amphibians. If the tank isn't clean, they die. As people get better about keeping tanks clean and develop practical ways to deal with amphibians' skin problems, those longevity records will increase.

I'm So Glad We Had This Time Together

The death of a pet herp can be expected, or it can be a shock. Sure, your iguana had a cold a few weeks ago, but he seemed to be recovering. You never thought your painted turtle would knock the filter head off the sponge filter and get caught by the filter intake and drown. Sometimes you have warning signs, and sometimes you find a lifeless body where yesterday you had a live herp.

If you goofed, you goofed. You can take steps to help ensure that this same thing doesn't happen again. You can send a note to your local herp bulletin, telling others of your experience so that they can take measures to prevent the same thing from happening to their herps.

If you have no idea what caused your herp's death, you can have your animal autopsied at a state lab. Your veterinarian is familiar with these labs, and will remove and preserve tissue samples and send them to the lab for you. Expect to pay about $100 for this service (call and find out ahead of time so you won't be shocked). But the results may not be useful, because state labs are set up for warm-blooded creatures, not amphibians or reptiles. You may never know what killed your herp.

Considering whether to euthanize your herp

There are valid reasons for having a herp euthanized. Boas get inclusion body (or "stargazing") disease, and there's no cure for this progressive neurological disease. Your iguana leaps off the sofa, damages his back, and loses the use of his hind legs. A dog chews off the back legs of your box turtle.

Or perhaps you have a perfectly healthy pet, such as a Burmese python, that's gotten too big. You can't keep or handle a snake that's 11 feet long, and nobody, absolutely nobody, wants it, at least not alive. The tannery in the next town over, however, would like the snake's hide. But that option sure sounds both mean and bizarre to you.

One of the biggest breeders of pet Burmese pythons told me he had no problems if people "harvest" their pets when they get too big. I'm not saying this is a good choice, and remember that you took on a responsibility and knew the risks when you got that big snake.

Sometimes euthanasia is your best choice, or, more accurately, it's the best choice for your herp. Your veterinarian can advise you here and handle this process with an overdose of anesthetic.(Freezing tropical species used to be acceptable, but this process has been termed painful and is no longer done.)

Facing reality: Dealing with the remains

This section is written for the hobbyist who has no large emotional investment in his or her herp. If you loved your herp and now he's dead and you're beside yourself with grief, skip this section because it will sound very cold to you. The death of a herp is an awful experience for people who were crazy about their pet. Veterinary colleges, thank goodness, usually have a grieving hotline staffed by vet students who can help you sort through the grieving process when your herp dies.

What do you do with your herp's body after the herp dies? Other than the loss of an animal you liked and enjoyed working with, you may have also incurred a financial setback. (If you owned one of those $750 snakes out there, the death of that animal is a financial and emotional blow.) But what does one do with the herp's corpse?

- You can offer the corpse to your local college or community college biology department, to use either as a preserved specimen or for teaching anatomy in herpetology classes. Doing so may make you feel you're doing something useful, that your pet is making a contribution for those animals who live after him

- You can bury the corpse, either in your backyard or in a pet cemetery.

- You can throw it away (but keep it frozen until the day of garbage collection, or the smell of even a double-bagged dead creature will bring raccoons to your garbage can and have neighbors regarding you suspiciously).

If you're seriously sad about the death of your pet, turn your depression and guilt into action. Do something for someone else — read to children at a school, help lead a singing session at a nursing home, or take the book cart around the local hospital. Some good can come from your loss.

He's Gotta Go: Finding a New Home for Your Herp

Despite your best efforts, maybe you can't keep your herp. Maybe you're moving to a new apartment, and the landlord is very serious about the no pets rule and hates snakes anyway. Maybe you've moved back home to take care of your parents, and they'll never allow your turtles, Joey and Joyce, to move with you. Maybe you're being deployed to southern Afghanistan.

You've taken good care of your pets, but you realize that this relationship is going to have to end. What do you do?

Finding a new owner

When you're looking for a new owner for your pet, you may end up giving your pet away to someone you know, giving him to someone you don't know, or maybe selling him. Your decision depends on how quickly you need to act and how popular your pet may be. Large pets, such as adult monitors and reticulated pythons, have a very limited market. Placing a corn snake is a lot easier.

Pull together your acquisition and medical records for your herp. You'll want to pass them on to the new owner, if only to impress on that person that herp keeping is not to be undertaken lightly.

Here are some ways to locate a new owner for your pet:

✔ Make an announcement at your herp society that you have a herp you can no longer keep and you're looking for a good home for it. You may decide to give the animal to someone you know within the society, or you may decide to sell him. If you're really serious about giving the animal away to someone you know, mention that the animal is healthy, but you realize that herps cost money. Offer to make a grant to take care of veterinarian bills for the first two years. You also may want to place an ad in your herp society's newsletter (these ads are often free for members).

✔ Ask your friends if they know anyone who's interested in buying or acquiring a pet herp. Forget mentioning anything about covering any vet bills. The approach changes here, because you're dealing with people you don't know.

- Call the newsletter editors for your local Sierra Club, Audubon Society, and natural history clubs, and see whether you can place an ad for selling your herp in their publications. Your ad may be accepted only if your herp is captive born. Again, forget about offering to pay for any veterinary expenses, unless maybe your sister sees the ad and calls you about adopting your pet.

- Put postcard notices on pet store bulletin boards and on the bulletin boards at feed stores.

- Call your locally owned pet store and offer to sell the animal to it. If you have something a bit unusual, such as an albino leopard gecko or an unusual rat snake, the store may be very interested.

- Place a "for sale" classified ad in your local paper or in a local college newspaper. You may get calls from people looking for free snakes; you probably don't want to deal with them. Use your best judgment when you met the people who come to your house to see your animal. Make sure that they're the best new owners for your herp. You don't want to find out they gave the animal away on their way home.

- Try selling online. I found some very good Bolivian boas that way — and I didn't mind paying the freight charges, not one bit. The Web site www.kingsnake.com is one place to start.

- Talk to the science coordinators for elementary and secondary schools in your city. A science teacher may want a herp for his or her classroom. Chances are, you'll have to donate not only the snake but also his housing.

Relying on rescue operations

Reptile rescue groups (and herpetological societies, for that matter) are operated by people who like herps and think that every captive herp deserves proper care for the herp's entire life. They screen the people who request herps, turn some of them down, and check up on placed herps to ensure that proper care is being given. In addition, they require that new owners return the herp to the rescue group if the owners eventually decide that they can't keep the herp. These groups function sort of as fairy godmothers to captive herps that are being discarded. Finding these groups online is fairly straightforward. Just type in "reptile or amphibian rescue" and add your state.

Providing for Your Herp If You Leave First

Some herps are very long-lived. But when you buy that red-eared slider or that White's treefrog, you probably never for a minute think that your pet may outlive you. The fact is, however, that death happens to everyone. You may live a long life and die of natural causes when you're 80. You could die in an auto accident when you're 30. So regardless of your age, you should have plans in place in case you're the first to go.

Making arrangements

If you die without making arrangements for your pet herp, your herp is left in the lurch. Not many people want to deal with your herp once you're out of the picture. They have other things on their minds (like what to do with the 230 assorted tanks, pumps, filters, heating pads, lights, and hunks of cork-bark you've been accumulating over the years). Unless you make arrangements, your herp is just another personal effect.

In some states, if your pet (or your pet collection, meaning the total value of all your herps) is worth more than $1,000, it becomes part of your estate, to be sold so that the income can be added to the estate.

Don't treat your herp as if he were a household good, to be sold at an estate sale along with your used sheets and garden hoses, or (even worse) offered in a "free to good home" ad in your daily paper. Make sure that you consider your herp's best interests.

The world is fraught with danger for herps who are suddenly ownerless. Who's going to make certain their tanks stay warm enough on the next cold night? Who's going to make sure your herp doesn't go to someone looking for free snakes to feed to *his* snakes? An owner of an ophiophagous (snake-eating) snake such as a cobra doesn't care that you kept your snake for 20 years, or that you caught him yourself on a rainy night in Georgia; he just wants a meal for his animal. Your charge deserves better treatment than that; he certainly never asked to be in a cage at your place, and he certainly can't hang around your front door, looking for the first opportunity to make a break for freedom.

Own up to your responsibility. Add a codicil to your will, stating where you want your herp to go, and if at all possible providing a hundred dollars or so the help with that herp's expenses. If you aren't going to make a will, for reasons best known to yourself (everyone is going to die someday, you know), at least copy and sign the document shown here, have it witnessed, and leave duplicates where they'll be found.

You may have a friend, a relative, or a neighbor who likes your herp almost as much as you do and who would take the herp and keep it forever — and that's great. You need to write down those instructions and include them in your will, or use the document in the next section. In case you don't have a friend like this, think about giving your animal to herp rescue groups or herp societies.

Creating a will

Here is some sample wording to help you provide for your herps in the event of your death; you need to change it if you're single. You may want to ask your lawyer to read it over and make suggestions specific in your case.

> *Instructions providing for the placement and care of my herps in the event of my death (if there are two owners, like husband and wife):*
>
> *If my spouse shall die before me, my herps are to be given to _____ _____ (name of herp or animal rescue group or herp society), a _____ (State) corporation, for placement with a responsible individual. If the _____ (name of herp or animal rescue group) is unable to take in my herps, or if my Personal Representative finds that _____ (name of herp or animal rescue group) has ceased to function as a rescue/placement agency, s/he shall then query _____ (a nearby, alternate herp or herp rescue group or herp society), a _____ (State) corporation, for placement of my herps.*
>
> *Pending transfer of my herps to the rescue organization: If necessary, my herps shall be housed and given good quality care by a member of a herpetology society or by a private caretaker. A reasonable weekly fee, based on current food costs and caretaker's time, shall be paid.*
>
> *A contribution of $100 for each herp shall be paid by my estate to the rescue organization that eventually places my herps with responsible individuals. Those assisting in the process shall be guided by the knowledge that the welfare of my herps is important to me.*
>
> *(Date) _____*
>
> *(Witness's signature) _____*
>
> *(Your signature) _____*

Call your local reptile rescue agency or your local herp society before you make these sort of arrangements for your pet. Tell the agency of your dilemma, and ask about naming it in your will as the one responsible for finding a home for your herp. The form included here states that your herp will be temporarily placed in the care of a responsible individual until the herp can be transferred to the rescue organization. For placement with a new, responsible owner, the agreement also states that a cash gift of $100 will be given to the herp rescue group/herp society for each of your herps.

In case you also own a warm-blooded pet such as a dog or a cat, pet rescue groups are available to take care of him, too. In both cases, if an animal rescue group agrees to take care of your pets, be as generous as you can to that group.

Why Turning Your Pet Loose Is Never an Option

Sometimes people think that turning an animal loose is the kind thing to do. They mistakenly believe that returning the animal to the wild, where the animal, now a free spirit, can return to the bosom of nature, dwelling happily forever in peace and harmony, is okay. Doing so is acceptable only if you have nature tamed, if food is readily available all year-round, if all the animals in this wilderness place are vegetarians, if hollow logs and other hiding areas are everywhere and not yet occupied, if no automobiles are allowed, and if the temperatures are always moderate (and all the offspring are above average, to borrow a phrase).

If you give me the location of such a place, I'll go there myself.

You already know it isn't legal to turn a non-native animal loose. You can incur city, county, state, and federal penalties if you turn your animal loose.

Setting your animal free isn't fair to the animal. For example, where is a corn snake going to find the white mice he's eaten all his life? Mice of any sort aren't all that common in the wild, and those that are there are nocturnal, secretive, quick, and evasive. They aren't white in color, either. Your snake is *clueless* about scenting, following, and striking a live rodent. He's used to his food just appearing every week or so.

Your snake hasn't undergone the survival of the fittest where the slow-to-react types don't live. Your snake was selected because he was pretty. He should starve to death in the wild because of that? If you're talking about an amphibian like a tiger salamander, how is that tiger salamander going to live, in your neighbor's pond? There are *big* goldfish in that pond, and they eat salamanders!

Your pet snake isn't going to be suddenly aware that the vibrations of human footsteps signal a big danger, so move out. He thinks those vibrations mean food. He's not going to slither out of the way, and if the snake on the loose is a boa constrictor, the human coming across your former pet isn't going to be friendly or pleased.

Lizards taste freedom — and possibly an endangered owl

Suppose, just suppose, that your former pet does very well after you turn him loose. In fact, he discovers a niche that's occupied only by what literally turns out to be dinner. In this case, the reptiles on the loose are Nile monitors (big, toothy lizards that eat rodents, birds, and other warm-blooded animals) in Cape Coral, Florida. They moved into the burrows dug by burrowing owls. Burrowing owls are a protected species, unique because these small owls dig out their own dwelling burrows in sandy areas. They mate for life. They're endangered because of habitat intrusion; humans build (or would like to build) where burrowing owls live.

Areas set aside for the burrowing owls suddenly aren't protected enough. The Nile monitors have moved in. What goes on in the darkness of a burrow is hidden to those of us with soft beds and day jobs, but the owls disappear. The burrows are secure places to hide. The monitors venture out at night, looking for food. They have no enemies. Few people know they're there.

Or suppose that you turn out a Nile monitor. When he goes looking for food in your neighbor's yard, your neighbor finds him on her back porch, eyeing her cat. She is terrified and upset — and she's a lawyer. Oh, man, are you in trouble. What were you thinking of when you turned that lizard loose?

Maybe someone calls animal control to pick up your animal. This agency ordinarily handles stray dogs and cats (and once in a while, stray livestock), but some of them respond to calls on stray reptiles. If the animal control officer can find the animal, he'll put a noose on it, pick it up, and take it to the shelter. The animal will be set up in a cage of some sort, away from the dogs and cats, and animal control will try to place the animal with a new owner.

But not all animal control departments pick up reptiles. Some may simply refer you to your local state wildlife and game commission, or they may tell callers that they don't have anything to do with stray reptiles.

Save yourself a lot of trouble. Owe up to your responsibility for your herp. See that he goes to a new, responsible owner if you no longer want him — and take him there yourself.

Part IV
The Birds and the Bees, and Legalities

"Look at the bright side. We found a nice, warm environment where it looks like the skinks are going to mate."

In this part . . .

*I*f you're buying the animal so you can breed it and make lots of money, hold on. Few people actually make money when breeding herps and selling the young. This part explains factors you should consider before you put the male in with the female, from dealing with hibernation and day length to city regulations. I discuss ways to presell your expected offspring, and I explain the legal aspects you need to know about. You can also find easy ways to set up and feed the offspring.

Chapter 14

To Breed or Not to Breed: That Is the Question

In This Chapter

▶ Considering whether breeding is worth the effort

▶ Marketing your hatchlings

▶ Looking at the legal issues

*W*hen you get serious about keeping herps — meaning that you have more than one cage and you show up at a herp society meeting with dues money in hand — the questions change. No longer are you asked, "What are you keeping?" Instead, fellow herpers ask you, "What are you breeding?"

You don't have to breed your herps to be a serious herper. You don't have to feel guilty if you only keep single animals — one of this, one of that — instead of sexual pairs. But if you're interested, even vaguely, in breeding your herps, this chapter may give you some ideas about the process.

In a way, breeding herps is a bit like learning to drive a car. It isn't enough that you can start the car. You're not a good driver until you can get from point A to point B safely within the speed limits. If you're going to breed herps, it isn't enough that you can get two frogs of the same type but opposite sex interested in each other. You also have to market the young so they get good homes.

The phrase "good homes" sounds corny, but the point is that a market must be available for what you produce. People must want the creatures that now exist because of your meddling, or your efforts are not just pointless — they're a waste. Don't expend your efforts and your resources (broadly speaking, the world's resources) on producing pets that won't have homes.

Thomas Edison vowed, early in his career, not to invent something without a commercial application. You listen to your Uncle Edison, and do the same.

Deciding Whether to Breed

There's no sense in trying to breed something you don't like. Some of you may want to breed because you enjoy working with the animals and any money you make is not the focal point. Others of you may want to breed herps for a vocation, producing tens of thousands of different animals. No matter which category you fall into, you have to enjoy the animals, or you'll resent like crazy the time and money involved. Your significant other must also feel the same way you do, or your relationship will pay the price.

When you care enough to do the very best

Of course, you care about the little baby herps that take their first breaths in your snake room. You'll tend to them, put them in their own cage so you can monitor their progress, and put in a garden or go out and buy or scrounge food for them. (Grocery stores may give you their slightly wilted vegetables.) You'll check the temperature in their enclosure a dozen times a day, and you almost pass out when you notice the readout says 119 degrees, until you realize that the probe has fallen on top of a light bulb, resulting in an inaccurate reading. If you have tadpoles, you'll change their water everyday and squint yourself cross-eyed, watching for any signs of fungus. If you have turtles, you'll buy an expensive weighing scale and weigh the hatchlings (see Figure 14-1) daily until you realize that alarming weight loss shown by the prettiest one only meant he relieved himself in his shallow drinking pool.

Figure 14-1:
A hatchling peninsular cooter peers out of the egg.

Watching the young herps during the evening hours can be more interesting than anything you ever watched on television, and you may find yourself hoping they won't go to sleep too early. You begin asking your friends and other herp society members whether they're interested in some of your young herps as soon as they get old enough to leave. You seek out other successful breeders for tips on better caging, fresh food sources (many a tortoise-raiser has a pot of two of tortoise greens growing on the kitchen windowsill), and new developments in lighting. You also talk with other breeders about exchanging stock to bring in a new bloodline — pretty soon, you're hooked. You're a breeder.

When are your new babies old enough to sell or give away? Here are some herps and the signs that they're ready for a new home:

- **Tortoises, turtles, and lizards:** When they're eating steadily
- **Frogs and salamanders:** When they've metamorphosed into tiny adults and are feeding
- **Snakes:** When they've made their postnatal shed and eaten at least twice

Don't be surprised if you feel a bit of a twinge when you think about these young herps actually going out your door. Because you care about these young, you may actually think about keeping some of them (bad idea) or all of them (very bad idea). You shouldn't keep any of the young, unless you're going big-time and are acquiring additional breeding stock. Remember that every animal needs to be housed, cleaned, and fed. You'll have to develop a sensible attitude about not keeping the animals you produce, and make plans to move 'em out.

Suppose, for purposes of illustration, that your first breeding was sort of a lucky break and an accident. You had some brown anoles together in a tank, and they bred. The female laid the eggs (you saw her), and you incubated the eggs in place in the tank. The eggs hatched, and since then, you've spent your evenings placing the tiny anoles in their own plastic shoe box and making sure that the box gets enough heat and light. You also make sure that the babies can get out of the heat and light when they want to. You find and purchase a culture of fruit fly larva, wait anxiously for them to change into adults (it takes maybe three days), and then tap in two dozen or so adult fruit flies twice daily and watch to see who eats and who doesn't.

The young thrive. You have zero deaths, your local pet store snaps up your "captive-bred" (wink, wink) brown anoles, and you go home with cash in your pocket. "Hey," you think as you pull into your driveway, "this was easy. Maybe I should do more of this. That ten bucks is going to come in handy. If I set up more tanks, and each pair produces maybe twice a year, I could make some money. I've got a lot more shoeboxes."

Understanding your motives

Brown anoles are a common feeder lizard, meaning they're considered an inexpensive and readily available food for lizard-eating snakes (Oops. I could have been gentler about how anoles are used. Not many people think of them as captivating little gamins in their own right, although I *did* meet one person who proudly kept a pet brown anole in a 40-gallon tank, back in 1975.) It just makes sense to produce an animal that people will value.

If it's money you want . . .

If you want to make money from breeding, remember that you won't make actual money on breeding until you get production up. You can trade a couple of your young to a pet store for credit on another tank, or for another pair of leopard geckos, but that's not the same as cash. Once you have the basics of breeding down pat, the only difference in raising ten babies or a hundred is the cost of food and housing (and considerable time on your part).

If money is your goal, you'll need to find a herp that you like, one that has more than two eggs or six young per clutch. You may think that you need an animal that isn't already widely available, but the more popular herps, such as corn snakes, appear to produce steady sales.

Corn snakes are produced on a grand scale by commercial breeders like The Gourmet Rodent. The Rodent, as it's called, produces thousands of corn snakes a year. This breeder produces all color morphs, including the albinos, and sells most of them to a pet store chain and the rest at expos. The Gourmet Rodent also produces and sells frozen feeder mice, most of which they ship directly to the chain's various stores. The chain gets both snakes and snake food from one source. The thinking is sound. Once a customer buys a pet snake, he or she returns to the same store to buy mice to feed that snake. The Rodent has a solid relationship with that chain. The chain isn't going to buy any corn snakes from anyone else.

Breeding for fun

Kathy Love is another breeder of specialty corn snakes. She's been in the business for more than 20 years. She doesn't produce snakes in the numbers of The Gourmet Rodent, but she does produce a thousand or so a year. She sells directly to the consumer. She enjoys working with corns, she enjoys selling to people who like corn snakes, and she enjoys going to expos.

The majority of breeders breed their animals because they love doing it. They really like their animals, they take very good care of their animals, and they regard breeding as a sound way for others to enjoy herps without taking any animals from the wild.

There's room for both

Both types of vendors — those in it for the money and those who simply love the animals — enjoy the role they play in breeding herps and putting them in the marketplace.

You may be able to develop relationships with your local pet stores to buy your corn snakes, but they're going to want the right to buy just what they need (which may mean no sales for some months). Even if you have a relationship with your local pet stores, they won't turn down a hobbyist who walks in and wants to sell his baby corns for $2 each.

Winning the popularity contest

You can thumb through a year's worth of *Reptile* magazines, and check out the ads to see what's popular in the herp market, or you can stroll through a couple of pet stores (or one expo) and look at what's available. Doing so will tell you what sells now — and what part of your competition will be if you choose to breed and sell the same thing.

Competition from breeding ranches

Sometimes an imported animal, even from as far away as Africa, is cheaper than what you can produce in the United States. The United States imports some 100,000 baby ball pythons a year (all wild-caught). They cost the importer about $3 or $4 each once they cross our borders. I don't know of many people who want to set up a breeding colony or even just a few cages to produce a snake that will only bring $3. Captive corn snakes bring in more than that, and they aren't fussy eaters!

Ranched herps can keep the prices of popular herps low. Ranching herps generally means catching the gravid (pregnant) female and keeping her until she lays her eggs or births her young and the young are sold. Such practices are typical for imported baby chameleons and blood pythons.

One rancher in Sumatra buys wild-caught blood pythons for the snakeskin market. Gravid females are retained until their eggs are laid and hatched. A portion of the more strikingly marked babies are kept for the pet market, but this is just an incidental part of the business. Sumatra has a set number of blood pythons allowed to be exported each year. For the current level of 4,000 pythons, there's no differentiation between live blood pythons being exported for the pet market and for blood python skins. This single snakeskin operation is so large it could fill the entire export quota annually. Before you decide to breed blood pythons, think for a moment: Do you think you could produce baby blood pythons for the same low prices as these ranched babies?

Gazing into your crystal ball

While you're evaluating what's out there, think ahead. When you get production up, three years from now, can you count on prices being the same as they are now or demand for the animal being at least the same as it is today? There's enormous pressure to produce things cheaper, even if that item is a living animal, so you can't be assured that prices tomorrow will be as high as they are today.

But wait, you say. I can *do* production. For example, maybe you know that Burmese pythons produce a lot of eggs. That would help you get production up, wouldn't it? Yes, Burmese pythons do lay some 60 eggs at a time, and the young are beautiful. But Burms get big. Many municipalities are getting nervous about big snakes, and they're passing ordinances against Burmese and sometimes any snake over 8 feet long. Sometimes these restrictions are disguised as efforts to stamp out salmonella by forbidding reptile ownership. You may not be legally able to even possess a Burmese python in your community. Many pet stores no longer sell Burmese pythons. As the recorded voice on your phone says, please make another selection.

Before you breed (a herp), talk to the owners of pet stores in your area and to the dealers and vendors at expos. Ask them what's selling for them and what they wish they had more of. Ask them what stands in the way of their selling more herps. Contact the specialty clubs, such as the Global Gecko Society, about the direction they see gecko ownership moving, and what they think the up-and-coming gecko species might be. Talk to representatives from PIJAC (the Pet Industry Joint Advisory Council) about the trends they see in herp ownership and in herp regulations. Listen to what these people say. (PIJAC is a lobbying organization for the pet industry, and your friend and mine. Contact it via its Web site, www.PIJAC.com.)

Does your location make a difference?

Think about where you're living if you want to breed herps. Living three hours away from the nearest good-sized airport may be a help in discouraging unwelcome in-laws, but shipping your herps to wholesalers will take up an entire day.

Time is a factor if you want to sell at an expo — just ask any of the vendors there. You have to drive there and then set up and sell, and drive back again. Somehow that mountaintop in southern Arizona may not be the best spot for you and your herps to live, because you're too far from anything.

Is your climate appropriate to the animals you want to breed? Temperature is one factor. Bert Langerwurf, who owns a large lizard breeding facility called Agama International, breeds animals that can deal with the Alabama winters without supplementary heating. Bob Mailloux, of Sandfire Dragons, breeds bearded dragons, a xerix (dry) species. He has facilities in California. You can certainly heat your facility, but you'll be competing with those people who don't have that expense. If your power goes off for a day or two because of a winter's ice storm, you may not be able to save your animals, and your business is over.

Humidity is another factor. Sand boas, those small nippy boas with their beady little eyes near the top of their head, are arid-land creatures. (Read more about them in the appendix.) They may refuse to feed or become reluctant feeders (and even more reluctant breeders) when kept in humid areas like the southeastern tier of states or the Pacific Northwest. You can partially dodge the humidity issue by using air conditioning in the summer and heat during the winter and by offering water just three days a week in a small dish. But you'll be competing with breeders who live in Arizona or Nevada, who don't have to worry about the suitability of their environment. They'll pay less to raise their animals than you will.

Preselling Your Animals

Pre-selling your animals — selling them before they're actually born — is a good way to reduce the virtual sucking sound of money disappearing as you set up cages, pay utility bills, adjust thermostats, buy feeders, and price advertising. Preselling is the only way to go if you're dependent on the income from breeding. But how do you sell something that doesn't exist yet?

You set up a plan based on what you think your production will be. It works a bit like affirmation: If you tell yourself you'll have egg clutches from every one of your female Florida kingsnakes, it may well happen. That means you'll have some 60 baby kings hatching out in April and May (see Figure 14-2). Remember that snake eggs in a single clutch hatch out within the same one to two-day period. You'll need 60 pinkies (new-born mice) for feed every week until the young are sold — and you realize you *have* to presell!

Before you can presell, you have to do a couple things:

✔ Make a list of sources of buyers of one of your animals. Include pet stores, expos, and Web sites. Don't forget to let the Boy Scout troop that you give a herp presentation to every year know that you have the perfect pet for them.

✔ Decide on a selling price for your animals, and leave room for a bit of negotiation on each one.

  You may need more than one price category — one for pet stores, one for expos, and a third for your retail customers. Charge your retail customers very close to what they'd pay at a pet store.

Figure 14-2:
Preselling
the more
unusual
snake
species,
such as the
striped-
tailed rat
snakes, may
be easier
than
preselling
common
species.

If you're selling retail, don't undercut (sell your herps for less than) the pet stores that buy from you. It's rude to undercut one of your customers, who won't stay your customer if you do this.

Pitching your herps to pet stores

When trying to sell your animals to pet stores, begin with bulk sales — pet stores that will buy more than one or two babies. Take a photograph of one of your litters, along with your business card, to the pet shops in your area. You can try the chain shops, but don't be surprised if they're not allowed to buy from you. (The home office may have already decreed that the home office handles all livestock buys and that they will buy only from approved vendors.)

Talk to the store manager or the owner. You can call in advance to see whether you need an appointment, but if you get the brush-off, you might just stop in to see who you should talk to. Someone calls out "Brad! Someone to see you!" and you're face to face with the store's buyer. No appointment needed.

Take only a minute or two of the buyer's time, because that person has a dozen tasks waiting in the back room. Hand him the photo of your snakes and your card. Tell the buyer that you're a local breeder and you'll have hatchling Florida kings in April and May. Ask whether he's interested in buying some kings and mention a price, which is slightly less per snake if they buy six or more at a time.

The buyer may say, "Yep, bring me six in April, but call first." At the very worst, all that can happen is you get the card and photo back with a "nope, not interested." Thank the buyer for his time, and go on to the next store. Check back every two months or so at the stores that turned you down. They may have had some staffing changes, and a new manager may be more receptive to purchasing your animals.

After the young have hatched, call the store to set up a delivery date and time. Deliver the young in deli cups or snake bags and take an imprinted invoice along with you. You may want to take an extra copy of the invoice, to have signed as a delivery receipt. Be sure that your invoice says "net 30 days," or you may wait a long time before you get paid. (Nothing personal here — the first rule of business is to operate as long as possible on the other guy's money.)

You may need to call to check on payment if those 30 days go by and no check has arrived in the mail. Nobody likes these calls, but you're in the business, and you already know what the first rule of business is. Your customer may point out that the snakes haven't sold. As gently as you can, let the customer know this wasn't a guaranteed sale purchase.

Your customer may tell you that he'll pay you "real soon" and order another half-dozen snakes at the same time. This will be a judgment call on your part. You can deliver another six snakes, but don't hand them over unless you can pick up payment for the first six.

If the payment for the second set of snakes is slow, once you collect, ask for payment with delivery. This is called a *pro forma* delivery. I bet your customer is already getting the same treatment from his other vendors.

Is this customer worth the bother? That's something that only you can decide.

Selling to clubs

Selling to herp club members may be an easy way to find good homes for your baby herps. If you're not already a member, you can find these clubs by calling your local natural history museum, science teachers in private and public schools, college professors or grad students in the biology department of a nearby university, or a staff member at a local nature center. The chamber of commerce may have a listing of local clubs and contact information, or your local pet store (particularly if the store sells herps) may have information.

Members of your local herp society may be your best customers, but these are canny buyers. You'll work for every penny you get from them.

They may expect to buy the animals for very little money, but at least you can insist on payment when they pick out the herp they want to buy. Bring the animals packaged individually in appropriate containers. For example, bring small hatchling snakes in deli cups. Potential buyers can examine them through the clear top without opening the cup (and without the snake escaping or somehow disappearing). Herp societies generally dedicate some time at the end of each meeting when individuals can stand up and mention they have baby herps for sale.

You'll have better success if you offer to donate to the club treasury a percentage of your sales that night. You can also be the speaker for that evening, talking about the variety of color morphs of kingsnakes or corn snakes or the interesting habits of leopard geckos, depending on what you've bred.

What you want to do is to present your product in such an interesting and fascinating light that the listeners say, "Now, that's exactly the sort of (snake, gecko, or frog) I'd like to have!" You just happen to have a half dozen or so with you, just to show as example, and you're surprised when someone asks the price. You recover quickly, say you're pleased and flattered, and mention the price and the donation factor.

This technique really works. I first experienced it when I went to a rock club lecture on agates, and that's why I now have about three pounds of assorted agates in my dresser drawer.

Getting exposure at expos

Expos are a fairly new phenomenon, but they've really caught on. You can find one near you (or far away — traveling is enlightening for the soul) through the events calendar in one of the reptile magazines, the events page on Web sites such as Kingsnake.com, or through notices in herp society newsletters. You can preregister and save some money sometimes, or you can simply register the day of the expo. Admission at the exhibit hall is generally $20 or less, but you may have to pay additional charges for special events.

Expos are such fun you ought to try one just once. Renting a booth may cost you anywhere from $50 to more than $200, but this is a very practical way to expose the fruits of your breeding efforts to many potential customers. The Daytona expo, for example, averages some 18,000 people over a two-day period. That's a lot of exposure — and maybe a lot of customers.

These customers have cash (great), checkbooks (don't take whopping big checks unless you know the writer and maybe not even then), and credit cards.

Your bank can get you set up to take credit cards, and you need this capability at an expo. People who charge things generally spend more money than if they pay cash or write a check, which is why department stores have their own credit cards. Make it easy to buy from you.

Breeders who don't have enough stock to fill a table generally talk a friend who has a table into selling their stock for them. You'll have to come up with a fair way to compensate for the table space, but remember that you're making her table more appealing as well.

Expos are subject to a late-buyer's syndrome. People may come to an expo and check out the vendors and chat you up on your prices, but they don't offer to buy, at least not until the end of the expo. Then they come by and offer you a ridiculous price for your stock. Vendors who have come a long way and spent a lot of money for their table, travel, and the other animals they've purchased there sometimes accept the lowball offer. This is a shame, because in so doing they devalue the animals that have already sold. Set your prices and decide how and if you'll deal with these late-buying cheapskates.

Making online sales

Web sites are an inexpensive and effective way to sell your captive-born herps. You can create your own site with the help of purchased software (FrontPage was one of the first and easiest-to-use software programs for creating Web pages, but now you have several to chose from), or you may use software that was installed on your computer. (For more information, check out *FrontPage 2002 For Dummies,* by Asha Dornfest, and *Creating Web Pages For Dummies,* by Bud Smith and Arthur Bebak, both published by Wiley.) In addition to your e-mail address, you'll need a URL address for your Web site, but that cost is less than $50 a year.

Don't use big detailed photos on your site (they take too long to download), and avoid using white letters on a black background (these are tiring to read). Keep your paragraphs short and succinct.

Check out some of the Web sites on Kingsnake.com, and note that they all prefer credit card sales to checks. There's a reason for this: A credit card sale is a guaranteed payment. People expect to use their credit cards for online sales; they don't want to wait for their check to clear before they can receive the animals they've purchased. One of the credit card services is PayPal, but if you've purchased items online you might already know about this service.

Adding photos to your site increases the time people spend on your site, and the more time someone spends on your site, the more likely she is to buy. A digital camera with close-up or macro capability can take photos of your animals. You can use a film camera (as opposed to digital); any photo developer can put your photos on a CD. You can then transfer the photos to your Web site.

Marketing through print ads

Buying ad space in one of the reptile magazines, whether a display ad or a classified ad, gives you terrific exposure. Using paid advertising at least places you among the players in the captive breeders' group. You may not be able to afford paid ads for your own herps, but if you wholesale your herps to a larger dealer, ask him or her to add a single line to the dealer's ad, for example, "featuring the Jones Line of corn snakes," using your business name. Maybe your wholesaler will do this for free; maybe you should offer a couple of free hatchlings as a thank-you.

The Legal Aspects of Selling Herps

You've thought through all the issues concerning herp breeding. You planned what you're going to breed; how you'll set up the caging in your basement; how long it will be before you can reasonably expect young (see some baby reptiles in Figure 14-3); how much the animals, equipment, and utilities will cost for the first three years; and how soon you can expand and use that big utility shed in the back. What else do you need to consider? Lots.

Figure 14-3:
After hatching, baby leopard geckos are placed in cages with food, water, dishes of calcium carbonate, and dampened pans of sphagnum and mulch.

Making your home business everyone's business

The home business issue (especially one that deals with live animals in some way) concerns every agency and every business that might possibly make a buck off of it, or at least that's how it may seem to you at first. The following list explains all the government agencies and others who have a special interest in your business:

- **Your municipality:** If you're running a business from your home, you're living in a residential zone, and your real estate taxes are different than they would be for a commercial area. You may not even have an occupational license. Call the licensing division and ask what sort of license you might need. Most cities allow home-based businesses to operate from homes, but don't expect the municipality to allow you to add outbuildings for raising herps if your area is zoned residential.

- **Your local building and zoning department:** If you add on to your structure, you need to get permits for the work. In Fort Myers, Florida, for example, any job or renovation that costs $100 or more is considered big enough to require a permit. Be sure that you're operating a business that is allowed in a residential area.

- **Your waste disposal company:** This business handles both your trash and your recyclables. In cities, you pay for garbage disposal as part of your water use fees. Counties may charge for trash pick-up, or you may need to contract with a private hauler, or haul your own trash to a central pickup area. A business is required to recycle whatever solid waste items can be recycled, and your municipality has contracted with a solid waste company to haul recyclables to the recycling center. You can haul your recyclables yourself, but unless you live in a rural area where there's no trash pickup, you can't haul your own garbage — and businesses pay more for garbage disposal than do private households.

- **Your state wildlife commission:** You probably need at least one permit to even own more than one or two herps, and another if you work with venomous reptiles. These permits give the state the right to inspect your facilities. In Florida, these annual permits are to "possess or sell," and anyone who buys a herp from you should ask to see this permit.

- **Your animal control officers:** With the rash of ordinances being enacted against pythons, boas, or constrictors over 8 feet in length, dangerous "wild" animals such as giant green iguanas, tegus, monitors, and turtles that may carry salmonella, municipalities are obviously trying to legislate protection for their citizens. When these dangerous creatures are in a residential area, everyone gets nervous and starts hitching up those big wide black belts they wear. Call animal control and ask them about regulations concerning animal ownership. They'll know the scoop in your area.

- ✔ **Your department of revenue:** If you're selling herps, you better be collecting and remitting sales tax for your in-state sales.

- ✔ **Your EMTs, police officers, and firefighters:** When they respond to an emergency call at your house, they don't want the surprise of walking into a room filled with herps. These people are the bravest of the brave, but a lot of very brave people are scared spitless of reptiles (but they'll RUN into a burning building!). The virtual information system, fueled in part by the state permit system for possession of reptiles, both venomous and nonvenomous, works better than you might expect. The 911 operator tells the EMT, police officer, or firefighters that a venomous snake permit or that a reptile/amphibian permit has been issued to your address. The EMT sticks his head inside your front door, but the first question asked is not, "Where is the patient?" but "Where are the venomous snakes?" That's the question I heard, and I was able to say with complete honesty, "Nothing hot here now," and the EMTs came the rest of the way in.

- ✔ **Your landlord:** If you didn't read the fine print on your rental or lease agreement, you may be in for a surprise. The issue of pets and animals is probably quite clearly spelled out, as are the penalties for violating the contract.

You ought to be concerned as well. The catch-all factoid is that the owner of an animal is responsible if his or her animal causes emotional disturbance or injury to another individual, a hard-to-define claim that could be very damaging.

Protecting yourself with insurance

Insurance companies are in the business of betting you, in effect, that nothing bad will happen to you while you're insured with them.

By paying the premiums, you in effect are betting the opposite. When something bad does happen, your insurer shrills, "Oh, no! How could you?" grabs back your policy, and promptly increases the size of your premiums.

Operating a home business without checking with your insurance company and paying higher premiums is like playing with fire. When something bad happens, the insurer hauls out the insurance contract and points to the fine print, which is literally printed in 4-point type. The 4-point type says briefly that if you lied at any point while obtaining or holding the insurance policy, the insurer can declare the policy void.

Even changes you may consider insignificant are not insignificant. Been thinking about opening a reptile T-shirt business, where you design the shirts and have them printed by a commercial firm in their place of business? You store the finished shirts in your extra bedroom and go to expos to sell them. What's so risky about that? Expect your homeowner's rates to go up.

People who own an animal considered wild or dangerous make their insurer's eyelids twitch. Wild animals have no function in a legal sense. This means that humans are always right, and the animal (and its owner) are always wrong. If someone comes into your house and unlatches the cage in which you keep your prized bullsnake, Theodore, and the snake bites the guy's nose, that action is grounds for a lawsuit. Maybe if you have signs up that say "Warning: Theodore will bite your nose off," the courts will reduce the size of the settlement, but your homeowner's insurance may not have to pay. That means you're stuck.

You can understand why insurance people bite their nails a lot and get grabby about policies.

Recognizing the danger of taking your herp out on the town

Another aspect of the no-legal-status-finding regarding animals is the public displays of animals considered dangerous or potentially dangerous. For example, the herper or herp society that allows others to handle a large or adult-sized tegu, monitor, or snake at a family animal day at a nature center isn't thinking clearly. You are legally responsible for any damage, emotional or otherwise, that animal may cause. The least you can do is to insist that the visitor wash his hands with a waterless cleanser before and after petting the animal. You don't want a child that smells like the hamster he's just handled putting his hands anywhere near a snake's face. The child is going to get bitten, and his parents will nail you to the wall.

If a child contracts a Salmonella infection two days after petting a tortoise or a snake at a reptile show, and if any of these animals swab positive for Salmonella, the animal and his owners are going to be found at fault. It won't matter that the child spent the day before playing in a sandbox and could have picked up a Salmonella infection there. It's easier to pronounce the animal guilty and sue the owner or the officers of the herp club.

Acting responsibly

You can't duck ownership, perhaps not even after your actual ownership ends. Giving or selling a snake, a large turtle, or a large lizard to a child who then does something irresponsible with it may come back to haunt you. You should have known the child was not a responsible adult. You should have known he'd do something stupid with the snake, because he's a child and you're an adult. Never sell or give an animal to a child without her parent's permission.

Chapter 15

Making Babies

Things have changed since the early days (the mid-1970s) when the keeping of herps as a hobby was in its infancy, and most herpers didn't know what they were doing. But reptile and amphibian hobbyists persevered and learned, and life in captivity (for reptiles and amphibians, that is) has become better. Herpers are now interested in herp wellness, in establishing longevity records, and in breeding herps. And although we still have a lot to learn about some species, by and large, we've come a long way.

Today herpers place a lot of emphasis on breeding. Dedicated hobbyists routinely produce species as diverse as red-tailed boas, corn snakes, poison dart fogs, green basilisks, spurred tortoises, axolotls, and tomato frogs. In this chapter, you find out about breeding — how to sex your herps, about working with the annual breeding cycle, and how to incubate eggs.

Breeding: It (Usually) Takes Two to Tango

The first thing necessary (usually) to breed herps is to have both sexes available (candlelight and soft music optional). Although it generally takes two to tango, don't despair if you have only one herp. Find another of the opposite sex, introduce the two (but don't forget the quarantine, if necessary), and hope for the best. (You can also read the tips later in this chapter to leave less to chance.)

Some species don't have two sexes! This holds true in many of the racerunners and whiptails, in some geckos, in at least one kind of snake, and in some salamanders. So you simply can't have a sexual pair.

Keep in mind that the females in some reptile species (not amphibians, apparently) are capable of sperm storage, so you could end up with a female from the wild that was bred one year (does this constitute wild sex?), and she may produce viable eggs or babies for another year, or two, or even three. No additional male contact is needed. But for the most part, if your intent is to breed reptiles and amphibians consistently over the long haul, you must have both sexes. The following sections present some of the other aspects that affect successful breeding.

Day length (photoperiod)

Simply defined, a *photoperiod* merely refers to the number of the hours of daylight best suited to the growth and maturation of an organism. In temperate areas, the fewest hours of daylight hours occur in midwinter and the most in midsummer. The increasing hours of daylight in the spring trigger physiological changes in reptiles and amphibians, not the least being the seasonal and temporary increase of size of the gonads.

Time of day

When it comes to herp reproduction, timing isn't just the time of the year — it may mean time of the day, as well. Most amphibians breed during the hours of darkness. Geckos and many snakes (especially those with vertically elliptical pupils) are also nocturnal. Although breeding may occur during the day, it most often occurs at night. Diurnal herp species (those active during daylight hours) breed primarily during the day.

Misting and other stimulatory mechanisms should begin in the late afternoon and continue into the early evening.

Temperature

Reptiles and amphibians are *ectothermic* creatures, meaning that they maintain suitable body temperature by utilizing external stimuli. Thus, providing and maintaining suitable temperatures for your herps are some of the most important things you can do. This is especially so during the breeding season and becomes even more critical when a female is *gravid* (pregnant) or during egg incubation.

Thermal gradients are of particular importance to gravid reptiles. Provide bred females with warmth and an adequately large hiding area. A basking area with an air temperature of 88 to 92 degrees is ideal for most colubrid snakes and many lizards. The basking area can be close to 100 for many boas, pythons, and live-bearing lizards.

Improper temperatures often result in aborted undeveloped egg masses or partially developed or deformed young.

Some thermoregulating gravid snakes assume strange poses. For example, the females of many boas and pythons may lie partially on one side or even upside down to better facilitate elevating their body temperature. (This sight is very disconcerting, even when you think you're used to it!)

Temperature is also an important factor during incubation of crocodilian, turtle, tortoise, and some lizard eggs. The reason for this is that the sex of many crocodilians, chelonians, and lizards is determined by the incubation temperature of the eggs rather than genetically.

For most crocodilians and lizards, females are the result of low incubation temperatures, and males are the result of high incubation temperatures. In turtles, females are the result of high incubation temperatures, and males the result of low temperatures. Just to keep things confusing, there are a few more reptiles (some crocodilians, turtles, and lizards) where females result from incubation temperatures at the hot *and* the cold ends of the spectrum, while the males pop out from the intermediate temperatures.

It is only when the nest temperature varies during the critical second trimester that both sexes are produced. The gender of snakes is not known to be affected by incubation or gestation temperature, nor is it thought to affect the sex ratio of amphibians. This phenomenon is termed TSD — temperature-dependent sex determination. All breeders of reptiles should keep this factor in mind when calibrating incubators.

Humidity levels and barometric pressure

Relative humidity and barometric pressure are known to affect the reproductive cycling and readiness of reptiles and amphibians. The exact whys and wherefores of the benefits of these weather-related factors are speculative at best, but they do seem to have the greatest effects in conjunction with suitable temperatures and rain.

It is during the passage of winter or early spring frontal systems — storm systems that elevate relative humidity and drop barometric pressure — that temperate amphibians emerge from their winter's inactivity. Of course, these weather systems often bring rain and moderating temperatures with them.

TECHNICAL STUFF

Aestivation, hibernation, and brumation

Aestivation is a period of warm-weather inactivity prompted by climatic conditions that are unsuitable for continued surface activity. *Hibernation* is just about the same, but occurs during cold weather. *Brumation* is the term that is often used for reptilian hibernation.

Contrary to common belief, neither aestivation nor hibernation is easy on reptiles and amphibians. These periods of dormancy are undergone because they're the lesser of two evils. In the one case, habitats, modified by excessive heat or lengthy drought, may be temporarily unsuitable for living. In the other case, the onset of the shortened days and colder weather of winter slows bodily functions of these ectothermic creatures and renders surface life impossible.

Whichever the case may be, the reptile or amphibian must seek a habitat with modified temperature and adequate moisture to continue life. This process isn't always easy on a herp, a fact that researchers have documented by showing certain creatures entering a hibernaculum and never again emerging.

When the climate changes for the better, reptiles and amphibians are wakened from sleep by drumming rains or altered temperatures (and probably a lowering of barometric pressure). They emerge from their temporary lairs to continue life. Their first few acts often include shedding the skin and then indulging in breeding activities.

Besides being a necessary, if harsh, survival technique, hibernation of wild reptiles and amphibians seems to be an integral part of the complex procedure of attaining reproductive readiness. Hibernation has been proven less necessary for herps several generations removed from the wild.

By hibernating captive reptiles and amphibians, however, a keeper is able to get a two- to three-month break from the tedium of day-to-day care.

But the effects of lowering barometric pressure with no rain, no temperature changes, and only moderate humidity fluctuations can be observed on herps kept indoors. Frogs, such as White's treefrogs and red-eyed treefrogs, normally quiet and relatively inactive, sitting in a terrarium on a living room table, often sit up and take notice and even begin chorusing when a strong frontal system passes. Many captive snakes and lizards begin breeding activities during the passage of frontal systems, even in temperature- and light-controlled rooms.

Determining the Sex

How do you figure out the sex of a reptile or amphibian? In many cases, they don't advertise their sexes plainly. And in some cases, the sexes have no external differences at all. In these latter, radiography may be needed to ascertain the gender. (At least *humans* need to use radiology; the animals already have it all figured out.)

Knowing your herp and his habits may also help you make a determination. Male herps of many kinds are more outgoing, more defensive, more territorial, and seemingly more alert than the females. But herps react "naturally" only when they feel safe and secure, so behavioral differences may not be apparent in animals in a small cage.

Fortunately, many reptiles and some amphibians display gender-specific sexual characteristics. These are almost invariably best defined during the breeding season and may be almost nonexistent at other times. The following sections take a quick look at some families, genera, and species that do show differences.

Lizards

The males of most iguanian lizards (anoles, iguanas, collared lizards, horned lizards, and so on) are larger than the females of the same species and in most cases are more brightly colored. If secondary characteristics, such as dewlaps, femoral pores, or vertebral spines, exist, they're larger on males than on females. Males have a distinctly broadened tail base as opposed to the narrow one of females.

Males of some skinks develop enlarged, colorful heads during the breeding season. The males of some skinks have orange or red irises as opposed to the (usually) brown ones of females. Male teiid lizards are more colorful and may have a spur of scales on each side of the vent. Male agamids are larger and more colorful and, if a crest is present, have larger crest scales than the females.

Turtles

A few general guidelines can help you determine the sex of turtles. Males of most species have large, heavy tails that, when extended, have the vent at or beyond the rim of the upper shell. The males of some species are much larger than the females. Male tortoises have concave bottom shells so that they can stay perched on top of the female during mating. Water turtles don't have this indentation, but cling to the females with their feet during mating. Some of the male sliders have very long claws on their front feet.

Crocodilians

The males of most are much larger than the females, but most differences are internal. Probing, the only effective means of sexing crocodilians, means literally sticking gloved fingers into the crocodiles's cloaca to feel for the male hemipenes.

Snakes

External sexual differences are often present, but are variable and subtle. In general

- ✔ Male snakes have larger (and usually longer) tails than the female. The tail is the portion of the body beyond the anus.

- ✔ The tail base of the male is widened.

- ✔ The males of some species have brighter color or patterns that differ somewhat from those of the females.

Boas and pythons have visible cloacal spurs (remaining vestiges of rear limbs) that are noticeably larger on males than on the females.

Probing is the most reliable method of sexing most snakes. The correct method should be demonstrated to you by an experienced hobbyist. The probe must be of the correct diameter for the size of the snake, and the probing itself must be done very gently, or the probe will pierce the wall of the cloaca or damage the hemipenes. Sexing probes are available from many reptile specialty dealers. On a female snake, the probe can be inserted into the cloaca only 2 to 5 or 6 subcaudal scales. In males, the probe can be inserted into the hemipenes 6 to 12 scales deep.

Here's how to use the probe:

1. **Hold the snake upside down and bend his tail slightly backwards.**

2. **Slide the lubricated probe under the anal plate and into the anus, push it far to either side, and then angle it toward the tail tip.**

   A small opening (the inverted hemipenis if the snake is a male, or a duct to a musk gland if the snake is a female) is present on each side.

3. **Slide the probe into this opening and push gently until resistance is felt.**

   Using a probe of the correct diameter is important so that you don't injure the snake during this step.

4. **Measure the depth of the insertion against the subcaudal scales and withdraw the probe.**

Popping is a method of everting the hemipenes of tiny newly born snakes that are too small to probe. Use this technique only for the first few days after birth, to avoid permanent damage to the snake. Here's how:

1. **Hold the hatchling snake upside down, with one thumb immediately anterior to the vent and the other thumb several subcaudal scales posterior to the vent.**

2. **Bend the tail slightly upward (opening the vent slightly) while rolling the ball of the posteriormost thumb (the one on the tail) firmly (but gently) toward the vent.**

   When this step is done correctly, the tiny hemipenes of the male will be forced to evert through the vent. Females, of course, have no hemipenes.

Frogs, toads, and tree frogs

These *anurans*, or tailless amphibians, may have external sexual differences at breeding time, but these are subtle at best, and may be absent at other times.

- The males of some species have dark throats, while those of the females are light.

- The throat of the males of many species distends into a single or double resonating chamber (the vocal sac) when the frogs are calling.

- The males of some anurans have heavy forelimbs and sharp or horny spurs on their thumbs, wrists, or chests.

Salamanders and caecilians

Salamanders are especially difficult to sex. Males of some lungless salamanders develop nasal *cirri,* fleshly downward projecting appendages from each nostril during the breeding season. Males of mole salamanders and newts develop enlarged (almost bulbous) vent or anal opening areas during the breeding season. But for the most part, sexual differences are internal, rendering the sexes difficult to determine externally. Most people buy a trio and hope.

Caecilians have gender-related differences in the shape of the ventral openings, but these are very difficult to determine. Your best bet is to buy three and hope for the best.

Gearing Up for Cycling

Reptiles and amphibians often just don't up and breed whenever the two sexes meet. The breeding sequence is an annual or semiannual event, triggered by a number of external and internal stimuli depending on the habitat. *Cycling* is the term used to describe getting a herp ready to reproduce.

In temperate areas, breeding often occurs in the spring, as photoperiods lengthen and temperatures warm. Some species also breed in the autumn and the female stores sperm until ovulating in the spring. The period of inactivity known as *brumation* (the reptilian equivalent of wintertime hibernation) plays a significant role. The breeding season of tropical herps is often instigated by the advent of the rainy season, and with it the concurrent elevation in relative humidity. In both temperate and tropical areas, falling barometric pressure due to the passage of a storm front, tropical depression, or thunderstorm also induces breeding.

Once these climatic phenomena are all in place, factors such as the herps' overall good health, genetic compatibility, and the availability of a receptive partner come into play.

Many hobbyists simply can't duplicate some factors that may stimulate breeding in the wild, such as amphibian breeding congresses. Entire populations of toads, tree frogs, and salamanders are induced by climatic conditions to enter into simultaneous breeding situations. The jostling, calling (where applicable), and other normal interactions of the individuals stimulate the breeding activities of the many. The gatherings or congresses are powerful inducements to breed. One or two pairs on their own may simply not breed.

You may be able to duplicate frog breeding congresses by playing a recording of their vocalizations to stimulate reproductive behavior. For North American frog calls, check with NatureSound (www.naturesound.com/frogs/frogs.html) or AmphibiaWeb (www.amphibiaweb.org/aw/lists/sound.shtml).

The good news regarding captive breeding is that once you have succeeded, successive generations get easier and easier to breed under your "artificial" conditions. Your captive-born young will breed with less finagling than wild-collected herps.

For successful breeding, your potential breeders *must* be healthy and have "good" body weight because many herps fast during the breeding season. And to ensure genetic compatibility, it is best to have all of the herps in any given breeding project hail from the same geographic region. (Some breeders advocate keeping the sexes separated during the cooling period to increase the response rate during the breeding season.)

During the winter months, cycle (or cool) your tropical reptiles and amphibians for a period of 6 to 12 weeks (many breeders suggest 8 weeks) to 69 to 72 degrees at night and 79 to 84 degrees during the day.

Rewarming your tropical reptiles and amphibians is easy. They may be warmed and have cage humidity elevated simultaneously. Increase and maintain a natural photoperiod. After a few days of being warmed, you may again offer food to those herps that have fasted.

After amphibians have been returned to normal day length and humidity, you can stimulate breeding sequences by frequent gentle misting or by placing the creatures in a hydration chamber (see Chapter 12).

If you have been maintaining the sexes separately, you can now place them together. If they're compatible, breeding may begin almost immediately, or it may not begin until the female has had a post-hibernation skin shed. The female's stimulatory pheromone production seems strongest at post-shed, and breeding is most apt to occur then.

Triggering the cycling of tropical herps

Things will go back to normal with the return of the rainy season and overall higher relative humidity. For tropical herps, cycling is triggered/governed more by humidity levels than by photoperiods.

For breeding tropical herps, here's your sequence:

1. **Decrease your herp's food supply.**

   For reptiles, stop feeding your potential breeders about two weeks prior to the beginning of their cooling period, but continue to offer fresh water. This allows the reptiles time to digest any meals and clear their gut before the cooling sequence, when digestion slows due to the cooler temperatures. Amphibians are able to digest foods at lower temperatures, but the sizes of their prey and overall meal sizes should be reduced.

2. **Reduce the photoperiod to 10 hours of daylight and 14 hours of darkness.**

   This is especially important for herps originating from several degrees or farther south or north of the equator.

3. **Reduce cage humidity.**

   You can accomplish this by increasing ventilation, reducing the size of the water dish, and/or removing live plants.

Cycling equatorial herps

If your herps are of an equatorial form that will have its cage temperature reduced only slightly, you may continue feeding them, but reduce the relative size of the meal and the frequency with which feeding occurs. Some will stop eating anyway, and certain species (boas and pythons among them) may continue to fast throughout the actual breeding season. A good general rule is, if your herp does eat, allow the cooled snake to digest its meal fully and to defecate before feeding it again.

A cage temperature reduction to 69 to 72 degrees at night and 79 to 84 degrees during daylight hours will usually cycle equatorial herps successfully.

Getting things started for temperate herps

Many breeders simulate hibernation conditions to help cycle their temperate-climate herps for breeding. The process is much like cycling for tropical herps, but in many ways it's easier.

Depending on how many herps are involved and the ambient wintertime temperatures where you live, cooling (the desired temperature is 48 to 52 degrees for 10 or 12 weeks) may be accomplished in several ways:

✔ By lowering the thermostat in the herp's room

✔ By opening windows and letting cool air in (this ploy is often used in central Florida and some areas of Arizona and California)

✔ By retrofitting a refrigerator to remain at 52 degrees.

Before you cool your reptiles, discontinue feeding two weeks prior.

Enhancing performance

No Viagra necessary. When herps are properly paired and cycled, most will breed almost on cue. However, sometimes breeding just doesn't seem to be progressing as planned. Here are a few ways that you may enhance the interest of the creatures in each other:

✔ Mist gently with tepid water in the evening.

✔ Put both breeders in new quarters (or as a friend used to do with recalcitrant snakes, place the pair of intended breeders in a large snakebag and take both for a ride in your car). I'm not quite sure why this stimulates interest, but it often does.

✔ Add an extra male to an existing setup. This is an almost surefire method of stimulating interest. But because of the possibility of male-to-male conflict (very serious in some species, including many of the skinks, boas, and pythons), always closely supervise this method of inducing breeding.

✔ A change of substrate type or addition of dead leaves sometimes works to stimulate breeding for snakes and monitor lizards.

Introducing Potential Partners to Each Other

When introducing one herp to another for the purpose of breeding them, does it make a difference whether you introduce the male to the female or vice versa? Depending on whom you ask, you'll find proponents of both schools. Actually, I have had equal success with both methods.

Take the overall nervousness and irritability of the potential breeders — and also the size of the cages — into consideration when making a decision. You may need to do some cage juggling (and cleaning, to disperse some of the odors). The least nervous of the potential pair gets moved, but if possible the newly introduced pair also winds up in the larger cage. See Chapter 10 for more info on moving herps.

You may not always face this dilemma, however, because you can maintain many species year-round in pairs or trios (one male and two females).

Remember that many reptiles are more irascible during the breeding season (see Figure 15-1). Herps that don't show any adverse behavior toward their keeper at any other time of year may become savagely aggressive at breeding time. This is especially true of large skinks, iguanas, and many snakes. Always approach your herps with caution at this time.

Figure 15-1:
A male iguana flares out his jowls and challenges an intruder during the breeding season.

Eggs or Live Young: How Long Will This Take?

Depending on geography, temperature, and the location of the egg deposition site, reptile eggs hatch in about 60 days. Any of those factors can shorten or lengthen the incubation time. Not all eggs hatch this quickly; a few turtles lay eggs that will overwinter before hatching. Live-bearing reptiles have the advantage of being able to thermoregulate, and this increase in temperatures helps the young develop faster than eggs that are laid.

Here's information on how some herps reproduce:

- Snakes reproduce either by laying eggs (oviparous) or retaining the eggs in the body until they hatch (ovoviviparous). A very few species, normally egg layers, have been known to occasionally produce live young (viviparous). Lizards may be either live bearers or egg-layers.

- Turtles all lay eggs.

- Crocodilians all lay eggs.

- Tuataras or rhyncocephalians lay eggs.

- Anurans are predominantly egg layers, but a few are viviparous.

- Salamanders or caudatans are also predominantly egg layers, but have among their ranks a few live-bearers.

- Caecilians, depending on the species, may reproduce by eggs or by live birth.

Eggs: General incubation and hatching techniques

Egg deposition by reptiles may occur between 25 and 50 days after breeding. The birthing of live young will take another two to three months. Incubation may last from as little as 11 days (rare) to 60 days (normal) or up to a year (some chameleons and tortoises). The eggs of some reptiles begin developing and then undergo a *diapause* (a cessation of development, often to await a bettering of climatic conditions). Development continues when climatic conditions improve.

Amphibians of many kinds lay their eggs as fertilizing occurs. Fertilization can be external, as when the male frog releases sperm, or internal, such as when the female salamander picks up the deposited sperm packets. Development of the embryo is often rapid, with the eggs hatching in one or two days.

In a few amphibians, the young don't emerge from the egg until they have undergone metamorphosis, so rather than a tadpole hatching, a tiny miniature of the adult frog hatches out. In those amphibians that undergo direct development, time spent in the eggs is understandably longer, sometimes two or more months.

Eggs are not always fertile. You can tell whether an embryo is developing inside by *candling* hard-shelled eggs (viewing the interior of an egg by holding a bright flashlight up behind it), which often reveals developing blood vessels and an embryo as a dark spot. Viable hard-shelled eggs also develop white, chalky shells. Amphibian eggs that are not fertile never exhibit any signs of development and fuzz up with mold a few days after deposition.

Sometimes the embryo dies in the egg. In the case of amphibian eggs, fungus and obvious deterioration occur within days of being deposited if the eggs are infertile or laid where they dry out. Reptile eggs, which may have either a pliable parchment-like shell or a calcareous (made of calcium), nonyielding shell, are less readable. However, eggs with pliable shells may collapse if not viable (but collapsing can also occur if eggs begin to dry due to insufficient moisture in the incubation medium). Infertile eggs often look discolored and develop a slimy feel.

Incubating amphibian eggs

Amphibian eggs don't need incubation in the usual sense. If given a choice, the female deposits her eggs in a site that will permit their development. If the eggs are laid in water and fertilized, the water must have a "flow" to it, as in a gentle current, to provide the eggs with oxygen and to carry off metabolic by-products or waste. If the fertilized eggs are deposited under a log or in a moist cranny in a terrarium, they need to be kept moist. Adding a bit of dampened sphagnum moss is one way to help keep the eggs moist; adding moisture to the ground where the eggs were laid is another way.

Incubating reptile eggs indoors

Once you think your female reptile is gravid (primarily evidenced by an increasingly fat body), buy an incubator (see Figure 15-2). You can buy a reptile egg incubator for about $45 or more, depending on the model and manufacturer. Have the incubator on hand so you can go into action once the eggs are laid.

Do not buy a chick egg incubator for reptile eggs unless you can alter the incubation temperature. The cheaper chick egg incubators are set at incubation temperatures that are too high for reptile eggs.

Figure 15-2:
You'll get a higher rate of hatching if you incubate your reptile eggs in an incubator.

Before the eggs come, you need to prepare a proper incubation environment:

1. **Place 1 or 1½ inches of the moistened medium in the bottom of a plastic shoe box or plastic container that will fit inside the incubator.**

   Moistened perlite or vermiculite has proven ideal incubation media. Moisten the material (for many species, that means about 4 parts of water to 5 or 6 parts of the dry perlite or vermiculite by volume). The incubation medium should be moist enough to clump when squeezed, but should not drip water when squeezed.

2. **Make a depression for each egg with a fingertip and place the eggs in the depressions.**

   The eggs should be one-half to two-thirds buried in the substrate.

3. **Once the eggs are in place, you may wish to cover the exposed tops with a paper towel to absorb any droplets of moisture that would otherwise condense on the eggs.**

4. **Put the lid on the container and place it in the incubator.**

   A shallow open dish of water in the incubator will help keep the relative humidity high.

If the medium is too dry or too wet, the permeable eggshells will readily allow the embryos to dry out or to become too wet. Either can cause the death of the embryo.

Following deposition (the laying of the eggs), you need to remove the eggs as soon as possible for incubation. Check the eggs daily during incubation. If the eggs begin to collapse, increase the moisture slightly by gently and barely misting the paper towel covering. If the eggs get turgid (firm) and slick, decrease the moisture.

As careful as you might be, you need to expect a certain percentage of embryonic mortality.

When the eggs are nearing full term, dimpling and a concurrent lack of eggshell turgidity are normal and to be expected. Some eggs may go full term, but if the embryo is weak, the egg may fail to hatch. You may be able to save some of these babies by carefully slitting the eggshell. If the baby within is viable, it may emerge within a day or two, but even with extra care, weak hatchlings often succumb within a few days following emergence.

Allowing natural incubation of eggs of outdoor reptiles

Reptiles maintained in outside pens may nest in much the manner they would in the wild. This is particularly true for temperate-area turtles, such as box turtles, or big lizards kept outdoors in a warm climate.

If the ground temperature and soil moisture content are suitable (research the needs of the species with which you are working), you may be able to allow natural incubation. Iguanas and most tortoises and box turtles seem to find nesting in sandy soil to their liking. You may want to encircle the nest with wire mesh to prevent hatchlings from hatching and scattering, and always assess the potential for nest predation by predators (for example, crows, moles, rats, raccoons, and domestic pets). However, I've had many successful hatchings of temperate turtles and lizards under these natural conditions.

Live young: Almost no work on your part

Dealing with those herps who give birth to live young is fun. The animal takes care of everything, and you don't need to provide an incubator or worry about moisture levels. All you need to do is to figure out how and what to feed the young (some of which are very small).

Caring for viviparous female reptiles

Many boas and natricine snakes (water and garter snakes), some lizards, and a very few amphibians bear live young.

After a gestation of about 120 to 200 days (temperature and other factors help dictate and alter gestation duration), a female will produce her clutch of 1 to more than 100 babies. Infertile egg masses and some dead babies may be produced with the clutch.

Just as incubating eggs need a certain temperature to develop, a gestating female of any live-bearing species must also have a suitable temperature regimen.

Provide bred females with warmth and an adequately large hiding area, and provide the thermal gradients that will allow your female to thermoregulate. A basking area with an air temperature of 88 to 92 degrees is ideal. A gravid snake will seek out and use a hot spot for thermoregulation. Improper temperatures often result in aborted undeveloped egg masses or partially developed or deformed young. Even a short period of improper temperature may result in aberrant patterns or other (usually unwanted) abnormalities. Excessive handling of a gravid female or adverse gestating temperature may cause the female to either abort or give birth to deformed babies. Handle the gravid female as little as possible, and make sure that suitable temperatures are always available.

Not all gravid females look gravid. Cage tops need to fit tightly to contain active unexpected young.

Caring for viviparous female amphibians

Very few amphibians now available in the pet trade are viviparous. However, the European fire salamander is one of the exceptions. As with most amphibians, this beautiful salamander requires coolness rather than heat. In most cases, room temperature is perfectly suitable for gravid females.

Taking Care of Mama

Whether the species is oviparous or viviparous, because gravid female reptiles often cease feeding for a variable period while gravid, the production of her clutch or brood can use much of her available energy resources.

Because eggs are often developed and laid within a few days, most amphibians are less prone to breeding-related weight loss than female reptiles. But it's important to replace the weight lost by a spent female. If the female has fasted for an extended period, offer her small but frequent meals at the start. After you have noticed that she is digesting meals well, you can increase her meals to normal quantities.

Chapter 16

Tending to the Young'uns

A gravid (pregnant) reptile or amphibian is a beautiful sight — it means that you've done something right (which may be just putting two animals together). The hard part is over, right? You've cracked the reproduction code, and you can sit back and relax.

Actually, your work has just started. You've done some research and you already know whether to expect eggs or live young; now, you need to put things in order so that your pet has a good place to lay her eggs or to birth her young. If you're going to incubate the eggs, you need to have an incubator on hand; if your pet lays eggs that require no incubation, you have a bit more free time to figure out how you're going to cope with the young. This chapter tells you what to expect, so you can take steps to keep your workload to a manageable level.

When the Young Start Coming, You'd Better Get Going

You've succeeded! You watched your prized female bearded dragon/lizard dig her nesting hole, and you remained on tenterhooks until she laid her eggs and covered the nest. You gathered those eggs and carefully incubated them. Today, some of the most helpless-looking baby lizards you've ever seen have begun emerging from the eggs. You watch, amazed. The babies wriggle free of the shells and before taking more than a step or two, collapse on the incubation medium and just lie there. What should you do?

Bring out that sizing bin — the temporary home for the babies while they feed and "size up." For beardeds, your best bet is one of the large Rubbermaid storage bins. The bins are too high for the babies to leap out of, you can clamp a UV light on the rim and point it downward, and the heavy plastic sides hold the heat in. Smooth out the substrate, ready the full spectrum lights, and hie yourself off for baby crickets. By tomorrow, you'll be up to your armpits in baby dragons, and they're going to be *hungry*.

Or, if you're a frog person, how about *this* scenario? You had a female horned frog and a male horned frog. Because of their size difference (females are often almost twice the size of males) and cannibalistic tendencies, you kept them separated — the proper thing to do. But then a series of strong frontal systems began parading through your area, and — *voilà* — papa frog began to voice his baa-ing call notes. You couldn't let this go by, so you placed the frogs together.

The next morning, instead of one very fat female frog (and no male), you have a pair of horned frogs still in the mating grasp and about 1000 gelatinous coated eggs. You're elated, but what do you do now? If you thought you'd have your hands full with 25 young bearded dragons, you better *really* be thinking about how you're going to handle 1,000 *very* predatory tadpoles!

Particularly in the case of lots and lots of frog eggs, most hobbyists select a number that they think they can deal with, count out those eggs, and dispose of the rest.

Briefs on Babies

Babies need caging and food, of course, and the reptilian types will need proper lighting. Babies grow fast, and including vitamins and minerals, most specifically vitamin D3 and calcium, is important. You can provide these vitamins and minerals to fast-growing herps in a variety of ways. See Chapter 12 for details on the use of vitamins.

Snakes

After the baby snakes have emerged from their eggs or from their mother, you need to house them in a container of their own. You can use another, separate, terrarium or a series of ventilated shoe boxes (⅛-inch air holes drilled in at least two opposing sides). If space is at a premium, shoe boxes are easier to handle, and you can stack them. Make certain that any container you use has a tightly fitting lid. For substrate, you can use mulch, but you'll find taking care of these tiny babies to be much easier if you use paper towels instead. Paper towels are absorbent; moisture from stools is blotted up, and the cage (and snakes) stay cleaner. You can layer the towels and provide multiple hiding areas that afford maximum privacy in a minimum of space. The water dish can be small; just make certain that if a little snake crawls into it, the dish is shallow enough for it to crawl out easily.

In order to keep track of which baby is eating and which is not, house only four to a shoebox or six to a 10-gallon tank. You'll need to split them up after the first six weeks to two months because they'll begin to grow as they begin to eat.

In comparison to some other herp species, raising baby snakes (at least the more commonly bred species) is a virtual snap. Seldom do the *clutches* (the groups of eggs laid by a snake at one time) of common pet snakes (rat, king, and pine snakes) number more than a couple of dozen. In contrast, a large Burmese python may lay 60 or more eggs. Rarely, some species may have more young, such as a Florida green water snake I once knew that was ready to birth 128 babies when she ran afoul of a car. For a snake of any species, a clutch of that size is extraordinary.

Normally, baby snakes are easy to care for, requiring only occasional but regular feedings. A once-a-week feeding will be plenty. Most baby snakes will take baby mice and baby rats; once in a while, you'll get a holdout that wants only lizards. In the case of garter snakes and water snakes, earthworms and minnows are the preferred prey.

A few kinds of snakes are cannibalistic. Among the cannibals are the kingsnakes and the milk snakes. The hatchlings of these are especially apt to eat cagemates, so these snakes are excellent candidates for solitary confinement. Deli cups work quite well.

Even noncannibalistic snakes may occasionally make a feeding error. Suppose that you're keeping a clutch of baby corn snakes communally, and you drop in a few pink mice (Pink mice, or pinkies, are newly born mice. At this stage, they're hairless; their pink skins give them their name.): All will probably be well, providing that each snake can find its own pinkie. A problem can occur if two baby snakes start on opposite ends of the same pinkie. When the two snakes meet in the middle of the mouse, one snake or the other probably won't stop swallowing. The result is one dead snake and one uncomfortably fat snake that'll probably regurgitate his fallen sibling a few days after eating it.

Don't let this happen. You can avoid this scenario in one of two ways:

- Keep the baby snakes separated from each other when you feed them.
- Feed the babies individually by hand (actually with forceps).

About the only thing different in the care regimen between a hatchling corn snake and a hatchling python or a neonate boa is related to size. A corn snake is pencil thin and about 11 or 12 inches long, and a baby boa or python is from 18 to 28 inches in length and relatively heavy bodied. Corn snakes require pinkie mice, and boas or pythons can eat larger mice or pinkie rats.

Lizards

If your sizing containers for your baby lizards are 20-gallon tanks or larger, you should be able to place a dozen or so in each container. Give them a slightly elevated sunning position (such as a flat rock) beneath the UV light, a tiny receptacle of water, and a base diet of baby crickets (see the appendix for more details on what to feed different types of lizards). Within days, you'll see growth — slow on some babies, remarkably fast on others. You'll also be able to watch the babies' behaviors — for bearded dragon babies, look for their first tries at the arm-waving appeasement gesture known as *circumduction.* The smaller ones use it on the bigger ones to say, "I mean no harm." As the lizards grow, you may see the largest and fastest growing babies show signs of aggression toward their smaller siblings. This is especially true of bearded dragons and blue tongued skinks. Be ready to move the bigger ones into another container, and you'll have to continually sort out the group in this manner until you sell them or each is in his or her own cage.

Keeping track of who's eaten and who hasn't, which cages needs to be sorted and which need cleaning, and when to buy another batch of baby crickets will keep you busy, but it'll be worthwhile. And if you're keeping beardeds, just when you think that you have the whole schmear worked out, you'll probably have another clutch of dragon eggs hatch. Dragons typically have four or five clutches of eggs annually for the first four or five years of sexual maturity.

Frogs

For frog-raising, think kiddie pools, tropical fish food, frequent water changes, and a thermometer. Frogs can lay as many as 1,500 eggs at a time! If you intend to raise as many of those tadpoles as possible, you'd better be thinking about setting up three or four or six kiddie wading pools in a temperature-controlled area, and you'd better be thinking about how you're going to feed all those hungry mouths and keep their space clean. And when metamorphosis starts, at that point, you're going to need a lot of deli cups.

If fed regularly and well, one tadpole is quite capable of changing a lot of perfectly good food (such as black worms or finely chopped earthworms) into quite a lot of perfectly toxic waste. Now multiply that by about 1,000, or whatever number of tadpoles you have: The result can be staggering amounts of ammonia and related undesirable waste products. So the only way to keep those tadpoles alive and growing is through the use of sophisticated filters and occasional partial water changes and filter cleanings. If you don't use filters, you need more frequent, almost-complete water changes.

But to keep things practical and sane, suppose that you picked out 100 eggs and disposed of the rest. Even if you only have a 50 percent hatch rate, you'll have 50 tadpoles. That's one kiddie pool, or one 150-gallon aquarium. That's a doable figure for your first batch of eggs. If you only have two or three tadpoles that you've netted up from a nearby pond, you can use a 20-gallon filtered tank and follow these guidelines. A thermometer will tell you the water temperature; the temperature of the water affects the time the tadpoles stay tadpoles. If your water temperature is in the low to mid 80s, the tadpoles will begin metamorphosing into froglets in a month or so (see Figure 16-1). Provide a land area when you see the hind legs emerge, so the froglets can hop out when their lungs take over for the former gills. Some frog species develop more quickly than others, and the last of the tadpoles should metamorphose within six weeks.

After the tadpoles have changed into small adults, plan on housing them individually. Most frogs will try to eat their siblings, and in crowded conditions, stress takes its toll. Deli cups work well for froglets, and a dampened paper towel in the bottom of the cup can be re-dampened or changed as needed.

REMEMBER

Two popular pet frogs have distinctive habits you need to know about if you want to raise the young. Here's the pertinent stuff (for more on these frogs, see the appendix).

Figure 16-1: Provide a land space for green treefrog tadpoles near the end of metamorphosis.

Horned frogs are voracious predators at all stages of their lives. Strong or bigger tadpoles eat weaker or smaller tadpoles. Newly metamorphosed froglets are even fiercer, trying to eat siblings of identical size and killing the siblings and, sometimes, themselves in the process. So keep each metamorph in a separate deli cup with a bit of water in the bottom, and feed each one individually (guppies or small crickets or bits of earthworm are good dietary items). Now, your job has changed. Instead of having to clean those six pools once or twice a week, you only have to clean 1,000 deli cups almost daily. See Chapter 10 for more info on deli cups.

Poison-dart frogs, one of the hottest groups on the amphibian scene, are comparatively easy to care for because they only have one or two dozen tadpoles. (Wow! That exhaled breath of relief almost blew me off this page!) Rarely does a female have more than two dozen eggs, and, often, the clutch numbers only six to ten.

Dart frogs are strange little critters. They lay their eggs on the ground, and then a parent carries the tadpoles piggyback — sometimes only one at a time — to a small, shallow receptacle of water. They follow this regimen in captivity as well as in the wild.

If you're concerned that your dart frogs don't know what they're doing when it comes to raising their young, the eggs can be actually be removed from the terrarium and hatched by keeping them moist in a petri dish. Tadpoles are easily raised in shallow water in individual deli cups. You must keep the water fresh and ammonia-free, but with so few tadpoles, doing so won't be a significant chore.

Feed the young tadpoles typical tadpole food, such as chopped black worms, pureed earthworms (the food preparation is getting to be more fun, isn't it?), and dry tropical fish food. (Buy a major brand, such as Wardley; the nutritional value is significantly higher.) Fruit flies and termites are excellent foods for metamorphs.

Salamanders

Salamander young look a bit like tadpoles, and they need much the same caging and food. The numbers are a little different, with only 50 to 100 or surely not more than 500 young per clutch. Although these numbers seem simple when compared to frogs, you'll probably want to select the number you reasonably feel that you can care for and dispose of the rest.

Salamander larvae have gills and are aquatic (see Figure 16-2). They need clean water with a lot of surface area (like a kiddie pool), so that the water can absorb more oxygen from the air. You can use a large aquarium with a filtration system and save yourself a lot of work. Dried tropical fish food is a very good base diet item; supplement it with chopped black worms and mashed up earthworms (fruit flies and termites are excellent foods for metamorphs).

Figure 16-2:
A larval tiger salamander has gills, lives in water, and eats tiny insects.

Salamanders usually breed in the spring, and the breeding is stimulated by the spring rains. Rising temperatures is another factor, especially in the aquatic salamanders. This doesn't mean 70-degree days, by any means — the mole salamanders in Tennessee head for their breeding ponds as soon as the spring rains hit, providing temperatures are at least 10 degrees. Suppose that you clean your salamander's tank one day in late winter. Rain is forecast, so you put in a larger water dish than what was in their cage. That night the rainstorm moves through your area, and your salamanders awaken and begin to move about their cage. The female begins to nudge the male, and by the time you go to bed, the male is depositing spermatophores on the bottom of that large water dish. The next morning, you awaken to find salamander eggs in the water dish.

If you move the eggs to a separate aquarium, one with filtration, and keep the tank clean, in about two weeks, the eggs will begin to hatch. You can watch them develop, and the growing larvae will be readily visible through the transparent jelly of the individual egg-capsule.

When the eggs hatch, decide how many young you can reasonably expect to raise. Separate them with about 10 young per 15-gallon tank. Again, water, water, and more water changes will be needed, unless each tank has a filtration system. If you have a filtration system, you'll only need to make partial water changes between each full tank change. Like the horned frog tadpoles, salamander larvae produce a lot of waste, and a lot of waste equates to frequent water changes.

Larval salamanders may be herbivores or carnivores (see the appendix for more on specific types of salamanders) The carnivorous types are often every bit as predacious as horned frog tadpoles, and some members of an egg clutch will become predatory/cannibalistic, while other members of that egg clutch are herbivorous. For the carnivorous types, bigger ones eat smaller ones, and smaller ones eat weaker ones. Be ready to separate the number you want to raise and put them into individual containers. Again, deli cups will come to your rescue for a while, but you'll have to be diligent about freshening and changing the water in each one. Diligent, by the way, means *daily.*

Blackworms and finely chopped earthworms (Uck! Will you have fun dicing those!) are excellent food items.

Turtles

Everyone loves baby turtles, and water turtles — the sliders, cooters, and related turtles and baby mud and snapping turtles — in particular. The mud and snapping turtles are a little easier to keep than the sliders, cooters, and other baskers, because they don't seem to be anywhere nearly as dependent on sunshine to regulate calcium use.

But people seem to want the more colorful and personable sliders, cooters, painted turtles, and map turtles. These are all silver-dollar-sized (or smaller) as hatchlings, and spectacularly pretty, being clad in bright greens, yellows, and reds. When the babies bite, they don't hurt.

The cooters, sliders, painted turtles, and the map turtles are all basking turtles. They love the sunlight and will sit basking, with their feet extended and toes splayed, for long periods (see Figure 16-3). When they get too warm, they simply slip into the water to cool off.

Figure 16-3: Covering a baby turtle's pen keeps out predators, such as crows and raccoons.

Origin of turtle names

Here's where some basking turtles got their names:

- **Cooter:** Derived from an African dialect meaning turtle

- **Slider:** Named for their habit of sliding quickly into the water when frightened

- **Painted turtle:** Named for the bright coloring on the marginal scutes

- **Map turtle:** Named for the maplike lines all over the shell

These little primarily aquatic turtles change dietary preferences as they mature. The cooters and sliders start off life as carnivores, eating worms, insect, snails, and a little bit of plant matter. Adults reverse the diet, eating primarily plant matter and some insects and snails.

Some species of map turtles also undergo dietary changes, but these are gender related. Babies of both sexes eat insects, worms, and snails. Males continue with this diet as they mature. Females of the broad-headed species tend to become *molluscivores* (mollusk-eaters, feeding on snails and freshwater mussels) as they mature. These forms develop immense heads with broad crushing plates behind the mandibles. Don't try to test their strength with one of your fingers!

The babies of all of these turtles are usually compatible. However, as they mature, they may begin tail nipping and even may bite the edges off a cagemate's shells. Watch groups carefully and be ready to separate them if necessary.

Chapter 17

Keeping It Legal

*O*beying all the federal, state, and local laws dealing with reptiles and amphibians can be harder than you think. Consider this scenario, for example. You've just spotted a pair of the prettiest toads you've ever seen advertised on the Web. They were angular but pudgy — and oh! Those colors! The amphibians were spectacular, but they were also expensive! They were advertised as rare, and the asking price was $750.

So you, a resident of Texas, agonize for a while, begin negotiations with the seller (in Washington), and eventually work out the details of the sale. The toads are soon in an artistically designed terrarium in a place of honor in your living room. Your new herp friends come to ogle the creatures, and one of them mentions that the local herp society is having a meeting next week. That's cool, you think. I'll go and meet other enthusiasts and tell them all about these toads. And that's when problems begin. (Actually, the problems began when you bought the toads, but you just haven't learned that yet.) You go to the meeting and are telling everyone about those toads when some old-timer interrupts, "Golden toads? You mean *Bufo periglenes?* Those are supposed to be extinct. They're from Monte Verde, Costa Rica, and they're a federally endangered species."

Soon afterward you answer a knock on your door, and a suited man greets you with palm outstretched, holding a wallet with a little badge. He introduces himself as a special agent with the law enforcement arm of the U.S. Fish and Wildlife Service, and he's there to talk about your toads. You explain that yes, you have some toads. No, you don't know what their scientific name is, but someone told you it was *Bufo* something, that they're from Costa Rica, and they're supposed to be extinct. The agent asks you whom you got them from, how you found them, and how they came to you. Satisfied with your answers, he asks to see your permits. Permits? For a toad? What's he talking about — what permits?

You need permits to purchase federally endangered animals in interstate commerce and to ship them across state lines. Additional permits are necessary to get the animals legally out of the country of origin. The bottom line is, if your toads are restricted in any way, and you don't have permits, you have a serious problem, as does your supplier, and if the authorities can find him, so does his supplier.

You can get into trouble with far less effort. Suppose that you go from your home in Florida to visit a friend in Georgia. While in Georgia, you just happen to see a corn snake crossing a busy road. Hating to see any animal run over, you find a break in traffic, park, hop out, save the corn snake, and run back to your car. Then you say, "What the heck. It's a neat snake. I think I'll keep it." You bring it back to Florida with you, and by so doing you break the Georgia state law that protects all harmless snakes. Even worse, by breaking that law and crossing a state line, you've also run afoul of the Lacey Act, a federal regulation that makes it a crime to transport wildlife taken illegally across state lines.

The collecting and selling of protected wildlife is big business today, and doing so illegally has big consequences. If you're not careful, you could wind up in court, get hit with a sizable fine, or even land in a federal slammer, and ignorance of the law is absolutely no excuse. To make things even more difficult, laws may be federal, state, county, or municipal. Try to keep a handle on that!

In this chapter, I explain all you need to know about the laws and permits that make up the legal labyrinth of the herp world.

Layin' Down the Law

In general, laws are in place to protect animals. But why animals need to be protected and what that protection involves (or what the law is designed to prevent) can be a bit unclear. Laws are proposed and enacted by either well-meaning people or by frightened people. For example, the city commission in Myrtle Beach, South Carolina, worried about salmonella, so it banned the sales of turtles within the city limits. A state representative from Missouri learned of the problem with invasive plants, so he wrote a bill that will eventually provide procedures for dealing with all non-native species, whether plant or animal (and these non-native life forms do not have to become established in the state to come under the jurisdiction of this bill). Federal and state laws often have at least a modicum of research to support them (even if this research is sometimes biased, if only from lack of knowledge). County and municipal laws usually have very little basis in fact, being instead the result of panic or misunderstanding.

Laws, no matter at what level of government they may be enacted, are always somewhat subjective. What's okay one year may not be okay another year. What one officer regards as a minor impingement on a law, another might consider a flagrant violation. It's your responsibility to research the laws that pertain to your geographical area because even inadvertent transgressions can have serious consequences.

The arm of the law is long. Laws cover such herp-related issues as

✔ Selling

✔ Collecting

✔ Keeping

✔ Transporting

Laws (depending on where you are) may also regulate how you can go about looking for wildlife for the purpose of observation, nonlicensed research, or photography. Many laws include language that covers not only their main topic, such as collecting or hunting, but also language that covers the very broad-based (and often open-to-interpretation) subject of harassment. And when it comes to harassment, it's up to an enforcement officer to decide whether stamping your foot to induce a snake to coil or to induce a lizard to stop moving so you can take a photo is harassment. Even something as seemingly harmless as using the flash on your camera, which may stop a toad from calling, might be considered harassment.

One of the very sad interpretations of harassment is that it can be illegal in the eyes of some enforcement officer (and in the letter of the law) for you to pick up and move a herp from a roadway to save it from being run over, but running over that same creature is considered incidental take and is legal. Some laws even regulate how you can hunt herps. A Texas law, for example, makes it illegal (a ticketable offense) to road-hunt, meaning to drive along a roadway and pick up herps you see in your headlights, but you can park on the side of the roadway and hunt the same area on foot, using a flashlight.

Laws are partially enacted to keep people considerate. Noise ordinances are enacted, for example, to keep you from having loud parties late at night. When a collecting law says you may possess only three of a species, it's to keep you from making a pig of yourself and wiping out a local population of herps. All you need to do is to show a little R-E-S-P-E-C-T for others, and you'll save yourself a lot of trouble.

Respecting private property

Treat "Private Property" and "No Trespassing" signs as gospel. A landowner has the right to put up no trespassing signs and the expectation that this request will not be violated. In fact, once those signs are up, to violate the order is to violate a law. Be courteous; ask permission to access posted private land, and if the request is denied, continue to be courteous.

Road hunting: Doing it right

Road-hunting is a tried-and-true method of covering a very great amount of habitat in a relatively short time. You choose the proper habitat for the animal you want, select the correct time frame, hop in your car, and drive. And you drive and you drive and you drive. And sometimes, if you're lucky, you'll find what you're looking for. Sometimes you're just looking. Sometimes you're collecting. If you're looking for corn snakes, evening driving is most productive. If you're looking for desert kingsnakes or amphibians anywhere, night driving is best. If you're hoping for a buttermilk racer, drive as the sun is beginning to warm the roads.

But don't grab a flashlight and leap into your car. Road hunting isn't legal everywhere (I know, for example, that it's forbidden in Texas and in Hendry County, Florida). Check out the laws in areas you think you might like to road hunt. The Web site for the Pet Industry Joint Advisory Council lists each state's laws (www.pijac.org), but the site doesn't include municipal ordinances). You have to check each county's ordinances to see whether road hunting is allowed. Check with the game and fish departments for the states you want to visit; their officers are up to date on the local ordinances as well as state regulations.

Road hunting can be dangerous. Today, you must share the road with an ever-increasing number of vehicles. In addition, to road hunt most effectively, you must drive somewhat erratically, swerving to miss herps on the roads and stopping suddenly to ascertain what you've just gone by. This behavior can make homeowners along the roads you travel nervous. It can set a police officer's teeth absolutely on edge.

Playing It Safe with Permits

A *permit* is a piece of paper issued by a municipality, a state, or the federal government that gives you permission to do something. You get a permit to put a storage shed on your property. You get a temporary permit to pick up but not keep herps when you want to photograph them. The fee you pay goes directly to the issuing agency. When you have a permit to photograph herps on a specific park property, you can pick up and position a herp for the purpose of photography. Without the permit, you're harassing the herp, a chargeable offense.

CITES permits

CITES is the acronym for the Convention on International Trade in Endangered Species. This agreement is a listing by concerned member nations of wild plants and animals that research committees feel are vulnerable to commercial exploitation. Despite the word "endangered" in the title, it's very different from the Federal Endangered Species Act. The many creatures listed in the documents generated by the convention may be traded internationally only under permit. Unlike the endangered species act, which lists species individually, the CITES regulations may list not only individual types but also entire families of reptiles and amphibians. Among some of the families are boas, tortoises, crocodiles, sea turtles, and giant salamanders. CITES permits are required for every shipment, and you get them from the U.S. Fish and Wildlife Service.

CITES has three listing categories:

- **Category I:** Lists species that are considered to be in imminent danger of extinction and are the most stringently regulated.
- **Category II:** Lists species that are neither threatened or endangered, but are vulnerable.
- **Category III:** Lists species of special concern — types for which it is felt that traded numbers need to be monitored, but which are not now in imminent danger or vulnerable.

After permits have been issued and the creatures have been exported and properly documented at the destination country, it's not necessary to continue documenting transactions for internal distribution. For example, suppose that a shipment of baby boa constrictors is ordered from a Colombian supplier by a Miami, Florida, dealer. Once the exportation permit has been generated by Colombia and the snakes have been documented as received by the U.S. Fish and Wildlife Service, the dealer doesn't need to further document the sale of snakes to his customers throughout the United States. However, CITES documentation again becomes necessary if the dealer chooses to make international shipments.

Federal permits

Federal permits are issued by pertinent agencies (such as the U.S. Department of the Interior, U.S. Department of Agriculture, Bureau of Land

Management, Bureau of Indian Affairs, U.S. Public Health Service, and perhaps others) to individuals doing bona fide research on otherwise protected federal lands. They're seldom issued for any other purpose. These federal permits are usually species-specific and locale-specific, not only for a given park but also perhaps for a specific area of that given park. You'll need a permit before you can disturb or harass any plant, animal, or rock on federal land. At present, a blanket, nationwide policy for the land use in national forests doesn't seem to exist. You may need to purchase day use or seasonal permits merely to park on the side of the road in some parks, but the same activity may be entirely unregulated in other parks. You can clarify land use practices by inquiring at each individual National Forest Headquarters.

The policies pertaining to land accessibility on Indian reservations is also fraught with complex and often overlapping concerns. Of notorious complexity, for example, are the uses allowed on the Tohona O'odham reservation in Pima County, Arizona. Always cross all the *t*s and dot all the *i*s on all federal permits.

When you do have a permit in hand, always make your presence and intents known to the various law enforcement agencies that oversee the area in question. Doing so can save many awkward moments and encounters in the field.

A regulation that many of the most casual herp keepers may run afoul of is one enacted several decades ago by the Public Health Service. This regulation, discussed elsewhere in this book (Chapter 12) prevents the sale of any chelonian with a shell length of 4 inches or less except for specifically exempted purposes.

State permits and licenses

You'll probably need a permit before you can disturb or harass any plant, animal, or rock on state land. You need to have permits to hunt for herps. In some parks, you need a permit just to go off an established trail, meaning, to wander around. You should always research what permits, if any, are actually needed and allowed on state-held lands.

But this isn't the end of state involvement. Many states require annual licenses to sell herps, sometimes to keep herps, and often to display herps. Some states, Florida among them, even have regulations pertaining to the size and construction of cages used for herps. The keeping of certain species of herps is often specifically disallowed except under specific permits. Among the herp groups most frequently micromanaged by state laws are crocodilians, venomous snakes, and giant snakes. Most states also have lists of fully protected species of special concern as well as threatened and endangered reptiles and amphibians. You need special and specific permits to collect, keep, or otherwise interact with these species.

Many states completely prohibit the collecting, keeping, and sale of either specific indigenous herps, or in some cases all indigenous wildlife. In many cases, these laws would disallow the keeping of a specific herp within the state in question, even if it were legally collected in a neighboring jurisdiction.

You can't avoid these problems by dumping your herp. Turning exotic reptiles and amphibians loose is illegal in all states. If you can't keep your herps any longer for some reason, find someone (a private hobbyist, a pet store, or a wholesaler) to whom you can give the creatures. In most cases, in most regions, nonindigenous wildlife cannot survive. In the areas where much of it can survive (such as southern Florida, southern Texas, or southern Arizona), adding non-native wildlife can wreak havoc with native species. Not only do nonindigenous species place unneeded stress on native forms, but released wildlife may transmit pathogens contracted in captivity to their wild brethren. Be cool, be smart, and be legal.

County permits

Counties enact laws that pertain to the keeping of herps deemed "harmful" — and harmful can mean anything the county commission wants it to mean. If you want county involvement in herp keeping, just act irresponsibly — such as by taking your "tame" snake out on a public beach or to any other busy unincorporated public area. Remember, that the creature you consider your pet is somebody else's long-time phobia.

Municipal permits

Suppose that you want to live in a specific area. You have the lot picked out, it's gorgeous, and you can't wait to build. When you move, you plan on going into herps big-time, breeding them as well as keeping them. You better check out your land use regulations first. Your interests are quite probably not the same as other community residents, and deed restrictions (strict restrictions that control how a property can be used) can be brought to bear. Even if you're prepared to go through channels to get an exemption for your site, if your neighbors don't want a "snake breeder" on site, there's no way you'll get that permit. The time to learn of this possibility is before you make a monetary commitment, not after. Public hearings for land-use exemptions are possible, but they may well not work out in your favor. Be prepared to live elsewhere.

Remember that the anti-herp laws enacted by municipalities are the result of pressures brought to bear on local politicians by local constituents. Most local anti-herp laws have no scientific basis; they're just the result of political pressure from people who fear herps (especially snakes) and who use the banner of "protecting citizens from being endangered through the thoughtlessness of other citizens." As you can see, this sort of attitude can result in restrictive laws. If your neighbors think emotional health is an actual legal term, then they can blame you for anything you do that they perceive as endangering their emotional health. If your neighbor is enough of a pain, he or she can sue you over just about anything. If the source of their emotional discomfort is the iguana cage they know is just over the fence, they can sue. If you keep snakes in a room with windows, where your neighbors may be frightened if they walked by your house and saw the snake if the window shade was up, they can sue you. If they and their legal counsel believe that their emotional health has been compromised, you're going to hear about it. You'd better have any pertinent local and state permits up to date; any negligence on your part toward necessary permits is going to be interpreted as a defiant effort to "sneak around" legislation passed by well meaning and law-abiding citizens.

Knowing Where to Go for Information

Now that you're reeling from the trouble you can get *into,* here's how you can stay out of trouble to begin with. Here is contact information for state and federal conservation offices.

State conservation offices

Every state has regulations governing the possession of pet herps. You may be required to buy an annual permit to own even just one frog. Call or go online to contact your state's conservation office (see Table 17-1), and comply with their regulations.

Table 17-1	State Conservation Agencies
Alabama	Alabama Department of Conservation and Natural Resources, Game and Fish Division Law Enforcement Section, 64 North Union Street, Montgomery, AL 36130-1456
Alaska	Alaska Department of Fish and Game, P.O. Box 25526, Juneau, AK 99802-5526
Arizona	Arizona Game and Fish Department Permits Coordinator, 2221 W. Greenway Road, Phoenix, AZ 85023
Arkansas	Arkansas Game and Fish Commission, 2 Natural Resources Drive, Little Rock, AR 72205
California	California Game & Fish Commission, 1416 Ninth St., Sacramento CA 95814, 916-445-0411

Colorado	Colorado Division of Wildlife, 6060 Broadway, Denver, CO 80216
Connecticut	Connecticut Department of Environmental Protection Wildlife Division, 79 Elm Street, Hartford, CT 06102-5127
Delaware	Delaware Department of Agriculture, 2320 South Dupont Highway, Dover, DE 19901
	Delaware Department of Natural Resources and Environmental Control, Division of Fish and Wildlife, Richardson and Robbins Building, 89 Kings Highway, Dover, DE 19903
Florida	Florida Department of Natural Resources, Office of Protected Species Management, 3900 Commonwealth Blvd., Tallahassee, FL 32399-3000
	Florida Game and Freshwater Fish Commission, 620 South Meridian Street ,Tallahassee, FL 32399-1600
Georgia	Georgia Department of Natural Resources, Special Permits Unit, 2070 U.S. Highway 278 SE, Social Circle, GA 30279
Hawaii	Hawaii Department of Land and Natural Resources, 1151 Punchbowl Street, Honolulu, HI 96813
Idaho	Idaho Department of Fish and Game, 600 S. Walnut Street, P.O. Box 25 Boise, ID 83707
Illinois	Illinois Department of Conservation, Endangered Species Project Manager, 524 S. Second Street, Lincoln Tower Plaza, Springfield, IL 62701-1787
Indiana	Indiana Department of Natural Resources, Division of Fish and Wildlife, Commercial License Clerk, Indiana Government Center South, 402 W. Washington St., Room W273, Indianapolis, IN 46204-2267
Iowa	Iowa Department of Natural Resources, Wallace State Office Building, Des Moines, IA 50319-5145
Kansas	Kansas Department of Wildlife and Parks, Route 2, Box 54A, Pratt, KS 67124-9599
Kentucky	Kentucky Department of Fish and Wildlife Resources, #1 Game Farm Road, Frankfort, KY 40601
Louisiana	Louisiana Department of Agriculture and Forestry, P.O. Box 631, Baton Rouge, LA 70821
	Louisiana Department of Wildlife and Fisheries, P.O. Box 9800, Baton Rouge, LA 70898-9000

(continued)

Table 17-1 *(continued)*

Maine	Maine Department of Inland Fisheries and Wildlife, State Station House, 41284 State Street, Augusta, ME 04333
Maryland	Maryland Department of Natural Resources, Tidewater Administration, Fisheries Division, Tawes State Office Building, C-2, Annapolis, MD 21401
Massachusetts	Massachusetts Division of Fisheries and Wildlife, 100 Cambridge Street, Boston, MA 022202
Michigan	Michigan Department of Agriculture, P.O. Box 30017, Lansing, MI 48909
	Michigan Department of Natural Resources, Stevens T. Mason Building, Box 30028, Lansing, MI 48909
Minnesota	Minnesota Department of Natural Resources, Endangered Species Permit Coordinator, 500 Lafayette Road, St. Paul, MN 55155-4001
Mississippi	Mississippi Department of Wildlife, Fisheries, and Parks, Museum of Natural History, 111 N. Jefferson St., Jackson, MS 39202
Missouri	Missouri Department of Conservation, 2901 West Truman Blvd., P.O. Box 180, Jefferson City, MO 65102-0180
Montana	Montana Department of Fish, Wildlife, and Parks, Law Enforcement Division, 1420 E. Sixth Ave., Helena, MT 59620
Nebraska	Nebraska Game and Parks Commission, 2200 N. 33rd St., P.O. Box 30370, Lincoln, NE 68503-0370
Nevada	Nevada Division of Wildlife, P.O. Box 10678, 1100 Valley Road, Reno, NV 89520-0022
New Hampshire	New Hampshire Fish and Game Department, 2 Hazen Drive, Concord NH 033301
New Jersey	New Jersey Department of Environmental Protection and Energy, Division of Fish, Game, and Wildlife, CN 400, Trenton, NJ 08625-0400
New Mexico	New Mexico Department of Game and Fish, Villagra Building, P.O. Box 25112, Santa Fe, NM 87504
New York	New York State Department of Environmental Protection, Division of Fish and Wildlife, Special License Unit, 50 Wolf Road, Albany, NY 12233
	New York State Department of Environmental Protection, State University of New York, Building 40, Stoney Brook, NY 11794

North Carolina	North Carolina Wildlife Resources Commission, Archdale Building, 513 N. Salisbury St., Raleigh, NC 27611
North Dakota	North Dakota Game and Fish Department, 100 North Bismarck Expressway, Bismarck, ND 58501-5095
Ohio	Ohio Department of Natural Resources, Division of Wildlife, 1840 Belcher Drive, Columbus, OH 43224-1329
Oklahoma	Oklahoma Department of Wildlife Conservation, 1801 North Lincoln Blvd., Oklahoma City, OK 73105
Oregon	Oregon Department of Agriculture, 635 Capitol N.E., Salem, OR 97310
	Oregon Department of Fish and Wildlife, 2501 SW First Avenue, P.O. Box 59, Portland, OR 92707
Pennsylvania	Pennsylvania Fish and Boat Commission, Division of Fisheries Management, Herpetology and Endangered Species Coordinator, 450 Robinson Lane, Bellefonte, PA 16823-9685
Rhode Island	Rhode Island Department of Environmental Management, Division of Fish and Wildlife, Washington County Government Center, Wakefield, RI 02879
	Rhode Island Division of Agriculture, 22 Hayes Street, Providence, RI 02903
South Carolina	South Carolina Wildlife and Marine Resources Department, Rembert C. Dennis Building, P.O. Box 167, Columbia, SC 29202
	South Carolina Department of Natural Resources, Dennis Wildlife Center, P.P. Drawer 190, Bonneau, SC 29431
South Dakota	South Dakota Department of Game, Fish, and Parks, Foss Building, 523 East Capitol, Pierre, SD 57501-3182
	South Dakota Department of Game, Fish, and Parks, License Office, 412 West Missouri, Pierre, SD 57501
Tennessee	Tennessee Wildlife Resources Agency, Ellington Agricultural Center, P.O. Box 40747, Nashville, TN 37204
Texas	Texas Parks and Wildlife Department, 4200 Smith School Road, Austin, TX 78744
Utah	Utah Department of Agriculture, 350 N. Redwood Road, Salt Lake City, UT 84116
	Utah Department of Natural Resources, Division of Wildlife Resources, Wildlife Registration Office, 1596 West North Temple, Salt Lake City, UT 84116

(continued)

Table 17-1 *(continued)*

Vermont	Vermont Fish and Game Department, Law Enforcement Division, 103 South Main St., Waterbury, VT 05676
Virginia	Virginia Department of Game and Inland Fisheries, 4010 West Broad Street, P.O. Box 11104, Richmond, VA 23230-1104
Washington	Washington Department of Fish and Wildlife, 600 Capitol Way N., Olympia, WA 98501-1091
West Virginia	West Virginia Department of Natural Resources, Division of Wildlife, P.O. Box 67, Elkins, WV 26241-0067
Wisconsin	Wisconsin Department of Natural Resources, P.O. Box 7921, Madison WI 53791-9414
Wyoming	Wyoming Game and Fish Department, 5400 Bishop Blvd., Cheyenne, WY 82006

Federal offices

When you have a question about interstate transport, regulations, and permits for importing herps, you need to go to the feds.

The U.S. Fish and Wildlife Service is charged with conserving, protecting. and enhancing fish, wildlife, and plants and their habitats for the continuing benefit of the American public. It is one of the agencies involved with issuing permits for use of federal lands, and also oversees the importing of herps (among other animals).

- U.S. Fish and Wildlife Service, Office of Management Authority, 4401 N. Fairfax Dr., Room 432, Arlington, VA 22203; Web site: http://offices.fws.gov/orgcht.html.

- U.S. Fish and Wildlife Service, Region 1 Office, Eastside Federal Complex, 911 N.E. 11th Avenue, Portland, OR 97232-4181. The Pacific Region includes California, Idaho, Nevada, Oregon, Washington, Hawaii. and the Pacific Islands.

- U.S. Fish and Wildlife Service, Region 2 Office, 500 Gold Avenue, S.W. Albuquerque, NM 87103. The Southwest Region includes Arizona, New Mexico, Oklahoma, and Texas.

- U.S. Fish and Wildlife Service, Region 3 Office, Whipple Federal Building, Fort Snelling, MN 55111-4506. The Great Lakes-Big Rivers Region includes Illinois, Indiana, Iowa, Michigan, Missouri, Minnesota, Ohio, and Wisconsin.

✔ U.S. Fish and Wildlife Service, Region 4 Office, 1875 Century Center Blvd., Atlanta, GA 30345-3301. The Southeast Region includes Alabama, Arkansas, Florida, Georgia, Kentucky, Louisiana, Mississippi, North Carolina, Puerto Rico/Virgin Islands, South Carolina, and Tennessee.

✔ U.S. Fish and Wildlife Service, Region 5 Office, 300 Westgate Center Dr., Hadley, MA 01035-9589. The Northeast Region includes Connecticut, Delaware, Maine, Maryland, Massachusetts, New Hampshire, New Jersey, New York, Pennsylvania, Rhode Island, Vermont, Virginia, and West Virginia.

✔ U.S. Fish and Wildlife Service, Region 6 Office, 134 Union Blvd., Lakewood, CO 80228. The Mountain-Prairie Region includes Colorado, Kansas, Montana, North Dakota, Nebraska, South Dakota, Utah, and Wyoming,

✔ U.S. Fish and Wildlife Service, Region 7 Office, 1011 East Tudor Road, Anchorage, AK 99503. The Alaska Region consists of the state of Alaska.

The liabilities of raising big snakes

You could be tempted to get into snake raising because of the money aspect. The simple math part *is* alluring. Suppose that you have a female Burmese python that you've raised as a pet for five years. She's now close to 15 feet in length and heavy bodied, a brute of a snake in fact. Your buddy suggests getting his 5-year-old male together with your female, breeding them, and splitting the profits.

This sounds like a good deal to you. After all, as big as your female is, she could have as many as 60 or 70 eggs! You build a bigger cage and put the two snakes together on a December day, and they breed. After a few weeks, you can tell that your female is gravid (pregnant) based on her actions (or rather her inactions —gravid females don't do much except eat and get bigger).

Fifty days later she lays eggs, 50 of them, all big, all apparently viable. You remove the eggs and put them in the incubator. Most (42 of them) hatch 60 days later.

You keep the babies until they shed the first time (the postnatal shed), and have fed once. (That's 42 mice at $1 each.) You scout around and sell 15 of the young to your local pet stores for $25 apiece. A reptile expo is coming up in another month, but between now and then, you'll have to feed your 27 remaining babies a couple of mice each. That's another $54.

You attend the expo and sell 17 of the babies for $50 each and the remaining 10 to a single individual on the last day for $30 each. That's $1,525. You deduct the cost of the mice and the expo table and split the take with your partner. You're still $625 to the good. Sounds pretty good, especially when you consider that most of these sales are in cash. (You don't want to take a chance on someone's check bouncing, after all.)

But things start to go bad locally. Three of the kids you sold the snakes to want to return the snakes and get their money back — their moms don't want the snakes in the house.

(continued)

(continued)

You tell yourself it isn't your problem that the snakes you've just sold will reach 12 feet in length in less than four years, or that a snake longer than 10 feet should be handled by two people because it can bite and constrict strongly. You tell yourself that the people who buy your snakes will just have to find out how to take care of them and how to house and feed them.

A Burmese python will soon outgrow mice as food. At a 6-foot length — easily reached the first year — a Burmese needs four rats ($2 each) every two weeks. As the snake grows, the owner can either buy large quantities of rats (which are available frozen in 100 lots that you store in your freezer) or begin feeding rabbits. But then that's where parents who haven't already stepped in often do. Cheap rabbits are $8 each, and Mom doesn't like the idea of feeding Thumper to a snake — even when Thumper is bought already prekilled and frozen as snake food.

One kid, Robby, has trouble persuading his mom that the snake is okay, even after a year. This snake is 7 feet long and doesn't want to stay in the screen-topped terrarium her kid bought for it (he piles books on top to keep the snake in), and she thinks he's already too big.

You may be able to duck taking the snake back, especially if Robby takes your advice and puts the cage down in the basement. But one day, about four months later, he calls you again, and he's worried. He tells you he's been cutting down on the food he offers his snake in a misguided effort to keep it small. "My snake got out of his cage. The basement window was open, and I think he's somewhere in the neighborhood. How do I find him?" Are you liable if the snake bites someone, or if he crawls into someone else's yard and makes a meal of the family dog?

You quite likely are. In this scenario, you'd better hope it's just the treasured dog that gets eaten.

Eventually complaints are going to reach the compassionate ears of the city council or county commissioners. A collective gasp of amazement is heard as all say in unison, "You mean someone is buying and selling pythons here? Here in our town USA? These things can be dangerous, can't they? Well, we'll put a stop to that!" The result is a ban on all snakes over 7 feet long.

Certainly the state gets involved as well.

Robby will face at least two civil charges: keeping a reptile without a permit and housing a wild animal in an unsafe manner. If he turned the snake loose on purpose (who'd admit to this?), he'll be charged with releasing exotic wildlife. Those are charges from the state.

If the snake attacks someone's dog or cat, you can expect the pet owner to file charges against Robby as well. Although charges have not yet been brought against the seller of a snake, once that snake has been sold, it could happen. The head of wildlife inspection for the state of Florida, Barry Cook, has said "If a firearms instructor gives me faulty instructions in handling firearms and I kill or injure someone else as a result, you can bet the firearms instructor is partially liable." You, as the breeder/seller of the snake, are in a delicate situation. Not only did you sell a potentially dangerous snake to a minor, but through your lack of instruction and your lack of a disclaimer, you've put other people at risk.

Meanwhile 41 other not-so-little time bombs are out there, and you hope fervently that no one remembers your name.

Part V
The Part of Tens

The 5th Wave   By Rich Tennant

"Hey! I think you've found a friend!"

In this part . . .

This part offers some useful tips on myriad topics. I tell you how to know when your herp needs to see a veterinarian. I describe ten U.S. zoos with fantastic herp collections that will really pique your interest. If you want to know more about reptiles and amphibians, I supply ten information sources that are interesting as well as useful.

Chapter 18

Ten Reasons to See Your Veterinarian

In This Chapter

▶ Respiratory problems

▶ Puffiness and bulges

▶ Refusal to eat

▶ Mechanical damage, unresponsiveness, and more

Sometimes, being a herp owner seems to require more knowledge upfront than you might have. You can discover a lot, however, about what to expect from your herp by watching him as he feeds, sleeps, moves about his cage, and interacts with you. Becoming familiar with herp behavior is a learning curve, but it's not a steep one.

But what happens if something goes wrong before your brain has time to receive and process all that learning? Suppose that you wake up and your lizard is lying on the floor of his cage, not on his branch? You squint at him and think to yourself, "Something's not right here. What's going on?"

Here's a quick list of symptoms that you ought not to try to correct on your own. Your veterinarian is your best friend, and she or he can help your herp and, in so doing, help you.

Don't ask your herp to pay for your laziness and stinginess with his life. You can ignore your own health if you choose (go ahead — eat hamburgers!), but not your herp's.

Rasping Breath and Wheezing

Reptiles are far more subject to respiratory infections than amphibians. In fact, I've never seen an amphibian with a respiratory infection (usually shortened to simply "respiratory" as in, "My snake had a respiratory, but he's much better now."). Respiratories are a typical manifestation of stress in new imports or in reptiles subjected to chilling. Damp cold, as typified by winters in the fog belt areas of the United States, seems to trigger a particularly chronic respiratory infection. Some respiratory problems can also be brought on by an excessive endoparasitic burden — again, usually triggered by stress. Reptiles can get along with their endoparasites, but when something alters that sometimes delicate balance, the parasites get the upper hand.

Typical symptoms of a respiratory infection are wheezing, bubbles visible at the nostrils, and a gaping mouth. Your reptile has the equivalent of severe pneumonia, and he's distinctly uncomfortable. By the time you see these symptoms, your herp has passed the point of being able to get rid of this infection on his own. Snakes have only one functional lung, so they have no backup at all. Take him to your vet, correct your pet's day/night cage temperatures, and (for arid-land species) perhaps decrease the humidity in the cage.

Swollen Limbs

Puffy arms and legs are one sad symptom of *metabolic bone disease* (MBD). With MBD, the bones in the body become weakened because there isn't enough calcium in the diet, and the herp hasn't been able to sun. In an effort to restore strength in the weakened limbs, the body adds fibrous tissue to the muscles. This extra tissue puffs up the limbs, and they look chubby.

With UV, calcium supplements, and a proper diet, the strength can be restored to the bones, but certain deformities, such as a curved spine and shortened jaw, are there to stay. Take your herp to the veterinarian, buy some UV lights, read up on this disease (see Chapter 11 in this book), and provide a better diet.

Prolapsed Cloaca

A *prolapse,* or emergence, occurs when the herp's *cloaca* (the multipurpose bladder that houses the male's penises and into which the kidney and intestine empty) protrudes through the opening of the anus. Sometimes, one of the male's sexual organs or the hemipenis will become everted and will protrude from the body through the anal opening. When the protrusion gets stuck outside the body, it's called a prolapse. This problem may be caused by dehydration and straining, constipation, retained eggs that the female is trying to expel, or a male's effort to mark his turf with seminal material. The everted tissue becomes stuck outside the body and begins to dry out, which results in tissue death. Amputation may be necessary, and a host of worse problems may occur.

If soaking the animal in warm sugar water for 20 minutes or so doesn't enable the animal to withdraw the tissue, it's heigh-ho, heigh-ho, off to the veterinarian you go. Sugar water draws the moisture out of the engorged tissue. As a result, the tissue may go back inside the body or will stay inside the body once you gently push it back in. Wash your hands before and after soaking your animal.

Bulge in the Lower (Female) Body: Dystocia

Dystocia is a fancy term for "the inability to deposit eggs." The condition is also called egg binding. It can be caused by dehydration, insufficient calcium levels (there we go again — calcium affects herps in many ways), stress, failure to find a satisfactory spot for nesting, eggs that are too large to pass out of the body, or malformed *oviducts,* the passage through which the females *oocytes,* or unfertilized eggs, move on their way to the cloaca.

Your herp may be temporarily overactive or very restless, as if seeking something she can't find, or she just can't get comfortable. Then she'll become lethargic and depressed, and she may stop feeding. This condition isn't something that your female can fix on her own. Don't wait. She needs analysis of the cause and correction, which is something your veterinarian knows how to do. She may need surgery.

Prolonged Failure to Feed

Some herps are reluctant feeders, and this habit can drive their owners right up the walls of their own caging. Why doesn't your herp want to eat? Maybe he doesn't like the food you're offering. (Quick, rifle through the appendix in the back of this book, and see whether your herp is one of the most popular herps of its order. I list typical food items there.)

Maybe you're keeping the herp too warm or too cool. Maybe (if he's a lizard or a turtle) he needs sunshine. Maybe he doesn't like you looking at him when he's thinking about eating. (My newly acquired MBD-iguanas, as badly as they needed proper nutrition, didn't like me looking at them when they wanted to eat. If I was there, they didn't eat, period. So I learned to give them food and leave the room.) Maybe the animal is already so sick that eating is way low on his list of things to do.

If it's wintertime and you're keeping a temperate species, maybe he's in his winter slow time. Many pet herps are reluctant feeders during the wintertime, even when you use bright lights and a longer day cycle in an effort to keep them feeding.

If, during warm weather and a natural long day cycle, a snake fasts for more than a month, a lizard for more than three days, a turtle/tortoise for more than a week, a frog or salamander from a temperate area for more than two weeks, or a frog or salamander from tropical areas for more than a week, take your pet to the veterinarian.

Mechanical Damage

Sometimes, a body part on a herp breaks, due to trauma. Damage can be as minor as a broken toenail or as serious as a broken back. The good news is that with proper medical care and a good diet, recovery is rapid and complete.

- ✔ **Cracked shell on a turtle:** This problem can be a real sleeper. Turtles can sustain considerable damage to their shells and survive. On the other hand, they can suffer a hairline crack and die from an infection. From the outside, you can't tell what sort of damage has been done inside. Don't take a chance. Take the turtle to your veterinarian; he or she has a host of ways to repair broken turtle shells.

- ✔ **Burns:** Herps can be burned by lying against exposed light bulbs or exposed heating elements, or by a hot rock that gets too hot. Their skin doesn't react to burns the way mammalian skin reacts. Your vet will treat the burn and deal with threatened infections. (Burn-damaged skin shouts "welcome!" to bacteria and other infectious agents.) You'll need to locate the equipment that caused the problem and remove it or shield it against your herp.

- ✔ **Bites:** Reptiles bite each other. They tend to get lively ("Get that thing off my leg!") during breeding season. Males fight, shoving each other around and adding biting to the action when shoving doesn't produce a clear-cut winner. Males hang on to the females with their teeth before and during copulation — when you don't have hands, you gotta make do.

  Intended prey can bite herps. For example, a chick designated as food may peck a herp, or a mouse or rat left in the cage may nibble a herp, which is why prekilled prey is recommended. Bite damage can be extensive, particularly if it occurs on the head or in an area of limited circulation, such as the tail. Infection is a typical result. Your veterinarian will assess the damage and fix what can be fixed; surgery may be needed.

✔ **Broken limb or tail:** Captive lizards, larger lizards in particular, may break a limb in the day-to-day routine of their lives, but this injury should not occur under your safekeeping. If your lizard has broken a limb, take the animal to the veterinarian and assess the diet you've been using. Your pet may be suffering from MBD, which weakens the bones and makes them subject to breakage.

Lizards lose their tail as a defensive mechanism. If a predator grabs a lizard's tail, the tail is a small price to pay to escape with his life. The lizards most famous for losing their tails, like the blue-tailed skinks in Albuquerque when I was a kid, have fracture planes in the bones of the tail. One sudden move on the part of the lizard, one touch by a suspected predator, and the tail is shed and wriggling (in case you're wondering, the blue color doesn't last). Other lizard species don't have these fracture planes, but their tails will break off if grabbed and yanked. It takes more of a tug to break the tail of an iguana than it does to break the tail of the blue-tailed skink, but both tails can break. Don't fret in either case. Bleeding is minimal; the stump heals over, and the tail regenerates, although it's always different from the original in appearance.

Fungus on an Amphibian or Turtle

Fungus spores are everywhere. Like salmonella, fungus is an opportunistic infectious agent. If the skin of an amphibian is damaged or breached, or if turtles are kept in dirty water that isn't changed regularly, the spores are right there, ready to move in, hatch, set up housekeeping, and pop out thousands and thousands of their own tiny spore babies to populate their new home. Cleanliness is next to godliness, so keep all herps that live in water under very clean conditions. Any signs of external fungus (you don't know what's going on *inside* the animal) need prompt evaluation and treatment.

Swollen Eyes on a Turtle

Swollen eyes are usually an indication of a vitamin imbalance and/or starvation. Clean the caging, offer fresh food and sunlight, and get an evaluation, diagnosis, and treatment plan from your veterinarian.

External Parasites

Ticks and mites are an irritant and can be dealt with by using anti-tick and anti-mite medications. If the problem is severe, or if your methods don't end the problem after two weeks of use, talk to your veterinarian. Ticks can harbor diseases that other animals can contract, so don't mess around with this problem. Remove and kill every tick, and if the problem is mites, treat your animal appropriately.

Unresponsiveness

Herps that are unresponsive are close to death. Sorry to be so blunt, but you need to know the truth. If your herp sleeps a lot, if he doesn't pull his leg back from you when you take it in your fingers and give a gentle tug, if he lies in his cage without moving or feeding, *you* get moving. The cause may be any of the following:

- **Starvation:** Either the herp hasn't been fed, or he's been offered the wrong foods and refused to feed as a result.

- **Avitaminosis:** Your herp is lacking one or more vitamins.

- **Temperatures that are too cool:** The animal literally cannot move; his muscles are shut down until he gets warmer.

  After a freeze in Florida, the ground under some trees is littered with anole corpses — they were in the trees, got too cold, couldn't hold on, and fell.

- **Dehydration:** The herp has too little moisture in his body. Either he hasn't been offered water he can drink, or he can't drink because he's been too cold, too long.

Whatever the cause, if your herp is unresponsive, take him to the vet pronto!

Chapter 19

Ten U.S. Zoos with Great Herp Collections

*Y*ou like herps; you think they're fascinating creatures. You have a couple cages, you've joined a herp society, and you've gone to a symposium or expo or two. While you're peeling off the gold star I've just stuck on your forehead, you may well ask, "Is there another way to experience herps?"

You bet, and this in a way is the easiest of them all. You become a herp-watcher, except that you get practical and go where you know you'll see herps. You go to zoos.

Zoos have been keeping herps for a looooooong time. Some of the zoos are okay, most are quite good, and the ones I list here are some of the best. I call this list the best ten zoos for herps, but don't restrict yourself to this list, because there are a lot more. These are just my ten quick-picks.

The criteria I used for this ten list are all over the map. Except for having devoted staffs (who work with and devote themselves to their charges in a way that all animal lovers should emulate), the zoos I list are not alike in any other way. Some are known for the size of their collection; some are known for their expertise with one type of herp; still others are great because they specialize in geographical collections, such as the herps of Madagascar or of their own state. A couple zoos depict herps as art objects. (And they are! Just look at the browns on a Gaboon viper!)

Visit these zoos. Don't hesitate to call and ask specific questions. (If you push the "O" button during the recorded message, you get a real operator who can connect you with the reptile house). If you know of some other great zoos for herps, let me know. My e-mail address is ask234@aol.com.

Bronx Zoo

2300 Southern Blvd., Bronx, NY 10460-1090; phone 718-220-2046; Web site
www.bronxzoo.org

This zoo features five spectacular amphibian exhibits, with lots of plantings,
and mixed species of reptiles and amphibians from the northeast United
States forest and Southeast Asia. Exhibit animals include dendrobates, atelopus, and axolotls. JungleWorld has a 77,000-gallon "river" with gharials, Asian
turtles, and fish. The Congo exhibit with the rock python lets visitors "see"
the heat they produce.

Cincinnati Zoo

3400 Vine St., Cincinnati, OH 45220; phone 1-800-94-HIPPO; Web site
www.cincinnatizoo.org

You can see some really choice herps here, including Komodo dragons. A
new mixed species exhibit puts natural neighbors of bushmaster, Schlegel's
vipers, and dart frogs together. Be sure to look for the hellbender/Japanese
and Chinese giant salamander display. Marlin, the American crocodile, was
brought to the St. Louis Zoo by Marlin Perkins some 40 years ago and was
recently trucked to the Cincinnati Zoo.

Dallas Zoo

650 South R.L Thornton Freeway (I-35E), Dallas, TX 75203-3034; phone
214-670-5656; Web site www.dallas-zoo.org

This zoo has a large collection of venomous reptiles and amphibians and a
big monitor collection. Recent successes in the breeding field include bush-
masters and perentie monitors. The tuatara exhibit is cooled to 50 degrees
(that's the way, uh-huh uh-huh, they like it — bring a sweater). On exhibit are
Species Survival Plan animals, including Chinese alligators, rock iguanas,
Aruba Island rattlesnakes, radiated tortoises, and Dumeril's boas.

Denver Zoo

2300 Steele St., Denver, CO 80205-4899; phone 303-376-4800; Web site
www.denverzoo.org

The Tropical Discovery area is a huge building — 22,000 square feet — and it houses the Komodo dragon. Big windows separate you from the dragons. Breeding program successes include the Komodo dragon and a crocodile monitor, both of which are on display in the reptile nursery.

Detroit Zoological Park

8450 West Ten Mile Road, Royal Oak, MI 48068-0039; 24-hour info line 248-398-0900, phone 248-398-0903; Web site www.detroitzoo.org

Two big display areas are featured here. The biggest and most astonishing building houses the National Amphibian Conservation Center, which houses some 65 species in naturalistic displays. The frog calls and overhead changing images of amphibians are a show by themselves. The second big building is the separate reptile and amphibian building, which displays 100 species and 450 specimens in closet-sized habitats. Don't miss the re-created pond outside of Orientation Theater.

Fort Worth Zoo

1989 Colonial Parkway, Fort Worth, TX 76110; phone 817-759-7555; Web site www.fortworthzoo.org

Komodo dragons, gharials, Malaysian painted turtles, and Philippine crocodiles are on display in a 3,400-square-foot display. The tortoise collection includes star, pancake, Burmese brown, and Egyptian tortoises, Venomous species include rattlesnakes, vipers, beaded lizards, and Gila monsters. The reptile house is divided into geographical regions.

Indianapolis Zoo

1200 W. Washington St., Indianapolis, IN 46222; phone 317-630-2001; Web site www.indyzoo.com

Eye-catching graphics at this zoo will help catch your interest, but watch that motion-activated giant spitting cobra — he spits water! The breeding project with Cyclura (rock iguanas) and blue iguanas has won American Zoo and Aquarium Association awards. The reptile display inside the Desert Dune exhibit depicts snakes as art. The Beautiful and Venomous exhibit displays some of the most gorgeous and deadly snakes in the world.

Philadelphia Zoo

300 West Girard Ave., Philadelphia, PA 19104-1196; phone 215-243-1100; Web site www.phillyzoo.org

The recently renovated reptile house has display areas for aquatic herps, crocodilians, reptiles, and amphibians. Be sure to look for the Hosmer's skink (from Australia), the shingleback skinks, the big reticulated python (16 feet), and the colony of prehensile-tailed skinks, some of which have been in the colony since 1973. The king cobra has been in this zoo for 24 years. Giant tortoises are on display outdoors during the summer.

Riverbanks Zoo & Garden

500 Wildlife Parkway, Columbia, SC 22940; phone 803-779-8717; www.riverbanks.org

One highlight here is the award-winning 20,000-square-foot Aquarium-Reptile Complex. The galleries replicate South Carolina, desert, tropics, and ocean habitats. The extensive tortoise collection features naturalistic enclosures. Check out the free-ranging leaf-tailed geckos (Uroplatus) in the tropics exhibit. Current breeding projects include threatened state amphibians (including the dwarf siren and the dusky gopher frog) and third-generation green tree monitors.

Toledo Zoo

P.O. Box 14013, Toledo, OH 419-385-5721; phone 419-385-5721; Web site www.toledozoo.org. Take the Toledo Zoo exit from Anthony Wayne Trail (SR 25), just west of I-75 in Toledo.

This zoo is known for its conservation work with the Virgin Isles boa and the Aruba rattlesnake. The tuatara exhibit has a trio just coming into sexual maturity. Frogtown, USA, a big native amphibian exhibit, depicts the diversity of amphibian life. About 650 specimens are in the collection.

Chapter 20

Ten Ways to Become More Involved with Herps

In This Chapter
▶ Looking into herp organizations
▶ Checking out Web sites and magazines
▶ Visiting expos and natural attractions

Here's a brief listing of some useful information that I'd wished I'd had years ago. (The fact that most of these places didn't exist 20 years ago changes nothing.) This chapter is designed to open doors for you and to help you find some of the truly astonishing resources that are Out There waiting for you to call, e-mail, or write them. Don't waste any time — the information you can gain from these places is worth the price of this book and ten others.

Herp Societies

Your local herp society may be a bit hard to find — most are strictly volunteer-operated, which means that some details, such as updating Web sites and addresses of the officers, slip through the cracks. They rarely use post office boxes, and unless they're sponsored by a museum, they're not likely to have a street address. You can try the Web, but when I used addresses I found online for mailings to herp societies in Florida, easily two-thirds were returned as undeliverable. (I don't know if this says more about the type of the people who live in Florida, or about herpers in general.)

Use the following tips to find a herp society near you:

- Ask around.
- Talk to the manager or the employees at pet stores.
- Call your local community college or four-year college and talk to one of the biology or zoology professors.

- Call your nearby zoo and ask to speak to one of the reptile curators.

- Contact the natural science person at your local museum.

- Ask your local chamber of commerce. (They collect information on local clubs — this sort of data adds value when someone is thinking about moving to an area.)

- Ask your local librarian, also known as your best friend in the *whole* world, is an incredible storehouse of information. When I wanted to know where to stay in Ajo, Arizona, a very tiny place, the local librarian kindly gave me her thoughts on where to stay, and she was right.

- Check with your veterinarian, or if you're really lucky, you have a local reptile veterinarian. She or he will *certainly* know about the local herp society.

After you find your local herp society, your search will be worth the effort because you'll meet a bunch of helpful people who just happen to enjoy the same sort of odd hobby that you enjoy. They'll be useful, too, with ways to obtain frozen feeder mice at bulk rates, suggestions on where to make bulk purchases on mouse chow (if you're raising your own), and information on good buys on new or used equipment of every shape and description. Of course, society members buy and sell herps to other members of the club at very reduced rates. Should you go on vacation, you've already got a pool of trained people who can herp-sit and won't think pinching apart earthworms is gross.

Reptile Veterinarians

Sooner or later, you're going to need a herp veterinarian, one with more specific and very specialized knowledge about reptiles and amphibians. You may have one in your area and not even know it; very few of them hang out a sign that says "Herp Veterinarian Inside. Come In."

The easiest way to find a reptile veterinarian is to contact the Association of Reptilian and Amphibian Veterinarians, P.O. Box 605, Chester Heights, PA 19017; phone 610-358-9530; Web site www.arav.org.

Your own general veterinarian is probably comfortable with the idea of treating herps, but may lack experience. Call her or him first to check. Most veterinarians constantly update their training, and exotics are part of that training. My veterinarian is a general practitioner, and she's been very good at treating my iguanas with prolapses, the two iggies I got with metabolic bone disease (MBD), and a wide assortment of other furred, scaled, and scaleless creatures. If I did not have the confidence I have in her, or if I had an expensive herp, I'd make the drive to my nearest reptile veterinarian.

Your Local Library

The best bargain in the United States is your local library. Not only does it have books you can check out and read for absolutely no cost, but your librarian is by nature a helpful person who is made most happy when he or she can help you find the information you're looking for.

Species-Specific Groups

These are just three examples of species-specific interest groups. But if you name an animal, you can probably find at least one group of fellow enthusiasts.

International Iguana Society
133 Steele Rd.
West Hartford, CT 06119
Web site: www.iguanasociety.org

Global Gecko Society
c/o Leann Christianson
4920 Chester St.
Spenser, OK 73084-2560
Web site: www.gekkota.com

Crocodile Specialists Group
c/o Dr. James Perrin Ross
Executive Director
Florida Museum of Natural History
Gainesville, FL 32611
Phone: 352-392-1721
Web site: www.flmnh.ufl.edu/natschi/herpetology/crocs

Web Sites

Let your fingers do the walking. The Web sites in this section are full of information for serious herpers and hobbyists alike.

- **Kingsnake.com** (www.kingsnake.com): This is one of the biggest Web sites that deals with reptiles and amphibians (the name fooled me at first). It's particularly good for its listing of reptile expos and symposiums.

- **HerpDigest** (www.herpdigest.org): This free site is updated daily with what's in the news with herps. If you want to be current, this is the site for you.

✔ **PondTurtle.com** (www.pondturtle.com): Frank and Katie Slavens's Web site includes longevity and breeding data. Frank began collecting longevity data on herps in 1976.

✔ **Max Planck Institute for Demographic Research** (www.demogr.mpg.de/): The Web site for the Max Planck Institute in Rostock, Germany, has longevity records for some 90 species of reptiles and amphibians.

✔ **VenomousReptiles.org** (www.venomousreptiles.org): This site will convince you that venomous snakes are not curiosities, not macho play-things, but living creatures who are far better off uncaged and away from people.

✔ **Anapsid.org** (www.anapsid.org): This site belongs to Melissa Kaplan, the author of *Iguanas For Dummies* (published by Wiley). She has loads of first-hand and dependable advice on herps. She's an expert on green iguanas, and the quantity of solid information on this site will help you make good decisions in herp care.

Journals

Journals are published by academic societies and organizations, and these publications can get pretty technical. But if you want to find out what new species have been described, new behavioral notes, and loads of chemical and physiological data, journals fill the bill. The following journals are my favorites — do check out their Web sites:

Copeia
American Society of Ichthyologists and Herpetologists
Robert K Johnson, Secretary
Grice Marine Laboratory
University of Charleston
205 Ft. Johnson Road
Charleston, SC 29412
Web site: www.utexas.edu/dept/asih

Herpetology Review and Journal of Herpetology
Society for the Study of Amphibians and Reptiles
George Pisani
Division of Biological Science
University of Kansas
Lawrence, KS 66405-2106
Web site: www.ssarherps.org

Trade Magazines

These magazines are for nonscholars, people who enjoy herps for fun instead of making their living from them (although it would be nice . . .). Each magazine listed here features thoughtful, well-written articles.

✔ *Fauna Magazine:* Published by a nonprofit organization, *Fauna Magazine* focuses on the world's most unloved, unknown, and unusual animals. Contact information: International Fauna Society, 135 Marcus Blvd, Hauppauge, NY 11788; phone 631-231-2914; Web site `www.FaunaSociety.org`.

✔ *Reptiles Magazine:* The survivor of about four different reptile/amphibian magazines in the United States, *Reptiles Magazine* just celebrated its tenth anniversary. Contact information: P.O. Box 58700 (subscription department), Boulder, CO 80322-8700; Web site `www.animalnetwork.com/reptiles`.

✔ *Reptilia:* For those with an international flair, this reptile magazine is published in four languages, and it covers arthropods as well. It has good information and great photos and is very useful. Contact information: Salvador Mundi, 2; 08017 Barcelona, Spain; phone ++34 93 205 01 20; Web site `www.reptilia.net`.

Herp Expos

What if you didn't have to leaf through reptile magazines to find new products? What if you could see a dozen new gecko species at a single site? What if you didn't have to make a dozen phone calls to locate data on endangered species? What if you could met a couple thousand other herpers in a two-day period? An expo can offer all this and more. Here are only a few of the expos.

✔ **Florida International Reptile Show:** This show is held each March at the Tampa (Florida) Fairgrounds. Contact information: Tony Cueto, phone 919-496-7872; Web site `www.reptilesandexoticanimalshow.com`.

✔ **The Hamm show:** Held each March, the Hamm show is the big show in Europe. Check out the Web site at `www.exotics.net/terraristika`.

✔ **The International Reptile Breeders Association (IRBA):** The IRBA hosts shows in California from May to December. Contact information: 5519 Clairmont Mesa Blvd. #279, San Diego, CA 92117; phone 619-445-9964; Web site `www.irba.com`.

 ✔ **The International Herpetological Symposium:** This symposium is held each summer in different host cities. Contact information: IHS, Stan Draper, P.O. Box 16444, Salt Lake City, UT 84116; e-mail sdraper7@attbi.com, Web site www.kingsnake.com/HIS.

 ✔ **The National Reptile Breeders Expo:** This expo is held in Daytona, Florida, each August. Contact information: P.O. Box 3838, Winter Haven, FL; phone 863-294-2235; Web site www.reptilebreedersexpo.com.

Adoption Sites

Adoption is a very good choice when you're looking for a specific type of herp, such as a corn snake or a green iguana, and you don't care how big the animal is or what age it is. As with the acquisition of any animal, just be certain you know what you're getting into; there may be a hidden reason why the animal is available. Some reasons are easy to accept, such as "it got too big" or "I can't afford the earthworms."

Most herp societies have a member or two who has an animal up for adoption at little or no fee to a fellow society member. Once in a while, a pet store has an animal summarily given to it, usually the result of a parental ultimatum.

To do an online search, type in "reptile rescue (your state)," and you'll have plenty of choices. You can also be more specific in your request. If you'd like a turtle, type in *turtle rescue*, and you'll get sites concerned with turtles; the same holds true for almost any herp group.

Volunteers run a lot of the adoption sites, which means that the site — and the adoption agency — may be here today and unreachable tomorrow. Always look for a phone number and talk to a living person before you make any decisions on adoption. This is particularly true if you're trying to give up an animal — to have someone else adopt it out for you. You certainly don't want your herp to go to some self-styled "rescuer" who will take it to a pet store or wholesaler and sell it.

Most adoption sites do charge a fee for the animal, and if you want the animal shipped to you, that fee is extra. Expect to pay anywhere from $15 to $30 or up for the animal adoption fee. Any air freight shipment will cost you about $60, which is what it would cost if you were buying the animal and having it shipped to you. You can save money if you look for an adoption agency within your own state because you can drive to pick the animal up.

Herp-Watching Locations

You know about birders, those people who will drive five hours one way to catch a glimpse of a particular bird. They don't need to fill cages to enjoy their hobby, and you don't either. Herp watching is just a refinement on nature watching, a sport you can enjoy with a minimum of expense and equipment. Haul out those binoculars (you can buy close-up focus binoculars that bring something such as a lizard or butterfly ten feet away into sharp view), pull out the road atlas, and plan your next vacation to include some time herp watching in the field. Here are some good spots to start:

✔ **Arizona Sonora Desert Museum in Tucson, Arizona:** You get a zoo, a natural history museum, and a botanical garden, all in one place.

✔ **The former Crandon Park Zoo site on Key Biscayne in Miami, Florida:** A wonderful array of native and non-native wildlife flourishes here. (Eyes right, please — I'm talking about *herps*.)

✔ **Okefenokee National Wildlife Refuge in southern Georgia:** Rent a canoe and go paddling, although you can easily see the gators from the Visitors Center.

✔ **Big Bend National Park in Texas:** This site offers great lizard and snake watching, although the landscape, in muted tones of olive, gray, coral, and ivory, will add to your enjoyment of the trip.

✔ **Boone, North Carolina:** This is a grand spot for salamander watching. You'll need to get out of the car and look into roadside ditches and springs (water literally oozes from every vertical roadside cut in the spring), but you can find few prettier places for rambling and looking. If you've never wandered into the woods at 2 a.m. looking for salamanders, this is the place to start.

✔ **Eco-tours *anywhere:*** Let someone else do the work for you when you want to herp watch. Go on an eco-tour, either in the United States or abroad. (Get your passport application at your local post office.) Generally speaking, eco-tours employ native guides and the tour company takes care of details such as transportation, food, and lodging. All you need to do is climb into the bus, car, or boat and start looking. This type of tour is a very practical way to see native herps and other wildlife that you wouldn't be able to find on your own.

Appendix

Species Account of Popular Herps

• •

Popular frogs and toads and what makes them popular

Australian green treefrog

Scientific name: *Litoria (Pelodryas) caerulea*

Area of origin: Australia and Indonesia

Diet: Insects and smaller frogs form the diet of this species in the wild. Insects are also the best captive diet. However, many hobbyists have learned that their Australian green treefrogs eat pinky mice as well. Feed pinky mice only occasionally.

Ease of care: The Australian green treefrog is a very easily maintained captive. The green is variable, sometimes being olive and sometimes bluish-green, but most times, the frog is jade green. The belly is white. They're not usually aggressive to each other, so you can keep several in a woodland or a semiaquatic terrarium. Although nocturnal, these frogs often sit on horizontal limbs or on the glass of the terrarium during the hours of daylight and are frequently quite visible. Once acclimated to captivity, the treefrogs often awaken and forage during the daylight when food insects are introduced to the terrarium, and they're normally very active on cloudy days during periods of barometric low pressure. Although a temperature of 65 to 95 degrees can be tolerated, the suggested temperature range is 75 to 85 degrees. As with all amphibians, treefrogs must have access to moisture to replenish that lost from their body during normal activity and metabolism.

However, Australian green don't do well in saturated atmospheres, preferring instead rather dry conditions but regularly utilizing a shallow water dish. An occasional gentle misting is also beneficial. Keep the terrarium and the provided water clean. The water must not contain chlorine or chloramine and must not have been distilled.

Habitat/caging needs: A woodland terrarium is suitable for these treefrogs, but an even simpler one serves as well. A vertically oriented terrarium best accommodates their arboreal tendencies. Although Australian green treefrogs aren't overly active, I suggest that you use a terrarium of either 15- or 20-gallon (long) capacity to house from one to three frogs. In both cases, this gives you a terrarium with a 12-x-12-inch bottom footprint and a 24-inch

(15-gallon capacity) or 30-inch (20-gallon long) height. If the terrarium is used vertically, the top becomes an open side and can be secured with a modified metal- or plastic-framed screen or mesh top.

The substrate of the woodland terrarium should be several inches of clean soil. You can just use a few layers of dry paper towels for the flooring. In both cases, provide a sizable but shallow dish of clean, chlorine- and chloramine-free water. Add mossy logs or driftwood (do not use cedar) for climbing. A vining philodendron or pothos *(Epipremnum)* adds beauty to the enclosure and provides visual barriers. The live plants also help maintain a high relative humidity.

Behavior: These large treefrogs (2 to 4.5 inches long) are primarily nocturnal, but they may be active on cloudy days. Males may voice their honking calls if you mist them at night.

These treefrogs quickly learn to accept food offered to them in forceps or impaled on the end of a straw.

Bumblebee poison dart frog

Scientific name: *Dendrobates leucomelas*

Area of origin: Venezuelan rain forests are home to this remarkable frog.

Diet: Tiny amphibians require tiny insects for their diet. In the wild, dart frogs eat all manner of leaf-litter insects, including, but certainly not limited to, termites and ants. Captives thrive on vitamin- and calcium-enhanced pin-head crickets, termites, white worms, fruit flies, and springtails. Commercial suppliers of all of these bugs, except for the termites, advertise in reptile hobbyist magazines.

Ease of care: If their basic necessities of tiny food insects, correct temperature, and cleanliness are met, this beautiful frog is one of the hardiest and most outgoing of the dart frogs. Dart frogs lose their skin toxicity soon after being taken captive. These are diurnal amphibians.

Habitat/caging needs: Dart frogs, collectively, are specialized amphibians of the neotropical rainforests and, as such, require rain forest terrariums in which to live. Rainforest terrariums are certainly more complex arrangements than the caging required for horned frogs or toads, but when properly done, these terrariums are so beautiful that building and maintaining one can be as rewarding as successfully maintaining the dart frog inhabitants. Basically, a rain forest terrarium is just that: a tiny replica of a bit of one of the most complex ecosystems known.

The substrate can be potting soil over and separated from a layer of pea-sized river rock by a sheet of air-conditioning filter material. Place live woodland mosses atop the potting soil. One corner of the terrarium (a triangle of about 4 inches on each short side) should be devoid of soil and plantings. Excess water will be siphoned from this corner. Consider using the following as cage furniture: attractive foliage plants, a few pieces of driftwood (or other benign, nontoxic wood), hide boxes (halved coconut shells are a good choice here), and a shallow dish (a petri dish is an excellent choice). Besides mosses, plants such as fittonia, philodendron, and peacock ferns are excellent choices and are available at most nurseries.

Keep the plants and substrate amply watered and remove the excess water by siphoning it from the corner of the terrarium left bare. Don't use distilled water or water containing chlorines or chloramines. The level of water must not be above the top level of the river rock. You can maintain the high humidity needed by dart frogs by keeping a glass cover on the terrarium. The inside of the terrarium should be humid and moist but not always dripping wet. The terrariums need rather strong lighting (consider a fluorescent plant-grow bulb) to induce healthy growth of the plants.

Behavior: Dart frogs are beautiful, but dart frogs are also territorial bullies. The agonistic behavior by a dominant example toward others in the terrarium can cause the ill health and even the death of subordinate frogs. Watch your frogs carefully to ascertain that all is tranquil in the terrarium. Ample visual barriers — plants, driftwood, and smooth decorative rocks — help keep frog tempers on an even keel.

All the frogs in any intended group setting should be about the same size. Putting all the frogs in the terrarium simultaneously usually helps lessen tensions. If one frog displays overt dominance, remove it to a small holding facility for a few days. Doing so allows the remaining terrarium inhabitants to quietly establish their own succession of dominance and places the removed frog at somewhat of a disadvantage when he is reintroduced to the colony.

Dart frogs have an unusual method of breeding. They lay their eggs in moist terrestrial locations where they hatch after fertilization. One of the parents (usually the father) then transports the tadpole(s) on his back to a small puddle of water into which the tadpoles slither and undergo development.

Horned frogs

Scientific name: *Ceratophrys* species

Area of origin: Members of this genus may be found over much of South America, from Colombia and Venezuela to Argentina.

Diet: Three species and two hybrid horned frogs are available in the pet trade. The diet of these voracious frogs is dictated by the frog's body size as well as the size of the adult. Juveniles of all, and small adults of others, usually eat large insects and other frogs. Large examples of the Chaco and the ornate horned frogs eat other frogs (including smaller examples of their own species), small reptiles, large insects, and an occasional small rodent.

Ease of care: Of the horned frogs commonly offered in the pet trade, the Amazon horned frog *(C. cornuta)* is often very difficult to acclimate. Be certain to see the very frog in which you are interested eat, preferably several times. All others — the Chaco *(C. cranwelli);* the ornate, also called the Argentine, *(C. ornata);* and the two hybrids (Chaco x ornate and Chaco x

Amazon) — usually eat readily, are easily cared for, and are very hardy. Do remember that a varied diet is healthiest for horned frogs. A temperature of 72 to 85 degrees is preferred.

Habitat/caging needs: Collectively, the horned frogs are quiet predators that indulge in wait-and-ambush hunting techniques. They burrow into the forest leaf litter or loose soils, leaving only their eyes exposed, and wait for a prey animal to approach closely. When this happens, the horned frog erupts from its burrow, seizes the prey in powerful jaws, and swallows it. Females, by far the larger sex, can overpower creatures much larger than the smaller males. Albinos of several species are now readily available.

Because they're normally inactive, horned frogs don't require large cages. Their very strong cannibalistic tendencies dictate that only one frog should be kept to each cage. A 10-gallon capacity terrarium will suffice for any single horned frog. The terrarium can be as intricate or simple as you choose to make it. In the case of a frog as large as an adult female ornate horned frog, simple is better. The terrarium may be bare and sloped slightly with a little water in the low end. This setup is a little more spartan than is recommended. You can create a very simple yet effective terrarium by placing two or three inches of moist, not sodden, sphagnum moss on the bottom of the tank. Rehydrated sphagnum is fine. The horned frog will burrow into this and catch its prey in a most natural way. You can place a hardy plant, inserted pot and all, in this terrarium.

Behavior: Horned frogs will attack not only a mouse but an intruding finger as well. And a bite from a large individual can hurt. Approach these frogs carefully. If you feed them from forceps, be very careful not to allow them to hurt their mouth by grasping the forceps.

Oriental fire-bellied toad

Scientific name: *Bombina orientalis*

Area of origin: Southwestern Asia. Other species of this genus also occur in Asia and Europe.

Diet: These small frogs have hearty appetites. They eat a comparatively prodigious number of small insects (both aquatic and terrestrial) and occasionally are able to catch tiny fish and tadpoles as well. Like wild examples, captives eat tiny fish and insects. They eagerly accept small crickets, waxworms, and pieces of earthworm (or entire small worms). Fire-bellied toads readily learn to accept food from forceps or from the end of a broom straw. They swim to the proffered food item, grab the food with obvious eagerness, and then stuff it into their mouths with their hands as they swallow it.

Ease of care: Fire-bellied toads are hardy and very easily kept. Although they are highly aquatic, they can be maintained in either a terrarium or an aquarium. They're seldom aggressive, and you can keep them in colonies where you can easily observe their interactions.

Habitat/caging needs: These little frogs are green (rarely gray) marbled with black on their back and red or red-orange marbled with black on the belly. Occasional captive-bred individuals lack the red belly coloring, having instead an off-white and black belly. Several fire-bellied toads can live colonially in a 15- to 40-gallon capacity setup.

If you keep these toads in a terrarium, the substrate should consist of up to several inches of clean soil or rehydrated sphagnum moss. Mossy logs or driftwood and hardy plants add to the beauty of the enclosure. The substrate should be moist but not wet. Many hobbyists place live woodland mosses over the soil of the substrate.

If you keep the frogs in an aquarium, you must provide a substantial amount of floating plants or floating plastic lily pads. The water (or terrarium) temperature should be at about 75 degrees. Filtration is helpful but not mandatory. Above-tank lighting is necessary to keep the plants alive.

Fire-bellied toads are entirely at home in such a fully aquatic setup. They swim well, clamber among the plants as they forage and bask, and may often be seen floating quietly in the open water, hind legs stretched out behind them.

Behavior: Fire-bellied toads are among the easiest of the tailless amphibians (anurans) to acclimate to captive conditions. They eat readily and don't require an awful lot in the way of support equipment. These frogs do have rather toxic skin secretions. It's a good idea to always wash your hands carefully both before and after handling any amphibian or reptile.

Red-eyed treefrog

Scientific name: *Agalychnis callidryas*

Area of origin: Primarily Central America

Diet: Insects. In addition to catching the normally seen crickets and flies, this beautiful nocturnal treefrog is adept at catching moths. Captives eat crickets and flies, and usually accept other insects, such as waxworms and freshly molted mealworms if presented carefully in forceps.

Ease of care: Red-eyed treefrogs are easily kept. Large numbers are now being captive bred annually. This treefrog is a member of the leaf-frog group, so called because they place their egg clusters on leaves overhanging the water. When the tadpoles hatch, they drop from the egg mass into the water, where they complete their development. Both adults and tadpoles are usually available. The large red eyes so typical of this nocturnal frog vary little. The barred blue sides, however, are very variable. From one to several of these treefrogs may be kept in a vertically-oriented woodland terrarium. These treefrogs prefer to sit quietly on the leaves of bromeliads or vertically on the terrarium glass rather than on limbs.

The red-eyed treefrog is of tropical origin. Although these frogs can tolerate a temperature of 65 to 90 degrees, the suggested temperature range is 75 to 82 degrees. As with all amphibians, these treefrogs must have access to moisture to almost continually replenish that lost during normal activity and metabolism from their body. They often sit for long periods in a shallow dish of water. Gentle misting will usually awaken even a soundly sleeping treefrog and induce a period of activity. The water used both in the water dish and the mister must not contain chlorine or chloramine and must not have been distilled.

Habitat/caging needs: Provide your red-eyed treefrogs a spacious terrarium. A woodland terrarium containing a sizable but shallow water dish is suggested. A tank of at least 15 or 20 gallons (long) capacity is the minimum size suggested. This size gives the frog a bottom space (footprint) of 12 inches x 12 inches. The height of the 15-gallon terrarium is 24 inches, and that of the 20-gallon long terrarium is 30 inches. If used vertically, the top becomes an open side and must be secured with a modified metal- or plastic-framed screen, wire, or solid top.

The substrate should consist of several inches of clean soil. Provide mossy logs or driftwood for climbing. The addition of green, woodland moss atop the soil will add beauty to the terrarium but isn't mandatory. A hardy plant or two completes the setup. Such plants as begonias, philodendrons, or pothos *(Epipremnum)* are hardy and usually readily available. The substrate should be moist but not wet. The live plants help maintain the high relative humidity that this frog prefers.

Behavior: Red-eyed treefrogs aren't usually an overly active species. Although they're capable of making long leaps, as often as not they walk slowly from place to place. Although when multiple males are present they may occasionally grapple, the outcome of this activity is usually not serious. However, be ready to intervene and separate the frogs if necessary.

Popular lizards and what makes them popular

Bearded Dragon

Scientific name: *Pogona vitticeps*

Area of origin: Noncoastal areas of eastern Australia.

Diet: The bearded dragons (actually there are a half dozen or so species but only the inland form is truly popular) tend to vary their diets based on their own size. Babies of large species (coastal, inland, and Nullarbor, [*P. barbatus, P. vitticeps,* and *P. nullarbor,* respectively]) tend to eat a diet high in insects, other arthropods, and gastropods, but as they grow, the lizards eat an ever-increasing amount of vegetation. All sizes of the smaller species (dwarf, western, Rankin's, and Mitchell's [*P. minor, P. minima, P. henrylawsoni,* and *P. mitchelli,* respectively]) seem more preferentially insectivorous. In captivity, try to induce all dragons to accept an omnivorous diet. A mixture of very finely chopped greens (collards, turnip, nasturtium, dandelion), dandelion, and hibiscus blossoms, squash, apples, and berries, provides an excellent cross-section of vegetation (do not feed spinach, a calcium binder, to the dragons), and king mealworms, crickets, roaches, and waxworms are all easily procured insects. Care should be taken to feed *only* proportionately small crickets to these lizards. Large insects, if swallowed entire, may cause tetanic seizures that can result in the death of the lizard.

Ease of care: Bearded dragons of all species, but especially the inland variety, are very easily kept lizards. Dry savanna and aridland lizards in the wild, these dragons require dryness and heat when captive. Inland bearded dragons are now bred annually by the thousands and have an immense and devoted following in the United States. Tailor the food insects to the size of the dragons, always keeping the insects proportionately small. Full spectrum lighting should be provided. The temperature on the surface of the basking spot should be 110 to 125 degrees Fahrenheit. A thermal gradient is necessary.

Habitat/Caging needs: Despite being capable of bursts of considerable speed, inland bearded dragons are usually quite laid back in attitude and will thrive in a cage of moderate size. Start one to several babies in a 10- to 15-gallon capacity container, but the lizards grow quickly and soon need a larger cage. We suggest a cage having a floor space of no less than 18 x 36 inches (larger is better) for one or two dragons, and of no less than 18 x 48 inches for a trio of the lizards (again, larger is better).

Behavior: Adult male bearded dragons of all species are very aggressive toward each other and can't be kept together. Provided that they are not crowded, one male and one to three females are usually compatible. Dragons can climb but are primarily terrestrial. Cover the cage.

Inland bearded dragons are now available in a number of pretty and interesting colors. One of the most sought is the sandfire morph, a beautiful reddish-orange creature, the color of some of the red Australian desert sands. Other color variants are yellowish, whitish, or brown. The latter, with variably distinct lighter and darker dorsal markings, is most common. Male dragons are often more colorful than females, but even the brightest of dragons are very dark when cold. The common name of bearded dragon comes from the distensible throat of the male (but not all species of dragons have beards). The throat of the male inland bearded dragon blackens and is distended widely during territoriality displays.

The cage should be well ventilated, and cage humidity should be low. A very hot basking spot, preferably illuminated with full-spectrum lighting, is needed, but the cage must be large enough and provide a sufficient thermal-gradient for the dragon to cool when needed. A hot-spot temperature of 110 to 120 degrees Fahrenheit (a little hotter is acceptable) will allow the lizards to quickly elevate their body temperatures to optimum levels. It is then that all bodily functions are most efficient — from territoriality to foraging to digestion to reproductive behaviors.

Day Gecko

Scientific name: *Phelsuma* species

Area of origin: Primarily Madagascar

Diet: Several dozen species of day geckos exist. A few are quite small (3 to 4 inches in total length), many are of medium size (4 to 7.5 inches) and a few are relatively large (7 to 12 inches). These geckos all eat pollen, sap, and nectar, and suitably sized insects. Flies, termites, and many other insects are accepted. Captive day geckos eat small crickets, small waxworms, tiny roaches, and freshly molted mealworms. A honey-fruit mixture is a very important part of their diet. The formula for this is 1:1:1 honey, apricot baby food, and water. To this mixture, add a bit of powdered calcium-D3 and a drop or three of a liquid bird multivitamin. The amount of vitamin supplements will vary, of course, according to how much of the mixture you are adding it to.

Ease of care: Don't handle these lizards, just look at them. The skin is very delicate and tears free if the gecko is carelessly restrained. Provided that you are willing to meet their dietary needs, day geckos are hardy and long-lived captives. Many species are now being bred in captivity, some in considerable numbers. Hungry day geckos will chase insects down and all will soon learn where their dish of honey-fruit formula is placed. Day geckos also need fresh water. Some will drink readily from a dish, but may prefer to lap pendulous droplets of dew or rain from leaves, branches, or the glass of their terrarium. Day geckos may also drink water from an elevated dish if the water-surface is roiled by an aquarium air stone attached to a small pump. With their expanded, specialized toe pads, day geckos can readily and rapidly climb smooth surfaces such as glass.

Habitat/Caging needs: Day geckos are arboreal. Most are vivid Kelly green with orange spots or streaks on their anterior back. A very few are brown and one type is pale green. The terrarium for the day geckos should be vertically oriented and should contain some type of hardy foliage plant for the lizards to climb on and to drink droplets of water from. Bromeliads, orchids, and decorative ferns and aroids are all good choices. Vertical, diagonal, and horizontal twigs or limbs for climbing are also necessary. A 10-gallon capacity terrarium is suitable for from one to several of the small day gecko species. If you have one to several of the medium sized day geckos, provide a 15- to 30-gallon terrarium. The same number of the largest species should provide a 30- to 50-gallon capacity terrarium (or larger). The tank must be very tightly covered. Day geckos are very alert, very fast, and very adept at evading capture. They are best caught with a small fish net. Slide a stiff piece of thin cardboard or plastic over the mouth of the net to keep the gecko inside.

Behavior: Adult male day geckos are very territorial and aggressive, and the dominant male will quickly injure other males in the terrarium. Provided that they are not crowded, one male and one, two, or three females, are usually compatible. Unless they are of closely related species, day geckos in the same size range can be housed together. Males nod, bob, sidle, and wag their tails in an effort to intimidate each other.

No aberrant colors are known.

The day gecko cage should be well ventilated but the cage humidity should be high. Provide a basking spot, preferably illuminated with full-spectrum lighting and providing a temperature of 95 to 100 degrees Fahrenheit. The cage must be large enough to provide a thermal-gradient that allows the lizards to cool down when needed. Providing the needed gradient is easy, even in a fairly small terrarium, when you orient the warmed and illuminated basking spot near the top of the cage. Then the top of the terrarium is warm and the lower levels are cooler.

Leopard Gecko

Scientific name: *Eublepharis macularius*

Area of origin: India, Pakistan, Bangladesh

Diet: In the wild, the eublepharine (with eyelids) geckos eat insects and other arthropods. The diet in captivity includes crickets, waxworms, mealworms, and a very occasional newborn mouse. Because pinky mice have a very high fat content, give them as an occasional treat or to fatten a thin gecko. Not all leopard geckos eat pinkies, so don't be dismayed if yours refuses. The insects should be gut-loaded (fed healthy food just before being offered to the geckos) and occasionally be dusted with calcium-vitamin D3 powder. Leopard geckos wag their tails when stalking prey.

Ease of care: The three truly popular lizards in the pet trade today are the green iguana, the bearded dragon, and the leopard gecko. Of the three, the latter beautiful gecko is the least problematic and the least demanding. It is primarily nocturnal in its activity and so is readily viewable by owners returning after a hard day's work, which is a definite plus. Another plus for keepers with a mind toward conservation is the fact that the vast majority of these geckos (that are offered in the pet trade) are captive-bred. These little geckos are long-lived. A life span of 15 to 20 years is not uncommon.

Habitat/Caging needs: Leopard geckos do not require full-spectrum lighting. In fact, if their terrarium (or even the room they are in is brightly lit) the geckos are not apt to be active. Leopard geckos require very little else in support equipment other than cage, water, food, sunstrate, and a little under-tank heating. They are fairly small. Adult males range from 7 to 10 inches in total length. Females are somewhat smaller. This allows a terrarium of only 10- or 15-gallon capacity to serve as the geckos' home throughout their lives.

Leopard geckos are dry savanna and aridland lizards. In the wild they seem to prefer rocky soils. Captives require dryness and moderate heat (80 to 88 degrees Fahrenheit). Place an undertank heater beneath only one end of the terrarium to provide a thermal gradient. If necessary, leopard geckos can run quite fast for a short distance. However, they more typically move about their tanks in a slow, hand-over-hand manner. They can be lifted, but do not enjoy being tightly grasped. To pick one up, shepherd the gecko into the palm of one hand, cover it loosely with the other hand and move the lizard in this manner. They can bite (but usually don't) and may autotomize their tails if you grasp it. Start one to several babies of either or both sexes in a 10- to

15-gallon capacity container. However, as males reach sexual maturity, they begin fighting, which necessitates the removal from the group of all but one male. Visual barriers such as rocks or nonspinose aridland plants will usually help promote peace among the remaining geckos. A shallow dish (such as a petri dish) of fresh water should always be available and a very occasional gentle misting of the cage is beneficial. A hidebox should be provided.

Behavior: Although adult male leopard geckos are aggressive toward others of their sex, they usually coexist with one to several females without incident. These geckos occasionally attempt to climb, but do so poorly and are primarily terrestrial. Nevertheless, you should cover the cage.

Although captive geckos do not hibernate, even with a heated tank-bottom, they often become more quiescent and have a reduced appetite during the months of winter.

Leopard geckos are now available in a number of pretty and interesting colors. Albinos (most of these have pale yellow, not red eyes), leucistic, blizzard, yellow-blizzard, high yellow, orange-banded, and normal, are among the colors now most often seen. Other colors are being developed. Hatchling and juvenile leopard geckos usually have stronger patterns but paler colors than the adults.

Spiny-tailed Agamid (Uro)

Scientific name: *Uromastyx* species

Area of origin: Near East and North Africa

Diet: About six species of spiny-tailed agamids are now available in the pet trade. These lizards derive their name from the whorls of greatly enlarged, spiny scales that encircle the tail. The diet of all is the same. Most species are of moderate size (8 to 12 inches) but the Egyptian spiny-tail may occasionally exceed 2 feet in length. The spiny-tails are omnivores, but eat a preponderance of vegetation. In captivity these lizards will eat a mixture of very finely chopped greens (collards, turnip, nasturtium, dandelion), dandelion, and hibiscus blossoms, squash, apples, and berries. They also like wild-bird seed, and adults crunch up the halved dried peas and lentils used for soups. Feed the spiny-tail king mealworms, crickets, and waxworms, which are all easily procured insects. Take care to feed *only* proportionately small crickets to these lizards. Large insects, if swallowed entire, may cause tetanic seizures that can result in the death of the lizard.

Ease of care: Provided that they're given desert dry, brightly illuminated cages, and sufficient heat (the hot spot should be between 115 and 130 degrees Fahrenheit!) spiny-tailed agamids are easily maintained and can live for more than a decade. Most of the spiny-tails now available are wild-collected, but an increasing number are captive-bred. Dry savannas and aridlands are the natural habitats of the spiny-tailed agamids. Provide full spectrum lighting. During the lizard's daytime activity period, the temperature should vary from the 120 degrees Fahrenheit or so of the hot spot, to room temperature at the distal end of the tank. The thermal gradient is necessary to allow the lizards to quickly elevate their body temperatures so that all bodily functions are most efficient — from territoriality displays to foraging to digestion to reproductive behavior. They also need to be able to cool down when necessary.

Habitat/Caging needs: In the wild, spiny-tails construct home burrows to sleep in or if frightened. Captives should be provided with a deep earthen substrate and have partially buried *home-caves* built into the design. A home-cave can be as simple as a narrow cinder block laid on the very bottom of the tank with the center holes oriented horizontally and mostly buried by the substrate. Resting that heavy cage furniture securely on the glass bottom of the tank or propping it up is important so that it cannot settle on and injure the lizards if they burrow beneath it. Although often nervous when first acquired, when they're made to feel secure and become used to the various motions around them, these lizards usually become quite laid back. Start one to several babies in a 10- to 15-gallon capacity container; but remember that these lizards grow quickly and will soon need a larger cage. We suggest a cage having a floor space of no less than 18 x 36 inches and recommend larger when possible for one to three adults. Our favorite desert arrangement is a terrarium of 24 x 72 inches (and of 150-gallon capacity). Climbing facilities are not necessary. These lizards are not escape artists, but cover the cage just to be on the safe side.

Behavior: Like the males of most lizards, adult male spiny-tails of all species are very aggressive toward others of their own, or of closely related, species. However, provided that they're not crowded, one male and one to three females of the same species, or two groups of distantly related species (example, a pair of Mali and a pair of Indian spiny-tails) are usually compatible.

The colors of these lizards may be dull Eqyptian and Indian uros, *(U. egyptia and U. hardwickii)* or variably bright. Niger uros *(U.geyri)* may be orange, yellow, or very bland in color. Moroccan uros *(U. acanthinurus)* may or may not have highlights of orange, yellow, or green. Mali uros often have bright yellow backs. Ornate uros may have combinations of turquoise, chartreuse, and tan. The males of the brighter-colored species often are more colorful than the females.

Veiled Chameleon

Scientific name: *Chamaeleo c. calyptratus*

Area of origin: Yemen

Diet: A chameleon that eats vegetation as well as insects? Indeed, this beautiful creature does just that. The veiled chameleon eats leaves and blossoms in addition to the insect diet so typical of the other chameleon species. In captivity, the veiled chameleon eats the leaves of the fig *Ficus benjamina* (a tree that also provides the lizard with ideal arboreal pathways), romaine, turnip, dandelion, and nasturtium greens, and the blossoms of dandelions, nasturtiums, and hibiscus. They also eat crickets, flies, roaches, waxworms, and mealworms. Veiled chameleons simply bite off pieces of vegetation and chew them in lizard-like manner, but catch their insect prey on the sticky-tongue in the traditional chameleon-manner. Provided that you move slowly, these lizards often accept food from your fingers or from forceps.

Ease of care: Chameleons are look-don't-touch lizards. Although this is unquestionably the easiest of the chameleons to keep, we still cannot quite bring ourselves to call it *easy,* because this lizard must have a certain degree of specialized care. The veiled chameleon is adept at finding and catching food insects but is less adept at finding water. Chameleons prefer to drink droplets of dew or rain from leaves or branches, and many insist on lapping pendulous water droplets in captivity. Create these droplets by sprinkling water on the plants or twigs in the cage. Chameleons may drink water from an elevated dish if the water surface is roiled by an aquarium air stone attached to a small pump, but you must monitor the lizards to ascertain whether their water needs are being met. Veiled chameleons are an aridland species, but seem capable of tolerating both low and high cage humidity as long as ventilation is ample. The bundled, opposing toes of chameleons allow the lizard to tightly grasp the twigs and vines along which it normally moves. However, they hold so tightly to their support that if you try to pull one free you can damage its feet. This often results in difficult to treat infections.

Habitat/Caging needs: Like most true chameleons, the veiled chameleon is persistently arboreal. It changes color, but not as dramatically as some species. Adult males, which vary in length from 14 inches to 22 inches, are prettily banded in yellows, tans, greens, and blues. They bear an immensely tall head crest. The females are duller and smaller.

The terrarium for the chameleons should be very well ventilated and of vertical orientation. Climbing limbs are not a luxury but rather a necessity for these lizards. The terrarium should be proportionately large and we strongly urge that a hardy foliage plant such as a *Ficus benjamina* be incorporated into the terrarium design. Plastic screen cages are now made specifically for chameleons. A 15- or 20-gallon capacity cage is big enough for one or two babies, but a 75- to 100-gallon capacity is needed for one or two adults. These cages have zippered doors on both ends.

Behavior: Chameleons move slowly and methodically, using their feet and their prehensile tail to retain a tenacious grip on their supports. These are among the most solitary of lizards, but given sufficient space and plenty of visual barriers, a pair may coexist. Notice that we say "may." Watch the lizards carefully and be ready to intercede whenever aggression is manifested. Adult male veiled chameleons are so antagonistic that they can't even be allowed to see each other, or they become so stressed that their health is impaired. These lizards assume their brightest coloration during territoriality displays and courtship. Males flatten their bodies laterally, sidle in strut, and refuse food. Chameleons are diurnal. A basking spot should be provided near the top of the cage. Using a full-spectrum bulb, a temperature of 95 to 100 degrees Fahrenheit should be maintained. The lower levels of the cage should be cooler.

Popular salamanders and what makes them popular

Axolotl

Scientific name: *Ambystoma mexicanum*

Area of origin: Central Mexico; eliminated over much of its range in the wild.

Diet: Aquatic insects, tadpoles, smaller salamanders, worms, and tiny fish form the diet of wild salamanders. The diet in captivity is very much the same as in the wild. Captives eat all manner of worms. Larvae are very cannibalistic, and if kept in groups, these salamanders should be nearly identical in size.

Ease of care: This salamander is very easy to care for and is bred in untold numbers in captivity. However, because of cannibalistic tendencies, don't mix different sizes in the same tank. Even with this precaution, axolotls are very apt to bite off tail tips or the limbs (more rarely a gill stalk) of tankmates. Although these wounds may sound frightful and the axolotl's appearance may be disconcerting to their keepers, the axolotls quickly regenerate the missing parts and are not disfigured for long. Axolotls don't require a heated tank, thriving at a wide range of temperatures, but preferring coolness over warmth. A water temperature between 65 and 75 degrees is ideal.

Habitat/caging needs: The axolotl (pronounced axe-oh-lot-el) is a fully aquatic salamander that doesn't normally transform (metamorphose). These salamanders are larvae throughout their long lives (they are called obligate neotenes), yet they attain sexual maturity. They have occasionally been forced to metamorphose (through thyroid manipulation), but the trans-formed adults seldom do well. Axolotls routinely attain a length of 8 inches and some may exceed 10 inches in length. They lack functional eyelids, have three pairs of bushy gills, and look like a salamander having a bad-hair day. These salamanders are bred in several color morphs. The normal coloration is a muddy brown. Albinos (white with pink eyes), leucistic (white with dark eyes), and piebalds (black-and-white splotched) are as common as the normal coloration.

For a single axolotl, a 7- to 10-gallon aquarium will suffice. Should you be keeping more than one, a larger tank is better because it doesn't force the salamanders to remain in such close proximity. If they can keep some distance between each other, there is less chance of injuries from bites.

Although axolotls can easily live in very simple aquariums, a well-filtered aquarium containing aquatic plants can be a true showpiece. Anchor rooted or bunched plants into a substrate of aquarium gravel or small river rock. If your aquarium is large enough, you can use driftwood and ornamental rocks as accents and visual barriers. Without filtration, you must watch the water quality more carefully, but even with strong filtration, partial water changes will be periodically necessary. The tank should be covered.

When you need to move or handle your axolotl, do so with a large, soft net, just as you would a fish. Get the salamander back into the water as quickly as possible. In all cases, the water must be chlorine- and chloramine-free.

Behavior: Although axolotls are often sold in aquarium stores as a community tank species, they're not really well suited for such an existence. They eat smaller fish, and many fish will pick at the salamander's gill filaments, causing the amphibians distress and injury. Axolotls become particularly frenzied while feeding, and it is then that most injuries occur. Chopped fresh minnows and earthworm segments are immediately detected by scent when they're dropped into the tank. Although the foraging instinct kicks in immediately, the actual finding of the food item usually seems more a matter of accident then intent. When actively foraging, the axolotl will snap at anything with which it come in contact, be it prey or tankmate. Because axolotls are permanent larvae, they're able to regenerate injured or amputated body parts throughout their lives.

Eastern newt

Scientific name: *Notophthalmus viridescens* complex

Area of origin: The several subspecies of this interesting salamander are found in eastern North America, in fog-shrouded woodlands as well as in ponds, lakes, and their environs.

Diet: The various eastern newts are all small salamanders that eat a variety of small insects, worms, and other invertebrates. Captives eat fruit flies, springtails, termites, and tiny worms.

Ease of care: Newts are small and hardy. Unlike other salamanders that merely transform from larvae to the adult stage, the eastern newts, which are aquatic at both ends of their life, undergo an intermediate, often colorful, terrestrial stage. When in this stage, the newts are referred to as efts. The three subspecies most often seen in the pet trade are red-spotted newt *(Notophthalmus v. viridescens),* the central newt *(Notophthalmus v. louisianensis),* and the broken-striped newt *(Notophthalmus v. dorsalis).*

Whether they're in their terrestrial stage or their aquatic stage, newts are easy to keep, providing that their food and temperature requirements are met.

Habitat/caging needs: Efts are the terrestrial intermediate stage of some eastern newts. An eft's color is usually quite a bright red, but some are tan. If terrestrial conditions are particularly hostile (such as during a drought), newts may forgo the eft stage.

Efts thrive in a woodland terrarium. The terrarium should contain a substrate of several inches of clean soil. A shallow dish of cool, clean water should be present. Hiding areas of mossy logs or flat rocks should be provided. Some moss atop the soil and a hardy plant or two will complete the setup. You can find many ideal terrarium plants at local nurseries or from Web sources. Keep the soil moist (not wet) and change it every few months. Don't use soil that contains insecticides or herbicides, and choose one without filler material.

These amphibians don't require a heated terrarium. In fact, a terrarium temperature of 65 to 75 degrees is perfect for them. Most salamanders are escape artists, so cover the terrarium tightly.

Both larvae and adult newts require aquatic setups. A well-filtered aquarium containing aquatic plants can be a beautiful addition to any room, as well as an ideal home for one to several newts.

You can anchor rooted or bunched plants into a substrate of aquarium gravel or small river rock. If your aquarium is large enough, driftwood and ornamental rocks can be used as accents and visual barriers. Without filtration, you must watch water quality more carefully, but even with strong filtration, partial water changes are periodically necessary. In all cases, the water must be chlorine- and chloramine-free. Cover the tank tightly.

Behavior: Newts are often sold in aquarium stores as a community tank species. They are, in fact, one of the best adapted species for such cross-utilization. They're small and very interesting, and they won't bother fish larger than newborn live bearers. Keep the water temperature at the coolest end of the range acceptable to your fish. The greatest problem may be that newts don't forage as effectively as fish. You must be certain that the newts are getting their fair share of the food. Blackworms, tubifex, and enchytraea are ideal aquatic newt foods. These and many other aquatic newts will also accept prepared reptile "sticks" (Reptomin), trout chow, fish pellets, and frozen foods marketed for tropical fish.

Fire salamander

Scientific name: *Salamandra salamandra*

Area of origin: This spectacular salamander is of Eurasian distribution. It occurs both in woodlands and in semiarid areas, but in the latter, it is largely restricted to the vicinity of potholes and watercourses.

Diet: This salamander attains a heavy-bodied 6 inches in length. It eats many kinds of suitably sized, non-noxious arthropods and worms.

Ease of care: This salamander, in all of its numerous subspecies, is primarily terrestrial in habits, seeking shallow water only to birth its young. The live babies may be either gilled larvae or, at high and cold elevations, may be retained by the female until they have metamorphosed into small adults. No salamanders in the Americas have this mode of reproduction. Despite the fact that this creature looks more like a slimy-skinned salamander than a rough-skinned newt, it's in the newt family. Like the newts, the skin secretions of the fire salamander are particularly noxious. These animals have well-developed, toxin-producing parotoid glands.

If you give fire salamanders cool terrarium temperatures (60 to 75 degrees), they're among the hardiest of the tailed amphibians or caudatans. Like most amphibians that produce virulent skin toxins, the fire salamander is less secretive than less toxic species. They may be diurnally active on cool, damp days.

If properly cared for, captive fire salamanders may live for a half century. They readily accept food that is offered while impaled on a broom straw or held in forceps.

These salamanders have been captive bred for many generations. They're quiet, nonaggressive captives, and you can keep several in a communal terrarium without incident.

Habitat/caging needs: These salamanders are beautiful and heavy bodied. Most are clad in a skin of ebony and have a variable number of yellow spots or streaks on their back. Some few fire salamanders may be almost a solid yellow-orange in color. One subspecies has a jet-black body and a russet head.

The fire salamander will thrive in a cool woodland terrarium with a shallow dish of fresh water. The terrarium should contain a substrate of several inches of clean soil. Hiding areas of mossy logs or flat rocks should be provided. Some moss atop the soil and a hardy plant or two add beauty and a completed look to the setup. Cover the setup tightly.

Keep the soil moist (not wet) and change it every few months. Don't use soil that contains insecticides or herbicides, and if you use commercial soil, choose one without styro beads or other such filler material. Like all amphibians, fire salamanders derive their moisture necessities by absorbing water through the skin and mucous membranes. Impurities, many of which can prove fatal to these salamanders, will be absorbed with the moisture.

Larval fire salamanders are occasionally available in the pet trade. These must be sized and allowed to metamorphose in clean, cool, chemical-free, shallow water. They eat tiny worms (such as blackworms) or finely chopped pieces of earthworm. They may also accept prepared reptile "sticks" (Reptomin), trout chow, fish pellets, and frozen foods marketed for tropical fish.

Behavior: Few amphibians are any more colorful or hardy. If they're burrowed down into the substrate, you may be able to induce them to be surface active by gently spraying the surface of the substrate with cool water.

Marbled salamander

Scientific name: *Ambystoma opacum*

Area of origin: This pretty little salamander is found in hardwood and mixed forests over much of the eastern United States.

Diet: The marbled salamander feeds on leaf-litter insects (such as cutworms), sowbugs, and earthworms.

Ease of care: At 4.5 inches in length, this is one of the smallest, prettiest, and most secretive of the mole salamanders. Most live well in captivity but burrow so persistently that they're seldom seen. Marbled salamanders can be taught to accept food that is offered while impaled on a broom straw or held in forceps. Marbled salamanders aren't responsive captives, but they have been known to live for decades. A terrarium temperature of 65 to 75 degrees is preferred. Marbled salamanders derive their moisture necessities by absorbing water through the skin and mucous membranes. Impurities, many of which can prove fatal to these salamanders, are absorbed with the water. These salamanders have not yet been captive bred. They're quiet, nonaggressive captives, and you can keep several in a communal terrarium without incident.

Habitat/caging needs: The marbled salamander is one of the most terrestrial of the mole salamanders. It's a denizen of moist (not wet) woodland habitats. Unlike most other members of the family which breed in the water, the female marbled salamander lays her eggs in a soon-to-be-flooded depression on land. Autumn rains flood the depression, the eggs hatch, and from that point, their development is normal.

Because these salamanders are small (and are not often surface active), from one to several can be kept in a 7- to 10-gallon capacity terrarium.

The terrarium for a marbled salamander should be a replication of the salamander's woodland habitat. The terrarium should contain a substrate of several inches of clean soil. Provide hiding areas of mossy logs or flat rocks. Some moss atop the soil and a hardy plant or two will complete the setup.

Keep the soil moist (not wet), and change it every few months. Don't use soil that contains insecticides or herbicides, and if you use commercial soil, choose one without styro beads or other such filler material. Despite their bulky appearance, salamanders can climb. To prevent their escape, keep the terrarium tightly covered.

If you happen to start out with larval marbled salamanders, you need to keep them in an aquarium. For these, follow the suggestions mentioned for the waterdog, later in this section.

Behavior: Marbled salamanders are very secretive. They're surface active only at night, and then not often. You may be able to induce them to be surface active by gently spraying the surface of the substrate with cool water.

Tiger salamander

Scientific name: *Ambystoma tigrinum*

Area of origin: The several subspecies of this impressive salamander are found over much of the United States, southern Canada, and northern Mexico. Few tiger salamanders are bred in captivity. The salamanders you see in the pet stores have been taken from the wild.

Diet: In the wild, this salamander eats any type of smaller animal life that it can overpower. Captives eat crickets and other insects and worms.

A plea for dietary prudence: Over the years, tiger salamanders have become favorites of hobbyists because of their brilliant colors, complex patterns, and voracious appetites. Feeding tiger salamanders a diet of pinky mice caught on years ago, and continues today. However, strong evidence indicates that a high-fat diet can cause serious health problems for any herp, including these salamanders. Pinky mice are high-fat prey items! Feeding your tiger salamander an exclusive diet of pinky mice (or even when lab mice are a high percentage of the diet) can quickly cause obesity and may eventually cause the development of corneal lipid opacities that will eventually blind the salamander or cause lipid buildups on other organs. A variety of natural prey items is the best diet for a tiger salamander.

Ease of care: Many tiger salamanders are acquired accidentally. Aquarists often buy waterdogs (see the description later in this section), not realizing that these will sooner or later metamorphose into a land-dwelling tiger salamander. Although the adults are no more difficult to keep than the larvae, they do require a different housing setup. Tiger salamanders (a half-dozen subspecies exist, varying from bright to dull in coloration) are 10 to 12 inches in length when adult. They're members of the mole salamander group, a family of salamanders noted for their burrowing propensities.

Tiger salamanders very quickly learn to accept food that is offered impaled on a broom straw or held in forceps. Despite a sedentary lifestyle, many tiger salamanders become alert pets that will live for decades in captivity. A terrarium temperature of 65 to 75 degrees is preferred. Unless the tank is tightly covered, your salamander is apt to escape.

Habitat/caging needs: Despite seldom being thought of as predators, tiger salamanders do forage for insects and worms on cool, wet nights. Exactly how they spend their underground time is a matter of conjecture. These salamanders emerge to breed in nearby ponds during cold winter or spring rains. Albinos of several subspecies have been found.

Tiger salamanders don't require large cages. A 10-gallon capacity terrarium will suffice for from one to four salamanders. The terrarium can be of intricate woodland design (see the red-backed salamander descriptions for suggestions) or very simple. You can put together a very simple yet effective terrarium by placing two or three inches of moist, not sodden, sphagnum moss on the bottom of the tank. You can use rehydrated dry sphagnum if live sphagnum isn't available. The salamander will burrow into this and catch prey in a most natural way. A hardy plant, inserted pot and all, can be placed in this terrarium. You *must* keep the terrarium scrupulously clean, meaning frequent rinsing/replacing of the sphagnum and cleaning and careful rinsing of the tank surfaces.

Behavior: Tiger salamanders spend much of their time burrowed deeply in the substrate. They may often be induced to the surface by misting the terrarium with cold water. Most will bite a finger if you approach them carelessly. If you feed your salamanders from forceps, be very careful not to allow them to hurt their mouth by grasping the forceps.

Popular snakes and what makes them popular

American Rat Snake

Scientific name: *Pantherophis* (formerly *Elaphe*) *obsoleta* (complex)

Size: This is a complex of large, interesting and beautiful snakes. Adults often exceed 4.5 feet and occasionally attain 7 feet (and very rarely, 8 feet) in length.

Area of origin: Eastern United States and extreme southern Ontario, Canada.

Diet: Dietary needs of the snakes in this species group change with age. Although hatchlings may accept nestling rodents, lizards and tree frogs figure prominently in their diet. And although Baird's rat snake *(P. bairdi)* and the Texas rat snake *(P. o. lindheimeri)* routinely eat lizards throughout their lives, as they grow they add a greater percentage of rodents and birds to the equation. The adults of the more easterly races of rat snakes prefer to eat rodents and birds and largely drop lizards from the diet. When in captivity, most hatchlings of both species and all subspecies can usually be induced to eat nestling lab mice, and the adults of all types thrive on appropriately sized lab mice.

Ease of Care: These are easily cared for, hardy snakes that are captive-bred annually by the thousands. Most examples adapt well to the readily available diet of laboratory mice and tolerate variable temperatures well, requiring only a daytime hotspot of 85 to 95 degrees Fahrenheit for basking; normal room temperature is otherwise sufficient.

Habitat/Caging needs: All of these rat snakes thrive in rather simple quarters. We urge that the largest terrarium or cage possible be provided. Several babies, which are only 8 to 12 inches at hatching, may be maintained in a 10-gallon capacity terrarium. Two or three adults will live well in a 40- to 75-gallon terrarium. Climbing limbs (at least three or four times the diameter of the snake's body) or an elevated flat shelf, a water bowl, and one or more hideboxes should be provided. The substrate may be of aspen, dry leaves, newspapers, or another simple and readily obtained medium.

The eastern rat snakes — the black, the gray, the Everglades, and the yellow — are better adapted to high humidity than Baird's and other western rat snakes. However, all are adaptable, and as long as the substrate is dry and the cage is not so damp that moisture condenses on its walls, most rat snakes thrive as captives.

Behavior: The black rat snake *(Pantherophis o. obsoleta),* the gray rat snake *(E. o. spiloides),* the yellow rat snake *(P. o. quadrivittata),* the Everglades rat snake *(P. o. rossalleni),* and Baird's rat snake are pet trade staples. The common names referring to color are quite descriptive of the ground color of the adults. The yellow rat snake is yellow(ish), the black rat snake is black(ish) and the gray rat snake is gray. The Everglades rat snake tends toward a rich orange ground color, and Baird's rat snake is orangish overlain with an opalescent patina. The yellow, the Everglades, and the Baird's rat snakes are patterned with four dark longitudinal stripes. The gray rat snake is strongly blotched, and the black rat snake may bear blotches or be almost all one color. Designer colors (albinos, hypomelanistic, patternless, etc.) of all but the Baird's rat snake are readily available. The hatchlings of all have variably dark blotches against a pinkish-gray to tan ground color, with those of Baird's rat snake having a particularly busy pattern and those of the Everglades rat snake having the lightest color.

Rat snakes, powerful constrictors all, can be defensive at times. This is especially so of those collected from the wild. As is so often the case, the hatchlings are often even feistier than the adults.

Ball Python

Scientific name: *Python regius*

Size: 3.5 to 6 feet is the normal size range for adult ball pythons. A very occasional example may near 7 feet in length. The very heavy girth of this snake makes it look considerably larger than it actually is.

Area of origin: Tropical West Africa

Diet: Although these snakes are rodent eaters, they're also a species that *prey imprints.* That is, they begin feeding on a certain species or two of rodents when they are hatchlings in the wild, and are reluctant to switch "brands" when taken captive. This prey specificity can make all but newly hatched imported ball pythons problematic captives. When acquiring a ball python, inquire whether it's captive bred or an import. In either case, it is always best to see the ball python you're considering actually eat (if possible, more than once) before making the purchase. Adding to the uncertainty, occasionally an imported ball python will feed once with avidity then never eat again.

Ease of Care: Ball pythons that feed are very easily maintained. If feeding, they are fine snakes for beginners. If a nonfeeding import, this snake species can test the resolve of the most experienced herpetoculturist.

Habitat/Caging needs: Because it is not an overly active snake species, the ball python does not require a particularly large cage. A baby or two can be started and partially grown in a terrarium of only 10-gallon capacity. One or two average-sized adults will require a terrarium of 40- to 50-gallon capacity (or a cage of similar size). Although ball pythons can climb, and occasionally will do so, providing climbing limbs is optional. Actually, an elevated shelf is more apt to be used than a limb. It is more desirable to have a properly furnished terrarium with a larger footprint than a tall cage with littler horizontal crawling space. Fresh water should be provided at all times. Provide a hiding box or two for this shy snake. A cage temperature of from 85 to 95 degrees Fahrenheit is ideal.

Behavior: The ball python (known as the royal python in Europe) is one of the most popular of the pythons.

This popularity is as much because they are inexpensive as for any other reason. The normal colored ball python (the wild morph) has an intricate, but usually regular, pattern of brown on tan. Pastels, albinos, caramels, and several other colors have now been developed through selective breeding.

Ball pythons are usually quiet snakes that are reluctant to bite. However, the occasional individual will strike and bite savagely. Use care; a bite from a large ball python can hurt. The European name, royal python, is derived from the snake's scientific name of *regius,* meaning royal or regal. The derivation of the common American name of ball python is equally easily explained. Merely glance at the positioning of one of these snakes when frightened. Curled into a ball, its head is in a protected position in the center of the coils.

Ball pythons have small clutches of large eggs. Hatchling ball pythons are similar to the adults in appearance. Color and pattern intensity of both juveniles and adults is almost identical. However, for their 10-inch length the hatchlings are a little more slender and they have proportionately larger heads. Because of their tendency to prey imprint, start your hatchling feeding on whatever food mammal you intend to give your ball python throughout its long life.

Common Boa

Scientific name: *Boa constrictor*

Size: Several types of boa constrictors are now available in the pet trade. Some of the smaller island or high-elevation forms are adult at less than 4 feet in length. The largest of the mainland subspecies may attain, or even slightly exceed, 10 feet in length.

Area of origin: Latin America, from Mexico to Argentina.

Diet: The natural diet of a boa constrictor depends on where it's from. Some of the smaller island populations feed primarily on frogs, lizards, and crabs in the wild. It may be the low fat intake of this diet that limits the growth of these boas to 3 or 4 feet, for captives, fed upon a diet of rodents grow quite large. Larger mainland forms that prey upon all manner of small mammals and unwary birds (as well as tegu lizards and iguanas) get very large and grow quickly. Captives usually eat all manner of small mammals well. Some of the very largest boas may do best on a diet of rabbits. Although boa keepers usually have few qualms about feeding mice and rats to their snakes, some folks balk at feeding rabbits to their snake. Consider this, and alternatives (several rats or a chicken) before acquiring the boa.

Ease of Care: Most boas are very hardy and easily cared for, but those of a large size should be approached and handled with care. If the boa is 8 feet or longer, always have a companion present when working with the snake — just in case of an emergency.

Habitat/Caging needs: The size of the cage is dependent on the ultimate size of your boa. Because these are heavy-bodied snakes, they rather quickly outgrow small terrariums. One or two neonate boas (boas are live bearing snakes) may be maintained in a 10-gallon capacity terrarium. The terrarium size must be increased as the snake grows. An adult boa of 7 or 8 feet in length needs a cage with a *footprint* (bottom dimensions) no smaller than 6 feet in length and 4 feet wide. Height is optional, but should be no less than 3 feet (higher if you provide an elevated basking shelf). This water, too, must be kept scrupulously clean. These tropical snakes should be kept at temperatures between 80 and 90 degrees Fahrenheit. One end of the cage can be cooler.

Behavior: Boas are possessed of a supple beauty and usually become quite tame and used to their keepers if handled frequently. Those from the northern sections and southern sections of the range usually have brownish-orange to orange tail markings and are quite dark in overall color. Those from the equatorial rainforests have blood red or maroon tails and strongly contrasting dark markings on an olive-tan ground color.

Some designations you're likely to encounter when considering a boa are Mexican, Hog Islands, Coral Island, and Colombian red-tail (all geographic races of the Colombian or common boa constrictor *[B. c. imperator]*). Guyana red-tail, Peruvian red-tail, Brazilian red-tail (all red-tailed boas *[B. c. constrictor]*) and Argentine boas *(B. c. occidentalis)*. More rarely, Peruvian West Coast boas *(B. c. ortoni)* and Peruvian black-tailed boas *(B. c. longicauda)* are available. Because they are now farmed in very large numbers, then imported by pet dealers, it is the Colombian boa constrictor that is the least expensive and most often found in pet stores.

Neonate boas are about 15 inches long, and are less colorful than the adults. The babies — especially those of the Mexican and Argentine morphs — may be very defensive but usually tame quickly. The boas from Colombian seem to be the most tractable.

Corn Snake

Scientific name: *Pantherophis* (formerly *Elaphe*) *guttata guttata*

Size: 30 to 72 inches

Area of origin: Southeastern United States; southward to and through Florida from the Pine Barrens of New Jersey to Tennessee and Louisiana.

Diet: Hatchlings may eat pink mice, but some require lizards. Adult corn snakes are rodent eaters.

Ease of Care: This is an excellent beginner's snake.

Habitat/Caging needs: One or two adults may be housed in a 20-gallon, long terrarium. From one to several hatchlings may be maintained in a 5- to 10-gallon capacity terrarium. Many kinds of substrate are suitable — aspen shavings, pine shavings, newspaper, and dried leaves are just four of the choices. Because these snakes are adept at escaping, the terrarium must be tightly covered. A hidebox for the snakes is essential. They prefer the smallest hidebox that they can hide in comfortably, so the size of the hidebox should be graduated upwards with the growth of the snake. Diagonally oriented or horizontal limbs will also be used as resting platforms by this snake. A cage temperature of 78 to 88 degrees Fahrenheit is fine for the corn snake.

Behavior: The corn snake is a variable and beautiful rat snake. In concordance with its usual coloration, the corn snake is often referred to as the red rat snake. At its best, the corn snake has a rich orange ground color, bright red blotches with wide black outlines, and a black-and-white checkered belly. It is a spectacular snake. Some corn snakes from southern Florida are steel gray with red saddles, and a naturally occurring population in southwestern Florida lacks red pigment, and instead is brown on gray or tan in color. So many designer colors of this snake have now been developed, that it is impossible to list all. The hodgepodge of genes now in captive breeding colonies almost assures that some new color or pattern will be developed annually. Among others, striped corn snakes are now available (normally this is a strongly blotched snake), and so are butter yellows, albinos (called amelanistic) of many varying gene combinations), caramels, and some that are ruby freckled. Corn snakes are oviparous.

Corn snakes are unquestionably the most popular pet snakes in the world. They are now available in more than 25 colors and patterns.

Like other rat snakes, the corn snake is a powerful constrictor. Although the corn snake is able to climb, and may at times be found high in trees, it is less apt to indulge in arboreal activities than many other rat snakes. Except when basking or foraging, you're more apt to find these snakes amidst debris in unused buildings or under ground-surface debris.

Baby corn snakes may be a little snappy, but most soon tame with just a little handling. The hatchlings are paler than the adults but intensify in color quickly with growth. At hatching these snakes are about 8 inches in length and proportionately slender. It is difficult to determine the true intensity of color that will be assumed by an adult by looking at the corn snake as a hatchling.

Eastern Kingsnake

Scientific name: *Lampropeltis getula*

Size: Although subspecies are found as far west as California, collectively, these large constrictors are referred to as the eastern kingsnakes. Seven well-defined subspecies exist, and several geographic color phases. The largest races may attain a length of more than 6.5 feet, but 2.5 to 4.5 feet is the more usual size.

Area of origin: The eastern kingsnakes are found in low to moderate elevations from coast to coast in the southern half of the United States and northern Mexico. These snakes are usually associated with riparian habitats.

Diet: Kingsnakes are noted for their catholic tastes. They eat all manner of animals from frogs and salamanders to small birds and small mammals. They also eat baby turtles, turtle eggs (which they are adept at finding and digging from the nest), lizards, snakes and their eggs (including those of their own kind), and even some insects.

Ease of Care: Kingsnakes are very prone to developing a difficult to cure (and often fatal) blister disease if they are maintained on a damp, or especially, a damp and unclean substrate. However, if kept dry and clean, kingsnakes are among the hardiest of snakes, and adapt well to a diet of lab mice. A basking spot with a temperature between 75 to 85 degrees Fahrenheit should be provided, but the remainder of the cage can be of room temperature (70 to 80 degrees Fahrenheit).

Habitat/Caging needs: Cleanliness is the keynote to successfully keeping kingsnakes — or any snakes for that matter, but especially kingsnakes. The eastern kingsnakes (and especially the eastern kingsnake, itself *[L. getula]*) can be large snakes of quite considerable girth, and adults should be provided with cages having ample floor space. For one or two kingsnakes, a tank of at least 40-gallon capacity is needed, and larger would be better. Be careful when keeping these in pairs. Remember that they can be, and often are, cannibalistic! Hatchlings, even more prone to cannibalism than the adults, can be kept in much smaller terrariums. The kingsnakes (and the related milk snakes, the latter also cannibalistic) are best and most safely kept one per cage. These are secretive snakes that seem to feel most secure if provided with a substrate into which they can burrow, as well as one or two hideboxes. They are not great climbers, so neither elevated shelves nor climbing limbs are caging necessities. However, a limb lying on the floor of the cage or a rock — in fact anything that serves as a visual barrier — should be considered. A dish of clean drinking water is mandatory. If your kingsnake decides to soak and bathe in this, do not allow the snake to remain in it for more than a few hours.

Behavior: Kingsnakes are one of the more difficult to read among the easy-to-keep snakes. When encountered in the wild, kingsnakes are quite apt to "S" their neck and strike if approached. This feisty attitude is easy to read. However, even some long-term captives will allow themselves to be lifted and carried without manifesting any signs of aggression. Then, when it is least expected, they press their nose against the side of your hand or a finger, open their mouth, and bite and chew. Handle them carefully and remain alert.

Although all of the kingsnakes are popular as pets, the California kingsnake *(L. g. californiae);* the desert kingsnake *(L. g. splendida);* the Florida kingsnake — previously known as Brooks' kingsnake *(L. g. floridana);* the Apalachicola Lowland kingsnake — often called the blotched or Goin's kingsnake *(L. getula),* a color variant with uncertain affinities; and the eastern kingsnake are the most popular. Color variants of all have been developed. Hatchlings look very much like the adults.

Popular turtles and what makes them popular

Greek Tortoise

Scientific name: *Testudo graeca* complex
Area of origin: Eurasia and North Africa

Diet: Although largely herbivorous, this complex of several species of tortoises is by no means exclusively so. Besides vegetation, they also forage on carrion, scats, and the occasional insect. Captives usually readily eat all manner of greens (romaine, collards, turnips, and dandelions), nasturtiums, berries and fruits, squash, and beans. Some high-quality commercial tortoise diet may also be offered.

Ease of care: Because of the variable (but often rather bad) health of the various "Greek" tortoises that are imported by the pet dealers (who sometimes give any common name to a reptile or amphibian they're trying to sell), these creatures vary from difficult to easy to acclimate in captive conditions. The sad part about tortoise acclimatization is that these shelled creatures do everything slowly — very slowly. This slow pace carries over into the health patterns of the complex of Greek tortoises and the reversal of declining health. Although when they are in good condition these creatures are easily kept, a certain percentage of them arrive chilled, starving, and dehydrated. Because these conditions can allow endoparasites to proliferate unseen, unexpected problems may manifest. If you want to buy one of these animals, watch its normal day-to-day actions (including its regimen of eating) for at least several days.

Habitat/Caging needs: The various members of this species group regularly attain a shell length of 6 inches, and may approach 9 inches. These tortoises prowl actively during the daylight hours, a fact that must be considered when you're designing their cages. One to four Greek tortoises should be provided with floor space of at least 3 x 6 feet. An earthen substrate is best, but artificial substrates will suffice. Choose a surface on which the tortoise does not skid when walking, which is easy to clean on a frequent basis.

The Greek tortoise is a denizen of well-drained savannahs and semi-arid plains. They become dormant during periods of cold or excessive drought. The tortoises thermoregulate by basking, in cool weather sometimes for long periods. These tortoises should have a low-edged container of water large enough for them to rest in that's easy to access and exit. The water dish should be easy to clean. The cage should be illuminated by day and be kept quite warm (85-95 degrees Fahrenheit) on one end or beneath a basking bulb. The opposite end of the cage can be a few degrees cooler. These tortoises may be kept in well-planted pens outside during the hotter months of summer. Be sure they can escape from the direct heat of the sun.

Behavior: At one time, the Greek tortoise was thought to be a single very variable species. They have now been divided into several species, but most are difficult to differentiate using external characteristics. All have similar regimens of care and all react to various stimuli similarly. New imports can be shy but often aren't.

Although certainly not colorful in the strictest sense of the word, the various Greek tortoises are pleasantly colored. The shell varies from olive-tan to almost creamy-yellow with black markings of variable size. The head, limbs, and plastron are similarly colored.

Juvenile Greek tortoises of both sexes and the females of any age may be maintained communally. However, adult males are usually aggressive toward each other and should be kept singly unless in a large outside pen with many visual barriers.

Greek tortoises ram their shells into each other during courtship. Males, during territorial aggression, also ram and attempt to overturn subordinates. In the wild, the tortoises can escape from each other when necessary. In captivity it becomes your job to keep an eye out for aggression and to intercede when necessary.

Hinge-backed Tortoise

Scientific name: *Kinixys erosa/Kinixys homeana*

Area of origin: Tropical West Africa

Diet: The forest *(K. erosa)* and the Homes's *(K. homeana)* hinge-backs are the species most often seen in the American pet trade. Both are very omnivorous tortoises. They feed on all manner of vegetation, including greens and fruits, on carrion, snails, worms, and whatever other edible (to them) animal matter they happen across.

Ease of care: At one time, largely because of the long period of poor care at the collection points, the hinge-backed tortoises were considered almost impossible to keep. Perhaps because of better conditions or quicker transfer to the ultimate dealers, problems no longer seem insurmountable, although they do still exist.

In captivity, these tortoises eat turnip and collard greens, romaine, berries, squash, mushrooms, tomatoes, apples, earthworms, waxworms, snails, tortoise diet, a little puppy chow, and many other things. Feed a well-rounded diet. Don't allow the tortoise to become spoiled and choose only one or two favorite items.

Habitat/Caging needs: Although most are somewhat smaller, hinge-backed tortoises may attain 10 inches in shell length. Although these tortoises are not overly active, you must still consider the size when you are designing a cage. An adult hinge-back should have floor space of at least 3 x 6 feet. An earthen substrate is best, but artificial substrates will suffice. Choose a surface on which the tortoise doesn't skid when walking, which also is easy to clean on a frequent basis. Both the forest and the Homes's hinge-backs are more closely tied to damp, sometimes swampy areas, than most other tortoises. They do not bask as frequently as savanna or desert tortoise species, relying instead on an ambient temperature suitable to sustain their activity. These tortoises should have a low-edged container of water large enough for them to rest in but of easy access and egress. The cage should be illuminated by day and be kept quite warm (80 to 90 degrees Fahrenheit) overall for these tropical tortoises. These tortoises may be kept in well-planted pens outside during the hotter months of summer. Be sure they can escape from the direct heat of the sun.

Behavior: The hinge, just posterior to the hind limbs on the upper shell (the carapace), makes the several species in this African genus unique amongst the turtles.

Collectively (there are several other species), hinge-backs are shy tortoises. Newly imported examples may withdraw into their shell and remain there, most literally, for hours on end. However, within a few weeks they become used to captive conditions and are more outgoing.

These tortoises are not colorful. Some shade of brown is usually the predominating color of the carapace, the plastron, and the soft parts. The center of each shield may or may not be variably lighter. An occasional example may even have lighter radiations (rays) on each carapacial shield. The forest hinge-backed tortoise has the rear marginals (the shields that edge the shell) very strongly serrate (toothed). The same shields of the Homes' hinge-back are more gently rounded.

Juvenile hinge-backs of both sexes may be maintained singly or in groups with no adverse interactions. Adult females are also usually compatible with juveniles or with other females. However, adult male hinge-backs can be aggressive to other males. More than one male may be kept in a large outside pen with many visual barriers. But if indoors with limited space, only a single adult male can be maintained in each cage, but large females or juveniles can be kept with him.

Hinge-backs ram their shells into each other both during courtship and in territorial aggression. In the wild, the tortoises can escape from each other when necessary. In captivity it becomes your job to monitor and intercede when necessary.

Painted Turtle

Scientific name: *Chrysemys picta*

Area of origin: Of the four subspecies of painted turtle, three are restricted to the eastern United States and southeastern Canada, and one ranges well into the western areas of both countries. The care is identical for all.

Diet: Although they do eat some aquatic vegetation, painted turtles of all ages eat a proportionately great amount of animal matter — insects, worms, tadpoles, tiny fish, and carrion. Captives will eat some greens (romaine, turnip greens, and so on), but should have a base diet of insects, chopped fresh fish, earthworms, good quality prepared aquatic turtle food, and a very little puppy chow.

Ease of care: Painted turtles are hardy, easily cared for, and small enough so that they're not awfully difficult to house. The quarter-sized baby that you see in a pet store will eventually attain a length of about 6 inches (western painted turtles, the largest race, may exceed 8 inches in length when adult).

Painted turtles are closely allied to the sliders, and like the sliders are a strong-swimming basking turtle. Ample swimming room, clean water, an illuminated and heated basking platform, and a healthy diet are important to these turtles.

Habitat/Caging needs: Painted turtles have brightly colored shell highlights at hatching, and retain these pretty colors throughout their lives. Each subspecies has a different highlight. When viewed from above, eastern and midland painted turtles look very similar. They both have olive-black carapaces edged with vermilion. The plastron of both is yellow. However, the plastron of the eastern painted turtle is solid yellow and that of the midland race has a dark central figure. The western painted turtle has an olive-green carapace and a bright red plastron with a dark central figure. The southern painted turtle lacks most of the bright colors that typify the other races, but has a bright orange stripe along the center of its carapace. Painted turtles are active, moderately wary, and strong swimmers. In the wild, they can be active in all but the very coldest weather. When the sun is bright, they bask for long periods, their necks half extended and legs and feet fully out with toes splayed. Males and females are about the same size. Like the sliders and map turtles, captive painted turtles need a brightly illuminated and warmed *haulout,* someplace that they can emerge fully from the water, lie quietly and elevate their body temperature. Basking is as much a necessity for these turtles as eating and swimming are. Like most basking turtles, painted turtles eat while in the water.

Painted turtles are active turtles. If kept indoors, they need a large aquarium. Painted turtles thrive in garden pools. Babies are tiny. One to several can be kept in a ten-gallon aquarium with room to spare. If kept indoors, a 40- to 100-gallon capacity aquarium is recommended for one to several adults. Because large turtles are invariable messy, the aquarium should have strong filtration, but frequent partial water changes are also mandatory. Provide an illuminated and warmed basking haulout (a full-spectrum heat bulb positioned above the haulout is recommended) of driftwood or firmly affixed plastic onto which the turtle can easily climb. The haulout surface should be nonabrasive.

Behavior: Painted turtles quickly become confiding, quickly associating the presence of a human with the availability of food. Although freshly acquired painted turtles may be nervous, they soon allow close approach and swim to the front of the tank. Painted turtles will try to bite if restrained. The pinch may hurt but seldom breaks the skin. Handle these turtles with care.

Slider

Scientific name: *Trachemys scripta*

Area of origin: Turtles of this genus now inhabit the northern United States to Brazil, with species on some West Indian islands. The care is identical for all, but we discuss only the yellow-bellied slider *(T. s. scripta)* and the common red-eared slider *(T. s. elegans).*

Diet: The dietary preferences of sliders changes with age. Although they do eat some aquatic vegetation, baby sliders eat a proportionately larger amount of animal matter — insects, worms, tadpoles, tiny fish, and carrion.

As they grow, these turtles become ever more herbivorous, and the adults eat mostly aquatic vegetation. Besides aquatic plants, captives eat romaine, sliced apple, berries, turnip greens, dandelion greens, some prepared aquatic turtle food, and a very little puppy chow.

Ease of care: Sliders are hardy, easily cared for turtles. Few people who acquire a baby slider realize that if it is properly cared for it will eventually have a shell length of 8 to 10 inches and a potential lifespan of well over half a century. However, to reach these sizes and ripe old ages, sliders do need certain things provided.

Habitat/Caging needs: As babies, the various sliders are often very brightly colored but most become dull, and some turn almost entirely black, with age. Baby red-eared sliders are a bright green above, with a yellow plastron with black spots, and the namesake red ear stripe. Baby yellow-bellied sliders are darker (often a blackish-green) above, yellow below with dark spots on the anterior half of the plastron, and have a large bright yellow cheek patch. Colors often obscure as the turtles age and grow, and males often are darker than the females.

Sliders (so called for the way they slide into the water when disturbed) are active, moderately wary, and strong swimmers. They are also inveterate baskers, lying in the sun with neck half extended and legs and feet fully out with toes splayed. Adult males and females are about the same size, having a shell length of 8 to 10 inches. As do all basking turtles, sliders need a brightly illuminated and warmed haulout where they can emerge fully from the water, lie quietly, and elevate their body temperatures. Basking is as much a necessity for these turtles as eating and swimming. And, by the way, in keeping with most other basking turtles, sliders eat while in the water.

Sliders are active turtles and need a large aquarium or, better yet, a garden pool. With an adult shell length of 8 to 10 inches, if kept indoors, a 75 to 100 gallon capacity aquarium is suggested. Babies, of course, can be kept in an aquarium as small as 10 gallons in capacity. Because large turtles are invariably messy, the aquarium should have strong filtration, and frequent partial water changes are also mandatory. Provide an illuminated and warmed basking haulout (a full-spectrum heat bulb positioned above the haulout is recommended) of driftwood or firmly affixed plastic onto which the turtle can easily climb. The haulout surface should be non-abrasive.

Behavior: Sliders quickly come to associate the presence of a human with the availability of food. Although freshly acquired ones may quickly drop into the water if surprised while basking, they soon allow close approach and swim to the front of the tank, usually splashing about at the water's surface in eager anticipation of a tasty offering. These turtles (even when long-term captives) will bite if restrained. Handle them with care.

A popular caecilian

Aquatic caecilian, rubber eel or Sicilian (a derivation of "caecilian") eel

Scientific name: *Typhlonectes natans* and *T. compressicauda*

Area of origin: South America

Diet: Earthworms, some pelleted fish foods, tubifex worms, and bloodworms

Ease of care: If you provide adequate hiding areas, these aquatic caecilians do well in captivity.

Habitat/caging needs: Start with a covered aquarium. Rather than a gravel bottom to the tank, offer two or three inches of clean sphagnum moss; if you place rinsed sphagnum into a partially or wholly water-filled aquarium, the moss will sink to the bottom over time. Terra cotta drainage pipes also provide roomy hiding spots. Suspend a potted philodendron or pothos with a clothes-hanger hook from the edge of the tank, with the bottom of the pot even with the top of the water. The roots will grow into the water, and the leaves will form a floating cover for the water's surface. A filter helps keep the water clean and provides a gentle water current.

Behavior: Make a point of offering food at one particular spot in the tank. The caecilians, whose sense of smell is very well developed, will soon learn that the approach of a human means food, and where to go to find that food. Use forceps or impale the food on a broom straw if you want to watch your caecilians actually take the food.

Index